AN IRREVERENT
CURIOSITY

AN IRREVERENT
CURIOSITY

In Search of the Church's Strangest Relic
in Italy's Oddest Town

DAVID FARLEY

GOTHAM BOOKS

GOTHAM BOOKS
Published by Penguin Group (USA) Inc.
375 Hudson Street, New York, New York 10014, U.S.A.
Penguin Group (Canada), 90 Eglinton Avenue East, Suite 700, Toronto,
Ontario M4P 2Y3, Canada (a division of Pearson Penguin Canada Inc.)
Penguin Books Ltd, 80 Strand, London WC2R 0RL, England
Penguin Ireland, 25 St Stephen's Green, Dublin 2,
Ireland (a division of Penguin Books Ltd)
Penguin Group (Australia), 250 Camberwell Road, Camberwell,
Victoria 3124, Australia (a division of Pearson Australia Group Pty Ltd)
Penguin Books India Pvt Ltd, 11 Community Centre,
Panchsheel Park, New Delhi – 110 017, India
Penguin Group (NZ), 67 Apollo Drive, Rosedale, North Shore 0632,
New Zealand (a division of Pearson New Zealand Ltd)
Penguin Books (South Africa) (Pty) Ltd, 24 Sturdee Avenue,
Rosebank, Johannesburg 2196, South Africa

Penguin Books Ltd, Registered Offices:
80 Strand, London WC2R 0RL, England

Published by Gotham Books,
a member of Penguin Group (USA) Inc.

First printing, July 2009
1   3   5   7   9   10   8   6   4   2

LIBRARY OF CONGRESS CATALOGING-IN-PUBLICATION DATA
Farley, David.
An irreverent curiosity: in search of the church's strangest relic in Italy's oddest town/David
Farley.
p.   cm.
ISBN 978-1-592-40454-4 (hardcover)
1. Jesus Christ—Circumcision. 2. Jesus Christ—Relics. 3. Calcata (Italy)—Church history.
I. Title.
BT318.5.F37   2009
232.9—dc22   2009003761

Printed in the United States of America

Set in Bembo

For The Magpie

Author's Note

Because I was not taking notes or recording every conversation that occurred during the researching of this book, some scenes were re-created from memory and some events have been condensed and/or rearranged.

"Avoid those who do not blush to write books about the circumcision of the Lord."

—Origen, as quoted by Guibert of Nogent

Chapter 1

THE PREPUCE, THE PRIEST, AND THE WARDROBE

Ａs Don Dario Magnoni draped the sacred vestments over his apple-shaped body, the pinch in his stomach blossomed into a knot. He had some bad news he'd been keeping from his congregation. He'd decided late one recent night, after polishing off a bottle of cheap Montepulciano d'Abruzzo, that this Sunday would be the day to tell them—after all, the New Year's Day procession was just weeks away. The reason for the knot of nerves was that he didn't know how he was going to make the announcement to his small audience. Church attendance had been decreasing since he arrived in the village in the early 1970s—now only a sprinkling of villagers regularly attended the Sunday mass—and Dario hoped the chilly December weather would keep more of the faithful from their weekly obligation. He straightened out his white chasuble and took a deep breath before sliding open the door that connected his house to the adobe-like church.

"This year," Don Dario began the announcement, "the holy relic will not be exposed to the devotion of the faithful. It has vanished. Sacrilegious thieves have taken it from my home." The priest paused, waiting for calamity to ensue. But the smattering of worshippers simply stared back at him in silence, a reaction Don Dario took as indifference.

The holy relic that Don Dario spoke of wasn't just the residuum of any holy human—nor was it just any body part. It was the *carne vera sacra*, "real holy flesh," as the people of Calcata admiringly referred to it. It was the foreskin of Jesus Christ, the only piece of the Redeemer's body that he could have conceivably left on earth after his ascension into heaven, jealously guarded over in this secluded medieval hill town for the past four and a half centuries.

But now in 1983 the relic was gone. And most likely for good. After mass, some of the parishioners retreated to a nearby bar. Amid the posters and scarves of the Lazio football team, the churchgoers sipped espresso and prosecco and shook their heads in disbelief. "Who would take our cherished relic?" someone said without looking for an answer. But ancient Giuseppina shook her tiny fragile fist in the air and said, "I know who took it—*they* took it."

The mystery of just what the Holy Foreskin was doing in the priest's house—in a shoe box at the back of his wardrobe, no less—and why and how it disappeared, kicked off the most cryptic case of relic theft in centuries. Who would steal it? And what would they want with it?

For the last century, the Church's official position on the foreskin was one of silence, set out in a decree on February 3, 1900. Pope Leo XIII stated that anyone who talked about, wrote about, or commented on the Holy Foreskin would face excommunication. The Church feared the relic was being sought out simply as an "irreverent curiosity." The people of Calcata could still hold their New Year's Day procession with the relic, but that would be the only time each year it would be on display—and it would have to be from a distance and without commentary. The decree also stated that the word *"prepuzio,"* foreskin, should no longer be used when referring to the object inside the reliquary. *"Reliquia,"* relic, or *"cosa,"* thing, would be just fine from now on.

But long before this "thing" had its quiet falling-out with the Church, Christ's foreskin was one of the most popular relics in Christendom. Saints pined for it: St. Catherine of Siena, the fourteenth-century Doctor of the Church and self-proclaimed spiritual bride of Christ, said she wore the foreskin around her ring finger; that same century, St. Bridget of Sweden claimed to have had a vision of the Virgin Mary, who told her that the Holy Foreskin (then kept in Rome) was the real deal. Several popes wrote about the pious prepuce and/or granted indulgences to those who celebrated it, including Leo III (birth unknown–816), Innocent III (1160–1216), Eugenius IV (1388–1447), Pius II (1405–1464), Sixtus IV (1414–1484), Sixtus V (1521–1590), Urban VIII (1568–1644), Innocent X (1574–1655), Alexander VII (1599–1667), and Benedict XIII (1649–1730). The thirteenth-century saint Bonaventure tried settling a theological dispute about the foreskin's existence. And many of the players in the sixteenth-century Reformation (or those who inspired it)—Jan Hus, Martin Luther, John Calvin, and Erasmus among them—have weighed in. While in Rome, nineteenth-century French writer Stendhal had hoped to visit Calcata to see it, and several other scribes have included it in their novels: James Joyce (*Ulysses*), Umberto Eco (*Baudolino*), Chuck Palahniuk (*Choke*), Jonathan Gash (*The Grail Tree*), and José Saramago (*The Gospel According to Jesus Christ*).

Christ's flesh and blood are central to Catholic belief. "Take, eat: this is my body," Christ said at the Last Supper, as recorded in 1 Corinthians 11:24. And thus the Eucharist, that tasteless wafer the priest gently places on the tongues of the faithful, was born as a substitute to the Savior's flesh. The Lateran Council in 1215, however, insisted—though not unanimously—that during the Eucharist ceremony, the wafer actually became the flesh of Christ once it arrived in the middle of the devotee's throat. That a piece of Christ's actual flesh—and his foreskin, no less—could still be floating around posed a theological dilemma (and, undoubtedly, some discomfort) within the Church over the centuries. But also, the enduring enthusiasm—among the laity and, at times, within the Church—for the Holy Foreskin is a reflection of the relic as the literal manifestation of the Eucharist.

It also made a lot of money. In the Middle Ages, a great relic meant pilgrims, which meant money, prestige, and power to those in control of a relic—whether it was an abbot, a prince, or even the pope. The foreskin of Christ was one of those cash-cow curios that packed in the pilgrims. So much so, it was eventually copied and forged all over Europe. Depending on what you read, there were eight, twelve, fourteen, or eighteen different Holy Foreskins in various European towns during the Middle Ages. Coulombs, a French village near Chartres, had one. Chartres also had one; as did the French towns of Metz, Charroux, Conques, Langres, Fécamp, and Puy-en-Velay. Auvergne had two. And the French weren't the only ones with a holy foreskin obsession. Pieces of pious penises could be found in Hildesheim in Germany and Antwerp in Belgium. Santiago de Compostela, the famed pilgrimage town in the far northwestern corner of Spain, had one too. And, of course, there was the foreskin in Rome (the earliest and the one that ended up in Calcata).

Relics in general, and the Holy Foreskin in particular, are products of another age, a time when saints were posthumous medieval rock stars, pilgrims their devout groupies, and monks their roadies. The quest for salvation pervaded the being of every devout European, and the supernatural and natural were one and the same; thunderstorms, large gusts of wind, and dreams were often seen as acts of God (or, at times, Satan). Piety was the prescription for life's pain. And one of the main ways to exercise this piety was through the saints and their relics. The saints, particularly the early martyrs, had gone through a kind of suffering similar to Christ's when he made his sacrifice for all of humanity. They had achieved, according to the faithful, perfection in their deaths. So, taking the Eucharist—a symbolic part of Christ's body—at an altar that housed the bones of the martyrs and saints was a heavily loaded spiritual experience that was grounded in the physical. Believers considered saints—the Redeemer's henchmen, VIP residents of heaven—to be present at their tombs and at the spot where their relics lay. Praying to a part of their body was like tugging at their pant leg: "Hey, I'm down here and I have a request."

In centuries past, the Christian faithful relied on relics to do things that medicine, the government, the lottery, and recreational drugs do today. Relics granted wishes. They gave fortune and restored health. They eased pain and sorrow. They even produced visions for the devout. The more miracles a saint performed via their relics, the more popular and valuable that relic became. In fact, miracles were expected. When a relic showed up in a town or monastery for the first time, worshippers would watch carefully for possible miracles. A dead relic (i.e., one that did not perform miracles) was useless. Having a miracle-spewing remain of a saint in your town's church, however, was like having the godfather's ear: Your wishes and desires could be granted. A group of medieval monks worried about a fast-spreading disease, for example, didn't lock themselves inside their rooms; they plunged their patron saint's bones in a vat of wine and then commenced imbibing, hoping it would make them immune.

The Holy Foreskin, an actual piece of Jesus Christ, was, of course, the grandest relic of all. Before the relic's arrival in Calcata, it had been kept in Rome's Sancta Sanctorum—the "Holy of Holies"—where it mingled with the heads of apostles, among other esteemed objects. But how did the *Santissimo Prepuzio*, "the most holy foreskin," quietly go from invaluable to verboten in the course of several centuries, culminating in the 1900 threat of excommunication? And did this have anything to do with its 1983 disappearance?

My wife, Jessie, and I had actually been to Calcata. We were spending a few months in Rome and had heard about a bewitching medieval village plopped on a hill filled with artists and bohemian types. During our daylong visit, the foreskin may have come up in conversation, but I must have quickly forgotten it. Then one day, while we were sitting at a French café a few blocks from our apartment in New York's West Village, Jessie brought up Calcata. For the last year, she'd had a yen for a big trip—not just a few weeks, but a long adventure.

"Remember that cool hill town we went to when we lived in Rome?" she said. "Weren't we briefly thinking about moving there? Maybe we should think about it again."

"I don't know," I said, hoping it would buy me some time. In the past few months, I'd already nixed Poland, Croatia, the Czech Republic, Spain, and Mexico. The idea of moving to a small hill town north of Rome filled with artists sounded romantic on paper, but I didn't really want to give up my New York life just yet. Working as a restaurant critic and a freelance writer, I'd spend my nights attending rooftop cocktail parties thrown by various tourist boards, eating lavish meals at expensive restaurants that someone else was paying for, and jetting off to Europe on assignment for weeks at a time.

But then she brought up the relic. "Remember, there was that bizarre relic in Calcata? The Holy Foreskin? You love stuff like that."

She suddenly had my attention.

"And don't you remember when we were there, someone told us that it was stolen? Now, *that* could be interesting."

When Jessie and I had been living in Rome four years earlier, I'd take visiting friends and family around the city, and at the end of the day they'd say, "Gee, I didn't really ask for the weird-relics tour of Rome, but it sure was interesting"; I hadn't even realized that my tour consisted of dragging them from church to church showing them the arm of St. Francis Xavier (in the Gesù) or the entire three-hundred-year-old body of St. Giuseppe Maria Tomasi (in the Church of Sant'Andrea della Valle) or the place that really got me off: the Church of Santi Vicenzo e Anastasio, directly opposite the Trevi Fountain, which boasts the hearts, livers, spleens, kidneys, and pancreases of every pope from Sixtus V (1585–1590) to Leo XIII (1878–1903).

My fascination with relics began, at least indirectly, with my childhood upbringing as a Catholic. There were no relics in my church, St. Peter Claver, named after the seventeenth-century Spanish missionary whose vocation was helping (i.e., baptizing) African slaves ("I am the slave of the negroes forever!" he proclaimed). In fact, there was almost nothing to stimulate the senses, making it a shining example of post–Second Vatican Council church. The Council (also called Vatican II), which was in session from 1962 to 1965, was focused on bringing worshippers into "active participation" in the church. This meant Latin was out and the vernacular was in. Though Vatican II didn't address architecture directly (just as it didn't address relics directly), the way churches were built after Vatican II dramatically changed. St. Peter Claver was a white-stone building dominated by a glass wall on one side, which let in natural light. Gone were the dark, imposing Houses of God, replaced by the more functionalist and modern Houses of the People of God. Entrances were more welcoming (i.e., walls of glass) and the altar was moved forward so the priest could be closer to the people. Though the matter wasn't specifically addressed in the Council, by the late 1960s, priests had stopped performing mass with their backs to the parishioners. The result of all these changes, however, was a Catholic mass experience devoid of magic and mystery. At least that's what it seemed to me when my parents would drag me to church every Sunday. I really only have two memories from my churchgoing days: having to bring my older brother's and sister's Led Zeppelin,

Ozzy Osbourne, and AC/DC albums to our afterschool cate-
chism so the teacher could show us the surreptitious Satanic influence and a play I once took part in on Christmas Day in which
I played one of the three gift-bearing kings. I zoned out during
the play and failed at my one obligation: Instead of putting the
ceramic goblet down in front of the crib along with the other
gifts, I held on to it until the very end.

But then something interesting happened: I took my first trip
to Europe. I was twenty years old, and save for alcohol-fueled
trips to Mexico in high school I hadn't been out of the country.
In California, it seemed like there was no history. Everything was
new and shiny and oversized. Europe was, in some ways, the an-
tithesis: The cars, restaurant portions, and even the dogs seemed to
have shrunk a few sizes. As a result, I became infatuated with all
things European, from the nonchalance to the palimpsest of history that played a role in the everyday life of people.

But it was the grand cathedrals that really mesmerized me
most: the Baroque interiors, the cherubs floating heavenward in a
partly cloudy dome, the larger-than-life sculptures of saints looking down, and the ornate altars. For the first time, I was inspired
by something inside a church. I wasn't ready to return to the
Catholic fold, but I could see the appeal of attending a mass for an
hour every Sunday. In the old churches and cathedrals of Europe,
God wasn't an abstraction; God—and his army of saints—were
everywhere in the form of paintings and statues.

And, of course, relics. There, on display (usually in a side chapel) were skulls and femur bones and pinky fingers and sometimes entire bodies. I was intrigued for other reasons too: These
weren't just the remains of saints; they were the curios of a different time and space of human thought and philosophy, when all
actions were attributed to God, a way of thinking that's been in
fatal decline since the industrial and scientific revolutions. Relics
represented a time when death was so near to us that we put it on
display.

I came back from that first trip to Europe infected with a new curiosity about the world. I had, in the words of the Church, an "irreverent curiosity." I got off gawking at relics—the more bizarre, the better. And this relic in Calcata sounded like the strangest and grandest of all.

Back at that outdoor café in New York, an eternity's worth of puns ran through my head. So did images of myself chatting up Italian priests and querying the Vatican about one of Christianity's most curious relics. *What if,* I thought, *I tried to find out who stole it?* Staring across the street as smartly dressed professionals raced for the subway to get to the office, I said, "Okay! Let's do it."

Jessie flashed me a look of surprise and I asked about the earliest possible date we could go. We ordered another round of cappuccinos and the planning began.

Before I stepped foot on Italian soil, I got in touch with an American woman I'd previously met who had lived in Calcata for years. Louise McDermott sold rare and out-of-print English-language books about Italy from her home in Calcata and seemed like an endless source of information. She sold me a few books via mail order, including a pamphlet-size book she had written about the history of Calcata. When I told her about my quest—that I wanted to find the Holy Foreskin—she seemed intrigued yet pessimistic. "The relic is the reason my husband and I moved here from Rome," she wrote to me in an e-mail. "But the Church and the people here are very embarrassed about it. I don't think you're going to get very far." On behalf of a scholar in California, she had recently paid a visit to Don Dario—the priest under whose watch the foreskin had disappeared and, perhaps, the only person who *really* knew what had happened to the relic. "He doesn't speak English, of course," she wrote. "He isn't very lucid. And to be honest, he tends to look upon the wine when it's red . . . or white or rosé, for that matter." And then, to up the intrigue, she added, "After lots of probing, it looks as if 'stolen' isn't the correct word; 'disappeared' is more likely."

But Louise seemed willing to help. In fact, in her last e-mail before I left she promised to do what she could to facilitate a meeting with Don Dario.

I felt good about what I was about to undertake. And through a generous local named Alessandro, I'd even secured a nice, small apartment smack in the center of the village. But a couple weeks before my departure, I received an e-mail from Alessandro: "First of all, I sadly want to inform you . . ." the e-mail began. My first thought, of course, was that the apartment I'd rented wasn't available or that he was going to suddenly jack up the rent. But it was worse. Louise was dead; she'd suddenly and unexpectedly died in her sleep. And, of course, with her went all her secrets and theories and historical knowledge about the Holy Foreskin and Calcata.

Chapter 2

A PIECE OF GOD

Calcata is not easy to get to. From Rome's Flaminio/Piazza del Popolo metro stop, you jump on a light rail for about twenty minutes before getting to the Saxa Rubra bus station. Buy your bus tickets (be sure to get round trip) and then wait for the big blue bus to arrive at platform number two. In the meantime, try to avoid the salty regulars who park themselves on a bench near the snack bar, nursing large Peroni beer bottles and trying not fall over.

The bus to Calcata goes north up the Via Cassia, one of the most important of the ancient Roman roads. Two thousand years ago it was trafficked with wagons and military officers on horseback moving between Rome and Florence. Today, the Cassia— the new Cassia, that is—swarms with buzzing Vespas and Fiat-driving maniacs who rocket up the highway like they were on a high-speed police chase. The bus turns off at Sette Vene and then twists and turns through a patchwork of low-rolling, villa-topped hills and olive tree groves. It then passes through the village of Mazzano Romano before descending into a valley, which today makes up part of a regional park called Valle del Treja. Calcata sits almost halfway between the Cassia and another ancient Roman road turned modern-day thoroughfare, the Via Flaminia; because of this, Calcata was largely inaccessible until about midway through the last century, when roads were finally paved to the village.

As the bus winds its way through the verdant forest and back up a hill, you come around the bend and then there it is: Calcata, an ancient hill town, a medieval island, magically suspended in the air. In French writer Roger Peyrefitte's 1955 novel, *The Keys of St. Peter*, the protagonist comes to Calcata on a pilgrimage to venerate the Holy Foreskin. When he's approaching the town, he says, "There are places predestined for certain relics." Take your first glimpse at Calcata, and you'll understand. The village, which sits like a cupcake on a high perch, surrounded by almost 360 degrees of sheer 450-foot cliff, is made from *tufo*, soft volcanic rock, the same type of stone on which it sits, giving the impression that the buildings had just sprouted from the living rock. From above, you can see the half-football-field-size village is liver-shaped. But from the approach on the only paved road, Calcata's precarious position atop the rock appears to have been guided by a divine hand, its church campanile and rook-like tower of its diminutive castle pointing heavenward while the dense but ramshackle cluster of tan two-story houses crowns the edge of the cliffs, cementing a long and uncertain relationship between nature and civilization.

There's only one way to get into Calcata: on foot, by walking through the thick stone gate. An ascending S-shaped passageway, which actually goes underneath the church, is barely wide enough to fit a golf cart and steep enough to give some of today's wheezing inhabitants a reminder that it's time to stop smoking. It was on this passageway's last curve (before a final stretch that climbs up to the piazza) that, in the mid-sixteenth century, the first of many miracles occurred: Donkeys and goats, used for lugging food and supplies up to the village, started planting their hooves into the cobblestones in front of the thick wooden doors of a storage cave in the passageway, forcing their owners to a halt; they'd bow their heads and then continue on their way.

Village livestock don't usually persist on doing curtsies at the doorway of a storage cave, so the local priest was compelled to unbolt the doors and have a look around inside. The cave, which today houses a shop that sells hippie clothes, was sometimes used for incarcerating criminals; it hadn't seen much activity in the thirty years since a German soldier was kept there after he wandered into Calcata in 1527 on his way back from sacking Rome. Kicking around piles of hay and gently upending barrels, the priest didn't expect to find much. But then he saw something. A glimmer reflected the light from his torch. He approached the corner of the cave and brushed away a pile of hay. And there, wedged halfway underneath an ancient pile of manure, was a small silver box. The priest bent down to pick up the container. Described as being "half the size of a palm long and three fingers high," the box contained three small sacks, each one tied with a red bow. The priest stuffed the silver box into his pocket, bolted the door to the cave, and quickly set out for nearby Stabbia (today known as Faleria), where a branch of the ruling aristocratic Anguillara family was based.

He presented the container to Maddalena Strozzi, onetime painting subject of Raphael and wife of Flaminio Anguillara, the patriarch of the family. The priest, along with Lucrezia Orsini (the widow of the blue-blooded family patriarch, Giovanni Batista Anguillara), gathered with Signora Strozzi in the castle's drawing room, curious about this surprise discovery in Calcata. Signora Strozzi slowly lifted the lid of the box, taking note of the three small silk-ribbon-tied sacks. She picked up the first one and placed it in the palm of her left hand. With her right hand, she stretched out the silk ribbon and squinted to read what was printed on it. It said the sack contained the big toe of St. Valentine. She pulled the ribbon off the sack and deposited the tiny bone into the palm of her hand. "*Oh, mio Dio*," said the priest, making the sign of the cross over his face and across his chest. She gently placed the sack containing the toe back in the box and picked up the second of the three. She straightened out the ribbon and read it out loud: a tooth and a piece of the jawbone of St. Martha, sister of Mary Magdalene. Again, the priest made the sign of the cross, and this time, after placing the sack back in the silver box, Signora Strozzi blessed herself too. She then placed the third sack in her left palm and cradled the worn ribbon in her cupped right hand. "I can't read it," she said. "It's faded." The priest inched closer.

"It looks like it says N . . . S. . . . ," he said, but couldn't make out the rest. Signora Strozzi lightly shrugged, not sure what to make of it. The priest suggested they might have a better idea if she opened up the sack. Signora Strozzi pulled on the silk ribbon, but with the ribbon between her index finger and thumb, she announced her hand had gone numb.

"We have to pray," the priest said. Which they did. And then she picked up the sack again and, hesitantly this time, tugged at the ribbon. Again her hand froze, this time more stubbornly than before. She tried one more time, only to suffer the same result. Finally, someone in the room suggested they needed a person of complete purity, a virgin. So Lucrezia Orsini called for Clarice, her youngest daughter, to come into the room. The seven-year-old was handed the sack.

"Try to open it," the priest said. Everyone in the room leaned in, their attention completely focused on Clarice's little fingers pinching the silk ribbon. She gave a slight pull and the ribbon came free. Everyone let out a gasp.

The priest, at first unable to collect his breath at the sight of this miracle, finally burst out, "N.S.G.! *Nostro Signore Gesù*, Our Lord Jesus!"

The small silver box that contained the Holy Foreskin and the other two relics had been the subject of a thirty-year search. Ever since the Sack of Rome in 1527 and the plundering of everything that was precious in the city, the papacy had been determined to reacquire all the holy objects that had been stolen by German and Spanish invaders, especially those that were taken from the Sancta Sanctorum, "the Holy of Holies," a chapel in the Lateran Palace in Rome that held some of Christianity's most esteemed objects. One of the most conspicuous pieces to have gone missing from there was the Holy Foreskin. Church authorities did have a vague idea of its whereabouts: When the Landsknecht, or German mercenary, who helped in the sacking was released from Calcata he headed back to Rome. He was ailing—from what, we don't know; either he'd fallen ill or was still nursing an injury from the sack of the Eternal City—and eventually checked himself into Santo Spirito Hospital in Rome. He lay there, knowing his time was nearly up. So, with a chaplain at his bedside, perhaps reading him his last rites, the Landsknecht confessed to the theft of the reliquary.

The problem was that he didn't know the name of the town he'd been imprisoned in. Nor did he know the exact location, muttering only something about its being north of Rome . . . with a small castle . . . and that the ruling family's name was something like "Ang-ew . . . lla . . . Ang-wee . . ."

"Anguillara?" the chaplain suggested.

The soldier nodded, and the chaplain immediately sent word to the Vatican. Pope Clement VII, still recovering from the shock of the ransack of his city, had a message delivered to Giovanni Batista Anguillara, asking that he diligently search his properties—Stabbia, Mazzano, and Calcata. The search came up with nothing. The soldier passed on a few days after his confession, and the Anguillara family eventually called off their search for the relic and moved on. The Lateran Holy Foreskin, as it was called to distinguish it from the other foreskins floating around Europe in the Middle Ages, was considered long gone.

But now, thirty years later, Maddalena Strozzi, Lucrezia Orsini, the parish priest of Calcata, and a few other members of the Anguillara family were huddled around Clarice, craning to look at the Holy Foreskin, which the seven-year-old had just emptied into the palm of her hand. Described as "dense and fuzzy" and the size and color of a "red chickpea," the relic was placed in a silver bowl. Immediately it began to ooze a sweet-smelling perfumed mist that within minutes had filled the room, and quickly crept into other parts of the palace. Flaminio Anguillara, the patriarch of the family, got whiff of it and wandered in to see members of his family praying around a silver bowl. The cloudy, perfumed mist crept beyond the palace and, as historical chronicles relay, engulfed the entire village of Stabbia for two days.

The Holy Foreskin, now in a new silk sack, was brought back to Calcata and placed in the Anguillara family chapel, which would eventually be extended into a full-size church in honor of the relic.

The obscure and isolated village of Calcata would soon officially be on the map. The devout from nearby towns of Stabbia, Mazzano, and Civita Castellana, having heard of the miraculous discovery, made their way to Calcata (and, in time, pilgrims on their way to Rome would deviate from the Via Cassia or Via Flaminia, navigating footpaths through the forests to get to Calcata in order to see this sacred spectacle of a relic). The most noteworthy early visit came from the nuns of the Sisterhood of St. Ursula, located in nearby Mazzano, who made a procession, candles and torches in hand, to Calcata, singing incantations the entire three-mile journey. When they arrived in the village, they knelt and prayed at the door of the chapel and begged the priest to let them in. He finally conceded, and as soon as he unlocked the door, the women made their way to the altar and began praying to the miraculous membrane. The altar suddenly became enveloped in a cloud of glittering stars. The parish priest ran up the campanile and began ringing the bell to alert the locals that a miracle was under way. The gathering crowd became so dense inside the church that the faithful climbed up on the roof of the chapel and tore away shingles so they could see the miraculous spectacle themselves, which is said to have lasted four hours. Witnesses, according to documents written after the event, were in tears and some claimed they'd been redeemed.

As the public excitement mounted, Maddalena Strozzi traveled to Rome to tell Pope Paul IV the good news: The Holy Foreskin had, at last, been found.

Chapter 3

OH! CALCATA!

After a transatlantic flight, a light rail ride, a few stops on the Roman subway, another light rail ride, and a bus journey snaking through the hills north of Rome, I found myself heaving my way up Calcata's ascending S-shaped passageway, passing right by the cave where the foreskin was discovered. Due to work obligations, Jessie had to remain in New York a couple weeks longer, so I'd made the trip alone. I climbed up to the piazza and, to bask in the triumph of my arrival, dropped my bags down on the ground and took a deep breath. Three cats sprawled out on the chunky river-rock of the cobbled square and lanes of Calcata, absorbing the sun's rays. Two- and three-story buildings with faded and chipped paint made up the L-shaped square. Three bulbous thrones fashioned from *tufo* huddled in part of the square. I could instantly feel the presence of absence, that for dozens or even a hundred generations, this space had been life's drawing room. Then I noticed an African man, slouching on one of the marble benches. "I'm looking for Via Garibaldi," I said in my near-halting Italian. He shrugged his shoulders and I picked up my bags and walked on, passing a freshly painted fresco of Jimi Hendrix on a house on the square. If I traversed every lane in the village, I'd eventually find my apartment. Probably in the next five minutes.

Which I did. Gisa, my new landlady, was waiting for me. She quickly showed me around the two rooms, loft sleeping area, and bathroom that would be home for my wife and me. I signed a contract, paid her the first month's rent, and she was gone. Here I was, having gone from New York City to a real medieval village in central Italy—a village with a small handful of restaurants and cafés, and no post office or grocery stores or cash machines.

As soon as I dropped my bags, I felt the emptiness inside my stomach. I hadn't eaten since the midflight meal hours ago. The few restaurants I'd seen on my way in to Calcata seemed to be closed for the afternoon, so I trudged up the steep footpath that connects Calcata to Calcata Nuova, the modern offspring of the medieval village. Located a half mile from the old village, Calcata Nuova sits on a high plain that was once fertile growing land. If Calcata, or rather Calcata Vecchia (Old Calcata), is mind-boggling in its extreme charm, then Calcata Nuova is mind-numbing in its uninspiring grid of streets flanked by three-floor cinder-block houses. Though the migration to the new village took place in the 1960s and '70s, there are still scores of unfinished three-story buildings, vacant structures wedged in between lived-in family houses. Flimsy metal sliding doors were open to reveal kitchens, and residents sat in lawn chairs in front, chain-smoking and probably speculating about the strange blond-haired fellow wandering around their isolated town.

Which frightened me more than a little. I had heard rumors that Calcata Nuova was not friendly to foreigners—and by that, I mean anyone who wasn't from Calcata Nuova—the people from Faleria and Mazzano, the two neighboring villages, included. A few years earlier, an Italian photographer and his friend were chased out of the village by an angry mob—led by the mayor—while trying to witness the annual September saint's day festival.

As I traversed the barren streets of Calcata Nuova, old people stopped and stared at me. Housewives came to the door to watch me pass. Little kids responded to my hello with a mousy, tentative ". . . Ciao." In the 1960s and '70s, the area around Calcata was frequently used to make spaghetti Westerns. And while that era is long gone, I suddenly felt like some black-clad cowboy who'd just entered a town in the Old West, expecting one of the town's gunslingers to challenge me to the draw. When I saw that the two food shops in town were closed, I gravitated to a bar where a cadre of ancient men were sitting outside on red plastic chairs. As I approached them, I tried rehearsing in Italian how to ask when the food shops might open. And kept an eye out for the quickest escape route.

"Ciao. Er . . . food shop. Open. Time. Do you know?"

No one responded right away. Instead, the men—who seemed to range in age between forty-five and sixty-five—looked around at each other.

"Nothing is open for another thirty minutes. At five o'clock the shop down the road will be open," one of the men finally said. He spoke perfect, but slightly accented, English. "I'm the only one around here who speaks English, so if you have any more questions, I'm the one to ask."

Maybe they felt sorry for me or thought I was mentally impaired, but this guy actually seemed nice. And I did have a lot of questions.

"I'm Mario," he said. Except for his right eye, which looked like it was slowly dripping off his face—as if he were a plastic action figure left in a car during the summer heat—he looked a lot like Woody Allen without glasses.

"And this is Piero and Giancarlo." They nodded at me.

"Do you know anyone around here who wants to learn English? I'm offering free conversation lessons."

This, I thought, would be a nice peace offering. I could learn a lot about the place just from correcting their speaking and hopefully avoid getting beaten up.

Mario answered my question about teaching English with another question: "Red or white?"

I just stared at him, not exactly sure what he meant.

"Wine. Red or white?" he repeated, his voice a little louder this time. "C'mon, let's have a drink," he said, opening the door and motioning me inside.

Two glasses of prosecco magically appeared in front of us, as we approached the bar. Mario explained to me that, in the sixties, he was married to an Australian woman and lived in Sydney for six years. He hadn't really spoken English since then, which surprised me because he spoke so well.

I told him that I'd just arrived and was living in the old town.

"Ah," Mario said, as if it all made sense to him now. "Some fucking idiot in the government," Mario said, looking to the floor and shaking his head, "deemed the old town dangerous to live in and all the people here had to move to this place and build a new town."

Who could have known that an earthquake in 1908, in the Sicilian metropolis of Messina, just across the strait from the "toe" of the Italian peninsula, approximately 450 miles south of where I was currently enjoying a glass of sparkling wine, would eventually have such an effect on the people of Calcata? The quake, which killed about 150,000 people and transformed the ancient city into a pile of rubble, created a paradigm shift in Italian town planning. Soon after, government officials began studying millennia-old hill towns all over the Italian peninsula, designating some as "dangerous urban centers" and slating them for demolition.

On June 27, 1935, almost twenty-seven years after the earthquake, Calcata was added to the list of towns to be destroyed. The residents were told they'd have to evacuate so their village could be razed. Which, at the time, might have been a good thing: The medieval village of Calcata was cramped. A mid-nineteenth-century census revealed there were 420 residents, making up eighty-four families, improbably living in seventy-nine houses on about a six-acre space. The Calcatesi didn't want to see their village destroyed, but more space was just too appealing. Besides, the government would pay for their move up the hill as soon as a new village was built; residents would get a new house, an actual driveway, and plenty of room to stretch their legs. As the former priest said of the old residents in a magazine article I'd read about Calcata, "They saw America up there on the hill."

But the wheels of change moved at a Mediterranean pace. A few decades and a world war went by before anything happened. In the mid-fifties, however, spurred by a new priest, Don Mario Mastricola, who lobbied heavily for the new town to be built in order to free his flock from the worsening conditions of the old village, the government finally put construction into gear. By 1969, Calcata Nuova was complete. With the exception of a few holdouts (mostly old women who refused to leave their ancestral homes and a clutch of abandoned cats), residents migrated up the hill to the modern town.

Calcata, this ancient and bewitching village, was nearly abandoned and just waiting for the government bulldozers and wrecking balls to arrive. But then something interesting happened: Artists and architects and bohemians and beatniks, perhaps hoping to retreat from urban areas like Rome, showed up instead, buying the houses from the old residents at cheap prices—the old residents, sitting in their plush new houses, wryly smiling at the idea of selling a condemned house to a hippie. The new residents went to work, fixing the plumbing, repairing cracks in the walls, and filling in holes in the cobblestone alleys. They opened restaurants, cafés, and art galleries; they sold accoutrements of hippie culture from blankets laid out on the cobblestones; they smoked a lot of dope and waxed philosophical about energy and whatever else made Calcata so groovy. They put on plays in the square and showed their art at self-curated exhibitions. The village, they felt, was all theirs!

Calcata had been resurrected. And the people perched up on

the hill, those living in Calcata Nuova, weren't pleased. Sure, they still liked their new village and their spacious modern houses, but these hippies were breathing new life into a place the government had once said was dead. If they couldn't live there, then no one should be able to—not to mention those long-haired freaks who'd gravitated here from God knows where. Fast-forward three decades: The artists and now-aging hippies lobbied to have the Messina Law rescinded, and property values in Calcata have skyrocketed. Houses that were sold for a few thousand dollars are now selling for a few hundred thousand dollars.

And especially since "America up on the hill" has become worse for wear and hasn't lived up to the promise it once held, it would be understandable if the people of Calcata Nuova felt at least a small amount of frustration about the turn of events in Calcata.

"Yes, there's some resentment," Mario said. "Definitely."

I looked around at the men in the bar, smoking, reading newspapers, looking not particularly content, and wondered if they were thinking about which bone in my body they should break first. I finished off my glass of wine in one large swig and eyed the clock on the wall. It was five minutes to five. I still needed to get to the grocery store and now might be a good time to make my exit.

"One thing you should know about me is that I say what I think," Mario said. "And people here like me for that. I'm volatile and if you make me angry, that's it." He sliced his hand through the air. "Also, I'm very drunk right now."

"Are you and your friends celebrating?" I asked.

"Celebrating?" he said, looking somewhat perplexed. Maybe he didn't know the word in English.

"Last night. I heard there was a big soccer match. Are you still . . . you know," I said, shaking an invisible pint glass to my mouth.

He looked down at the floor and pushed his lips forward. "I

don't fucking care about that," he blurted out. "We're like this all the time here."

Just then, I noticed a short, goateed man with brown shoulder-length hair standing among us. It was hard to believe, but he might have been more intoxicated than the others. More amazingly, after a brief exchange, of which I understood nothing, I found myself in his car. Just he and I. Capelló, as everyone called him—"big hair" in the Calcata dialect—made an immediate U-turn, despite the approaching cars from both directions.

As we headed down the very hill I had just trudged up thirty minutes earlier, Capelló told me in hard-to-comprehend Italian that he made wine. He didn't sell it, though. He didn't even want to sell it. He produced it simply for these occasions: to lure his buddies from the bar into his private wine cellar for some serious drinking.

His cellar, located halfway up the mountain between the two villages, was essentially a shack built into the hill. Two orange swastikas and a lightening-bolt-style "SS" were spray-painted on the wooden door.

"Are you a Nazi?" I asked, half jokingly.

"*Quasi*," he replied, smiling, his crow's-feet ever deepening around his eyes. I wasn't sure if he was joking, quasi-joking, or not joking at all. Remnants of posters clung to the wooden doors of the cantina, appearing like they'd been pasted over the Nazi signage and then ripped down.

Capelló swung open the doors, the early-evening sunlight revealing two plus-size plastic barrels and a few wooden beams raised up on blocks of *tufo* to serve as benches.

"Red or white?" he asked, nodding at the two barrels. Before I could answer he grabbed a white plastic cup, squatted down, and poured me a glass of red wine.

Just then Mario and Piero showed up and the party was officially on.

Capelló, I learned, was Calcata to the core. "The Calcatesi are so beautiful," he said, shaking his head and bunching up his lips in what looked to be a moment of instant drunken emotion.

"Were you born in the old village?" I asked.

"Yes, I was. Just like my parents. And their parents. And their parents . . . it's really such a shame that we had to move up here."

Rapid-fire Italian was now being exchanged between Capelló, Mario, and Pierro. Capelló pointed in the direction of the old village and then up to the new village. Throughout my short time with them, Mario would often translate what they were saying, since my Italian was barely good enough to ask for directions to supermarkets. This time he didn't. He didn't have to. I had a pretty good idea what they were talking about. And I felt a little bit uncomfortable. Besides my outsider status, I was one of those "invaders," one of the bohemians living in one of the houses that Capelló and his friends should be living in.

The German soldier who had inadvertently brought the relic to Calcata in 1527 popped into my head. He wasn't apprehended and incarcerated in Calcata for five-fingering the Holy Foreskin (and the valuable silver box that contained it) from Rome's Sancta Sanctorum—in fact, he didn't even tell anyone that he had it, knowing even further punishment would be in his future. He was imprisoned in a cave-cum-cell (where he stashed the relic) because he was an outsider. Imprisoning strangers was not uncommon in medieval villages. I wasn't here to commit a crime, at least I didn't see it that way. I was eager to get my search for the Holy Foreskin under way, and part of me wanted to fire a bunch of questions at Mario so he could ask Pierro and Capelló their thoughts on the relic—but now didn't seem like the best time.

When I thought about it, they hadn't actually asked me anything about myself. They knew I was from New York because I'd volunteered that information. But that was it. They knew nothing else about me—not that I was afraid of spiders or that I was born in Dubuque, Iowa, a town that's infamous because the first editor of *The New Yorker* once said the magazine was not going to be for "the old lady from Dubuque" (that was my grandma, by the way, and, yes, he was totally right). Nor did they know that in a matter of days my wife and dog would be joining me. They didn't even know I had a wife and a dog. Maybe if they did, they'd change their mind about what they were going to do to me, the latest barbarian to invade Calcata.

"Well," I said, putting my hands on my knees to push myself up, "I think the supermarket is probably open by now."

They seemed to have other plans for me, however.

"You just take it easy," Mario said, putting up the palms of his hands for me to stay seated. He was now standing toward the back of the cellar. "You haven't even tried the wine yet."

I took a swig and immediately understood why Capelló didn't sell the stuff. Meanwhile, Piero was lighting a candle. "Have you seen the cave yet?" Mario asked. "You must see it—it's very interesting."

Piero handed me the candle and stupidly I took it. I hadn't even realized there was a cave in this tiny room. I was already feeling like an invading bohemian, and now three possibly xenophobic local men had just handed me a candle and told me to descend into a cave because it's "interesting" down there? Great. I'd only been in Calcata for an afternoon and I was about to get the same treatment as the German soldier. And I didn't even have the Holy Foreskin on me!

I took a few steps forward into the blackness and Mario and Piero followed. Capelló stood in the distance, smiling and nodding at me. The candle hardly illuminated anything, save for the silver-dollar-size spiders that lurked just above my head. I kept shuffling my feet forward. And they kept following me.

It was cold when we got to the bottom. I moved the candle around and noticed a large cache of wine bottles.

"This is where the wine ages," Mario said.

We stood there for a minute, as I moved the candle around the subterranean cellar, viewing the pyramid-shaped stacks of wine bottles. "Looking at all this aging wine is making me thirsty," Mario said. "Let's go back up and get another drink."

I held up the candle to see Mario's face.

He looked at me, his one droopy eye gazing off somewhere else, and said, "I forgot, my friend: red or white?"

Chapter 4

THE FATHER
OF ALL FORESKINS

Don Dario had arrived for his new assignment in Calcata in the early 1970s by driving his tiny Fiat through the stone gate and up onto the square. He was a welcome sight. The village was in transition, finally ready to move up to the brand new town that had slowly been built. And with a new town they needed a new priest as well. Don Dario was replacing Don Antonio, a priest who had been pegged as the culprit for the continual disappearance of church valuables, including a life-size statue of the Virgin that had been adorned with precious jewels. Don Antonio had also shown a mercenary attitude toward the foreskin; though he wasn't supposed to show the relic to anyone, he'd happily march it out for tourists. As long as they'd pay him to see it (the going rate was ten thousand lira, or about five dollars).

Having spent his formative years in an isolated mountain town in the region of Le Marche, Don Dario was fifteen when a representative from the Church appeared one day asking if anyone wanted to join the ranks. Knowing it might be his only way out, young Dario was the first person to raise his hand; before he could say *"Oddio!"* he was whisked off to Assisi to be ordained as a monk. From there he moved on to a monastery in Spoleto. But he hated being there and soon enough was looking for a way out of town. With the ranks of priests growing thin, the Church began reaching into monasteries, and when Don Dario had heard about an open post in an obscure town close to Rome called Calcata, he once again was the first one to raise his hand.

And while Dario was pleased to be out of Spoleto, he had no idea what he was getting himself into; that he'd be the custodian of one of the most curious and controversial relics in the history of the Church. Despite succeeding a bad priest, Don Dario never built up a huge following with his flock. One of the reasons was because he obeyed orders from above (i.e., the Church). He was under strict instruction not to show the relic to anyone and only bring it out during the annual New Year's Day procession (formerly known as the Feast Day of the Holy Circumcision). When he'd process with the relic at the beginning of every year, the people of Calcata would nearly swoon; occasionally he let the faithful kiss the reliquary. The Calcatesi, it's safe to say, were enamored of their relic.

The Church likes to point out that the cult of relics had been active in other cultures and religions long before the birth of Christ. Five centuries earlier and thousands of miles from Bethlehem, for example, the Buddha took his last gasp and then made his way to Nirvana; his followers were waiting, freshly sharpened knives in hand, to distribute his remains throughout the Buddhist world.

Biblical scholars have pointed out a possible Biblical basis for relic veneration in 2 Kings 13:20–21 when a band of raiders had snuck up on some Israelites who were in the process of burying a man; in haste, they threw the body into Elisha's tomb and "when the body touched Elisha's bone, the man came to life and stood up on his feet."

But most relic scholars agree the cult of relics in Christendom didn't *officially* begin until almost a century and a half after Christ's death. Most historians date the beginnings of Christian relic ven-eration to the middle of the second century. That's when Poly-carp, bishop of Smyrna (in modern-day Turkey), got on the Romans' bad side for not partaking in a pagan festival. So, the Romans did as they so enjoyed doing to dissenters: They burned him.

After the pyre had cooled, Polycarp's followers scurried over and scooped up his remains, depositing them in a place where they could venerate their beloved bishop. In 156 A.D. one of his followers wrote (in what is called *The Acts of St. Polycarp*), "We adore [Christ], because He is the Son of God, but the martyrs we love as disciples and imitators of the Lord. . . . Then we buried in a becoming place [Polycarp's] remains, which are more precious to us than the costliest diamonds, and which we esteem more highly than gold."

And with that, the cult of relics began. The more Romans killed Christians, the more followers of Christ began sneaking off with the bodies of the martyred; in turn, the more relics they had for veneration.

Not that this made relic veneration acceptable in Roman so-ciety. Worshipping decomposing corpses wasn't only new and different to Romans—it was just plain weird. The prevailing Roman view of dead bodies was like our modern view of, say, rotting fruit. Once it turns, you want it gone before the smell and sight of it begins to assault your senses. The second-century A.D. Roman philosopher Celius wrote, "For what sort of human soul is it that has any use for a rotted corpse of a body? . . . Corpses should be disposed of like dung, for they are dung." Which is why the catacombs, essentially a Roman cemetery where the bodies of the early Christian martyrs were buried, are far out of the city (the most famous today being near the Appian Way). It's also the reason why the Vatican, built over the crucifixion and burial site of St. Peter, is where it is today; at the time of St. Peter's crucifixion, the Vatican Hill was an out-of-the-city necropolis, a place known, according to Pliny the Elder, for snakes and bad wine. Additionally, this is the place where executions were carried out and people were buried. (Today, Vatican City tourists can get a peek at Peter's bones by arranging a tour of the pre-Christian necropolis that rests underneath St. Peter's Basilica.) The cities of the dead were being transformed into the cities of the living as the new faithful began hanging out in cemeteries, thinking the closer they were to the supposedly divine, the better. For Christians, a martyr's or holy person's tomb was the place where that person's soul rested. As historian Peter Brown said in *The Cult of the Saints: Its Rise and Function in Latin Christianity*, ". . . the Christian cult of saints rapidly came to involve the digging up, the moving, the dismemberment—quite apart from much avid touching and kissing—of the bones of the dead, and, frequently, the placing of these in areas from which the dead had once been excluded."

Which is one reason Roman authorities soon found Christians and their love of lopped-off body parts to be pests. In 177 A.D., for example, Christians in Lyon begged a judge to give them the body of a martyred saint and not throw it in the Rhône. Eventually, they greased the judge's palms with some cash and the body was theirs. And seconds after St. Cyprian was beheaded in 258, his followers sprinted over, mopping up the blood spilling out of his neck with their clothes, and then ran away, leaving a crowd of Roman onlookers perplexed.

Five centuries later, relic veneration, once a strange and curious practice in the Mediterranean, had become obligatory for those who sought Christian salvation (which, at this point, was pretty much everyone in Europe). At the Second Council of Nicaea in 787, church leaders further ingrained the practice by passing a law that every church must have a holy relic at its altar. The punishment for not obeying this law was serious: excommunication. Coincidentally enough, this was about the same time missionaries began converting Germanic and Scandinavian tribes to Christianity. Relics were needed to keep up with the ferocious church-building going on in former heathen territory.

Where would all these skulls and skin fragments, bones and vials of blood, come from? Saints also had possessions. They wore clothes and jewelry. They touched things. There were the objects that had martyred them—rods, stones, and torture devices. So, eventually a system was put in place for classifying relics: A first-class relic was a body part of a saint; a second-class relic was a saint's possession; a third-class relic was an object that had touched a first-class relic; a fourth-class relic—the least valuable, but the easiest to produce—was an object that had touched a second-class relic: This could as simple as a piece of cloth that had been rubbed up against a saint's tomb.

At the same time eighth-century popes began changing the laws of the dead, now allowing the remains of humans to be moved from the catacombs that lie on the outskirts of Rome to St. Peter's and other Roman churches. There were thousands upon thousands of bones in the catacombs—the famed early martyrs were buried with other early converts—and when Rome was sacked by booty-hungry barbarian invaders in the fourth and fifth centuries, they ravaged the catacombs, hoping to find valuable possessions among the dead. They didn't find much, but they did ransack the underground chambers enough to erase any clues about whose remains were whose. Which meant that any bone from the catacombs could have been an early martyr's. The Church began transferring these relics to churches in Rome (after the Pantheon was converted to a church in the seventh century, twenty-eight cartloads of bones from the catacombs were delivered and placed under the altar); after which many of the unidentifiable bones that had been transferred from the catacombs were sent to northern monasteries and churches.

Which is when the relic-loving monarch Charlemagne, the French king whose reign over Europe made an indelible mark on the borders and culture of the continent, came into the picture. Charles, along with his allies in Rome, took the institutionalization of the cult of relics a step further by proclaiming that all official oaths should be done either in a church or with one's hand on a relic. Even his jewel-studded throne, located in Aachen, contained compartments and little drawers for holding relics; therefore everything the king said on his throne was an official oath.

Most important for us, he's credited—accurately or not—with resurrecting the Holy Foreskin. According to legend, the Holy Foreskin's miraculous rebirth occurred in the late eighth century when Charlemagne supposedly traveled to the Holy Land. As pious as he was powerful, the bearded monarch began praying in Jerusalem's famed Church of the Holy Sepulcher, the church built on the spot of Christ's tomb. That's when an angel (or, in some accounts, the actual hand of God) descended onto the king. Placed in front of him was something called the Holy Virtue. Before Charlemagne could look inside, a boy appeared on the right side of the altar. Claiming to be the Christ child, the boy said to Charlemagne, "Most noble prince, accept with veneration this small gift, which, it is sure, [comes] from my true flesh and my true blood." Charlemagne looked inside the package and found both a piece of the True Cross and the Holy Foreskin.

An alternative story of Charlemagne and the Holy Foreskin comes from the Grail legend of Parzival, which references a small silver casket in the Church of the Holy Sepulcher. In this box was a piece of the True Cross and the Holy Foreskin and it was given to Charlemagne as a gift for negotiating a deal with the Jerusalem-occupying Muslims to let pilgrims safely visit the Church of the Holy Sepulcher.

But why did Charlemagne become the chosen one, the fortunate receiver of the centuries-old foreskin of the Redeemer? The impulse to credit him in this fashion could go back to a precedent set by Constantine, the fourth-century Roman emperor who converted to Christianity after supposedly seeing a cross in the sky just before going to battle: a powerful ruler, anointed by God with a heavenly vision to rule. But it's also emblematic of the way holy relics are born. Relics are physical matter. They're pieces of flesh, chips of bone, articles of clothing. They're empty signifiers waiting for a definition. A sliver of wood, for example, is worth nothing unless it's billed as a piece of the True Cross. But now let's assume that piece of wood had come from, say, Charlemagne, or St. Helena, the mother of Constantine whose cross-finding mission to the Holy Land is the stuff of legend; suddenly the value of that sliver of wood is exponentially higher. Then miracles would be attributed to it, thus increasing the relic's longevity, livelihood, and power.

Relics embodied the philosophy of faith itself: If you believe it, it is so. It didn't matter that the wood Helena brought back might not have been the actual True Cross; nor did the possibility that she'd never brought back anything at all. The faithful believed it, and as a result—at least in their minds—miraculous things occurred because of it. So, when it came to the Holy Foreskin, the only remnant of the Christ remaining on the planet, the tale surrounding its supposed discovery should befit the importance of the relic itself. If there was a Holy Foreskin at all, God would have made sure that it was given to no one less than Charlemagne.

After his death in 814, Charlemagne Inc. was officially born. Everyone wanted a part of the Carolingian legend. Histories were invented that linked the founding of monasteries to him. Royals claimed ancestral links. Entire regions concocted tales about the king's travels and travails and battles in their areas (even his Holy Foreskin–finding mission to the Holy Land most likely never happened). For hundreds of years, Charlemagne's name gave credibility and, in many cases, special privileges to those who concocted a link to it.

Even today, some genealogists have claimed that all people of European ancestry alive today are descendents of Charlemagne.

And because the eighth- and ninth-century king of the Franks ruled over such a large swath of Europe, essentially uniting it, he's even credited with laying the foundations of the modern states of France and Germany and, some say, the European Union. Appropriately enough, he's often referred to as "the father of Europe."

In the late eighth century, a series of popes began courting Charlemagne. When the pious potentate arrived in Rome in 774, Pope Hadrian had city officials, schoolboys, and knights meet the budding Frankish king thirty miles from the city. They sang *laudes* to him, they carried large crosses and flags, as they escorted the king into the city, where the pope met him on the steps of the old St. Peter's Basilica. Twenty-six years later, in November 800, Charlemagne came back to Rome, this time the most powerful monarch Europe had seen since the days of the Roman emperors. And this time the pope, now Leo III, went into the Roman hinterlands to meet Charles himself (the two met at Prima Porta—perhaps for symbolic reasons, just to the north of Rome, the exact spot where Emperor Constantine had his famous vision of the burning cross in the sky).

As the story goes, on Christmas Day in the year 800, at the old St. Peter's in Rome, Pope Leo III crowned Charles emperor and officially resurrected the Roman Empire (which would now be called the Holy Roman Empire and would limp all the way into the nineteenth century before finally succumbing to modernity). And as a token of gratitude, Charlemagne gave the pontiff Jesus' foreskin (the one he'd received in the Holy Sepulcher), housed in a golden cross adorned with hyacinth; the pope accepted the gift with gratitude and then deposited the relic in the Sancta Sanctorum. Most histories of Charlemagne don't mention the foreskin gift when dealing with Charlemagne's coronation by Leo III, either because of embarrassment or lack of real evidence that it actually happened. In actuality, we know the Rome foreskin—the same one that apparently ended up in Calcata—was preserved in the Sancta Sanctorum from at least the late eleventh century, housed, as some sources say, with the umbilical cord of the Redeemer (with a tale attached that it, too, came from Charlemagne).

Medieval popes, some harboring suspicions about the authenticity of the relic, did an annual procession with the Holy Foreskin throughout the streets of Rome. Because the prepuce is so intrinsically tied to crucifixion—Christ's first bloodshed combined with a relic of his last, the alpha and omega—it's no surprise that the reliquary that held the foreskin was a cross. And every year, the pope would have the reliquary oiled and would then lead a procession with it from the Sancta Sanctorum to the nearby church of San Giovanni in Laterano. The procession didn't happen on the New Year's Day feast of the Holy Circumcision; instead, it was done on September 14, the feast day of the cross.

These were the foreskin's salad days, as it had unrivaled devotion. All that would change, of course—not just because the relic would be duplicated, but other mementos of the Holy Family would flood the market, eventually overwhelming the faithful, inspiring in some cases less faith and more skepticism.

Chapter 5

FAMILY JEWELS

I'd woken up the morning after my stint in Capelló's cave with the sting of subpar wine pinching my brain. I was anxious to start asking around about the foreskin, but I had no idea if broaching the topic was taboo. I felt like I'd barely escaped being locked up in a cave the night before with Piero, Mario, and Capelló (or Capellone, as he was also called by friends); I didn't want to bring further punishment to myself for inappropriately mentioning the relic.

I began my search in the Grotta dei Germogli. This wasn't just a random choice. Pancho, the owner and chef, was American (and thus spoke English fluently); he seemed the logical place to start. Besides, when Jessie and I had randomly met him in Calcata on the day trip four years earlier, he was charming and interesting and appeared to have an endless amount of information about the village. Plus he made amazing pumpkin gnocchi.

As the name suggests, the Grotta dei Germogli was fashioned out of a cave. Sections of the white cavernous interior were covered by colorful mosaics, some floor-to-ceiling, made by Pancho. When the place first opened, about ten years before I moved to

Calcata, it had been much more radical. Pancho had no prices on the menu. Instead, he'd just set a jar on the table and people could contribute what they wanted. The only problem, Pancho eventually found out, was that people were not only contributing minuscule amounts of money for whole meals, some people were even stealing money from the jar. The Grotta then evolved into the go-to place in the area for late-night debauchery. Kids from all over would come to drink and smoke all night. Occasionally things would get rough. Fights would break out. The police would be called. And Pancho's place started to get a negative reputation. Which prompted him to tone things down a bit and turn the cave into more of an eatery than a place to party. Of course, Pancho still would never admit the Grotta dei Germogli was a restaurant. That's partly because it's technically not one. Because of old zoning laws, certain spaces in Calcata are meant for certain functions. This cave, which was used to store wine and other things, tie up donkeys, and was—a few decades ago—the place where teenage boys went to masturbate, had never been cleared for commercial use. But Pancho slipped through a loophole, defining the Grotta as a "cultural association," a nonprofit organization to promote arts and culture. His mission was to promote healthy eating and offer the space as a venue for artistic ventures. Once you were a member, Pancho would tell people, you could use this space like your own.

I sat down on a stool and snuggled up to the bar, watching him cook for the night (open kitchens like the Grotta's are unusual in Italy). I felt like I could sit there for nights on end, listening to Pancho talk. And, in fact, I would. For the last ten years Pancho had been cooking up "bizarre" food in the form of Italian dishes with his own little spin on them: gnocchi with a tomato-curry sauce, chicken with peanut sauce, bruschetta with various toppings made from egg and nuts and cheese. Before he opened the Grotta, Pancho had lived in Rome and worked as a dancer, having been taken under the wing of a famous American dancer and choreographer. That dancer was Paul Steffen, now eighty-seven years old and also a Calcata resident. At one time in Rome, Paul had been—according to Pancho—"bigger than the Beatles." I had a difficult time with the idea that a dancer/choreographer could achieve such fame, so I jokingly asked Pancho if Paul's stardom came before the Beatles existed. "No, it was the sixties and seventies," he said. "At that time, there was only one TV channel—RAI—and Paul was their main choreographer. So the entire country was a captive audience to Paul's dancing."

I sipped on my wine and watched Pancho and his sous chef, Bea, skirt around each other like ballerinas, flipping sautéed meat in a pan, dishing pastas, and cutting bread. Rita, the Grotta's only waitress, was screaming about something and complaining of a headache. Meanwhile, I decided to take my first baby step in my quest. "Any idea what happened to the Holy Foreskin?"

Pancho stopped pouring coconut milk into a bowl of tomato sauce and rested the can on the counter. "Ah, yes, the Holy Foreskin," he said, and then turned toward Bea and Rita and asked in a sarcastic tone—as if this was a question that had come up a gazillion times—if they knew what had happened to the Holy Foreskin. Bea picked up a shriveled tortellini and held it above her head. In a dry tone, she said, "Here it is. Here's the Holy Foreskin," and everyone laughed.

"Well," Pancho continued, switching back to English, and putting the palm of his hand under his jawbone, "there's plenty of speculation. You should ask Patrizia. She's the Holy Foreskin expert. She's got some crazy theories about it that are quite intriguing."

Pancho continued, "The only problem is that she's really guarded in giving this information out. She jealously keeps it to herself. You wouldn't be the first person who has come to Calcata hoping to get foreskin info from her. And you wouldn't be the first person who left the village with nothing from her."

"Is there anyone else?" I asked. "Anyone who can help me get information about the relic?"

Pancho thought for a second and then turned to Bea, who was pouring a thick almond pesto sauce over a bowl of gnocchi, and spit out a couple sentences in Italian. "Don Dario," Bea said with dripping sarcasm.

I was desperate to find a way to get the priest to talk to me. But there was nothing to suggest that was going to happen. I knew he was a bibulous wine enthusiast, but showing up at his house with a couple bottles of Brunello and putting my faith in "in vino veritas" didn't seem like the shrewdest plan.

"You'd get Patrizia to talk before Don Dario talked to you. Some people know bits and pieces of the history of the relic and everyone has their opinion about it," Pancho said. "Don Dario not only would avoid talking to you about the relic, if he finds out you're trying to figure out what happened to the foreskin or that you're a journalist from New York, he's going to avoid you completely. Really," he added, "Patrizia might be the only one who has done research on it, but she will not talk."

I hadn't even met or seen this Patrizia yet, but I already envisioned her like the fortress town itself, all closed up and ready to spill a bucket of scalding wax on me as I stood, pen and notebook in hand, gently knocking on the oversized thick wooden door to the village.

I felt myself sinking. It seemed there were only a few people who knew anything about the relic: One of them was now dead and the other two I'd probably have to threaten with death in order to get them to talk.

"Maybe you should try finding another relic," Pancho said, in what was, I think, meant to be a joke and to lighten up my mood. "Aren't there other relics of Christ around?"

If the Holy Foreskin had been the *only* bodily relic of Christ, perhaps it wouldn't have eventually been so easy to dismiss. But there were other, sometimes awkward mementos that would surface. Like those of his mother, for example; like Christ, the Virgin also supposedly ascended into heaven, making bodily relics nearly impossible. Not that it stopped anyone from trying.

Beginning in the late eleventh century, men in Europe were encouraged by the pope (via a guaranteed ticket into heaven) to trek to the Holy Land to defend it from being overrun by heathens. The Muslims, a couple centuries earlier, had spread themselves throughout North Africa (and eventually got all the way into Spain). So, several crusades to oust them were hatched over the next couple centuries starting in 1095. The first mention of the Holy Foreskin's presence in Rome was in a document from the 1070s listing an inventory of relics in the Sancta Sanctorum. At the time, there were few Christ relics circulating around Europe. Nor were there many from the Virgin. But all that was about to change as troops stumbled home with booty.

At the end of the Fourth Crusade, about a century after the first, the relic scene in Europe would change forever. Crusaders stopped by Constantinople on the way back from the Holy Land and sacked the city, which had been the early-medieval epicenter for Christian relics. The city housed 3,600 relics from 476 saints, including the table that hosted the Last Supper, the Holy Shroud (likely not the same shroud that's in Turin today), the head of St. John the Baptist, the saw that cut the wood for Christ's cross, and a chart that had been used to measure Jesus' height growing up. In fact, so many recently returned crusaders were trafficking in relics brought back from the 1204 sack of Constantinople that Church bishops met in Rome in 1215 to try to put a stop to it. They were unsuccessful.

Many of the relics lifted from Constantinople ended up in private collections. One of the most eventful times of the year in fourteenth-century Prague was when Holy Roman Emperor Charles IV, who lived in the castle overlooking the city, carted out his private collection of holy curios for his annual relics show. Charles, an extremely pious monarch, owned a personal relic collection that was jaw-dropping in size. Pilgrims came from all over, congregating in Charles's eponymous square to pray and pay princely sums to see the parts of sanctified stiffs, especially the show's headliner: the breast of Mary Magdalene. A couple centuries later, the Renaissance prince Albrecht of Brandenburg had a stockpile of saintly remains so large that the indefatigable pilgrim could have racked up a remission from purgatory of 39,245,120 years.

The emergence of wealthy connoisseurs also contributed to the rise of the trade in dubious relics. With relics all the rage in the Middle Ages—saints' bodies were dug up, sliced, diced, and dispersed—each and every pious body part or secondary relic was up for sale. According to one story, a relic-seeking Spanish monk on a journey to find a relic for his monastery was accosted by a black market dealer with a very hot item for sale: the head of St. John the Baptist . . . as a baby. And venerated in both Brescia and Constance was the flaming cross that had appeared to Constantine upon his conversion in 313. It was not explained how a heavenly vision had been made manifest as a physical object.

But nothing could compare to the rapture worshippers experienced with relics of Christ and the Virgin. Christ's ascension into heaven, one of the key principles of Catholic belief, made the existence of first-degree Jesus relics nearly impossible. So for centuries after Helena's trip to the Holy Land, churches, monasteries, and kings were content with the endless procession of hokey secondary Holy Family relics that supposedly had been trotted back from Jerusalem and its environs. The Holy Manger, for example, could be seen at Rome's Santa Maria Maggiore. There was also the Holy Cloak, a piece of cloth that covered the baby Jesus; the Holy Baby Spoon; Holy Water Pots, used by Jesus at Cana (Calvin wrote that the liquor Christ produced was venerated in Orleans); the Holy Linen; and wooden carts said to have come from Joseph's carpentry shop that Jesus himself had lent a hand to build. In Genoa one could find a plate that once held

Christ's roasted lamb during the Last Supper; part of the table is still in the Sancta Sanctorum in Rome. A few pieces of very stale bread, part of the leftover bounty that Jesus had produced for five thousand hungry souls in the desert, could be found in the Eternal City. Rome was also home to the reed that held vinegar and was put to Christ's mouth as he was dying.

And that was just Jesus. Mary and Joseph were represented too. Two fifth-century aristocrats from Constantinople claimed to have discovered the Virgin's robe in a small village in Galilee. They took off with it and headed home. Later, Constantinople would claim to have the Virgin's shroud and the Holy Girdle. Other Holy Family secondary relics soon turned up: Joseph's Hammer; the Holy Tunic; a chair the Virgin reclined on; her combs, shoes, and handkerchiefs (part of the nearly 7,500 pieces of Phillip II of Spain's relic collection) materialized in the Middle Ages and were, apparently, causing miracles. Even her wedding ring was prayed over in Perugia. One of the most remarkable relics is the House of Loretto, said to be the house of the Virgin Mary. According to legend angels first carried it from the Holy Land to the Dalmatian Coast on May 10, 1291. As the skeptical historians G. W. Foote and J. M. Wheeler wrote, "But it was too precious a memorial of the true faith to be left there; and after a rest of three years, during which its angelic conveyancers were perhaps recovering from the fatigue of their first journey, it suddenly and miraculously appeared in the Papal state of Loretto, a few miles from Ancona."

But pieces of the True Cross commanded the most attention and the largest crowds. Slivers and small chunks of wood that were claimed to be parts of the cross were traded, willed, and sold throughout the centuries. The Venetians bought a piece for twenty-five thousand lire and then turned around and sold it for more to Baldwin I of Jerusalem in the early twelfth century. In 586 Gregory the Great gave a couple cross-shaped slivers of wood to Recaredo, Spain's first Christian king. Half of the cross was shown to the faithful on Easter Day in Jerusalem—until it was captured by the Persians (who also captured the city of Jerusalem) in 614. Thirteen years later, the Christian emperor Heraclius I recaptured it, an event still celebrated today as the Feast of the Triumph of the Cross on September 14. The chunk of wood was then brought to Constantinople (reportedly led by four elephants in front of the emperor's chariot) before finally making its way back to Jerusalem two years later.

The Persian emperor Saladin took Jerusalem in 1187, and Richard the Lion Heart asked him for the chunk of the True Cross in the 1190s. The queen of Georgia reportedly offered two hundred thousand dinarii for it. Both were denied and the True Cross was reportedly never seen again. But more parts would miraculously come forth—enough pieces to later launch a thousand quips from Protestant reformers, the most famous coming from John Calvin: ". . . if all pieces that could be found were collected together, they would make a big shipload. Yet the Gospel testifies that a single man was able to carry it."

There were at least twenty-nine locations that claimed to have at least one of the four nails used to crucify Christ: Aachen, Ancona, Arras, Bamberg, the convent of Andechsen in Bavaria, Carpentras, Catana, Colle in Tuscany, Cologne, Compiègne, Krakow, the Escurial in Madrid, Florence, Livorno, Milan, Monza, Naples, Paris, Rome's Santa Croce in Gerusalemme and Santa Maria in Campitelli, Siena, Spoleto, Torcello, Torno (on Lake Como), Toul, Trèves, Troyes, Venice (which had three nails), and Vienna.

That's a lot of potential piercings of Christ's body. Some of these nails could have been used to hold the cross together. Also, St. Helena took her four nails and divided them up into twelve pieces, which she gifted from time to time. And sometimes nails that had touched the real nails were confused for the real thing.

Not as prolific as pieces of the cross, but more widespread and well-trafficked than the nails, was the crown of thorns placed on Jesus' head during the crucifixion. There were allegedly up to seventy thorns distributed throughout Europe, along with a few thornless crowns (the thorns having been chipped off and gifted or sold). Louis IX, that great relic collector, apparently had a crown, which he acquired as a "gift," and, in return, gave a "gift" back in cash, so as not to be accused of the buying and selling of holy relics. But long before Louis, the crown of thorns first surfaced in the fourth century, the story being that the crown was yet another discovery of St. Helena. Like many secondary Christ relics, the crown of thorns found its way to Constantinople, where it rested alongside a piece of the cross, nails, the lance used to pierce Christ's side, the hyssop reed and the sponge used to quench his thirst, as well as a pair of the Holy Sandals. Today it (perhaps not the same one) can be found in Paris's Notre Dame Cathedral.

As the millennial anniversaries of Christ's birth and death came and went, there was a stronger emphasis on Jesus Christ the man. And not coincidentally, it was about this time that bodily relics of both Christ and the Virgin began to emerge.

The diversity and multitude of these early remnants strain credibility. His umbilical cord could have been saved. And, in fact, it was: The Sancta Sanctorum was, as mentioned previously, the home of the Holy Umbilical Cord. An abbey at Soissons boasted Jesus' milk tooth. Some strands of the Virgin's hair made an appearance in a few different places. So did relics like the Holy Tear (which some industrious follower of Christ must have swooped up in a vial just before it hit the ground). Don't forget about the two-for-one relic, the Holy Bib—complete with breast milk stains from the Virgin. In fact, vials of the Virgin's breast milk were popular medieval relics—Calvin later quipped that had the Virgin been a cow she couldn't have produced so much breast milk. There were at least sixty-nine claimants to vials of the beloved *latte.*

But no relic could elicit a stronger reaction among the faithful than the Holy Blood. The relics of the Passion were headline attractions in any relics show and the blood was the star. Though drops of Jesus' blood were sprinkled around Europe, Bruges was the best-known claimant. The locals began an annual procession with the Holy Blood after the Belgian city was saved from the marauding French, which began in 1203 and has lasted into the twenty-first century. Because the blood would liquefy for the faithful every Friday, Pope Clement V gave his official stamp of approval on the Bruges blood in 1310 with an indulgence—a remission of temporal punishment due for sins that have already been forgiven—to those who came to venerate it (after an unnamed blasphemy occurred later that year the blood became stubborn and refused to perform its weekly trick, only liquefying once more in 1388).

By the late Middle Ages, shrines to superstar saints and their relics had become ubiquitous. But starting in the early Renaissance, shrines to the Virgin and Christ were more popular than ever. And thus there was an even greater need for relics of the venerable duo. Coinciding with the Reformation, the Holy Foreskin would have another headlining era before it would be consigned to a footnote in Church history.

Chapter 6

THE STENCH OF MYSTERY

The day my wife, Jessie, arrived was a monumental one for me. So far, my search for the foreskin had yielded absolutely nothing. A familiar face, I figured, would be a very welcome sight. She brought Abraham Lincoln—our ten-pound miniature pinscher/ Chihuahua mix—with her and while she slept off her jet lag I took him out to get acquainted with Calcata. One would think this fortress town, with car-free lanes and alleys and just one exit and entrance, would be a heaven for unleashed dogs. It wasn't. The village had its own hierarchy of beasts, a few dogs competing for *capobranco*—head of the pack—status. Which meant that any other male dogs that got in their way, even ten-pound miniature pinscher/Chihuahua mixes, would be eaten. Gemma, the Belgian woman who ran the teahouse, was walking her dog one day when Puma, a pony-size Irish wolfhound, approached. Gemma picked up her dog and, as Puma lunged up, held her pooch even higher. It didn't matter: Puma managed to wrestle the canine out of her arms and, right in front of Gemma's eyes, disemboweled the dog. After the incident, Puma was kept on a leash full-time in front of his owner's apartment outside the walls of the village. Then there was Willie. He and his owner, Angelo, the so-called village burglar, were possibly the most detested duo in Calcata. Willie, who was at least half wolf, was practically a serial killer, having butchered a half-dozen dogs.

Another threat to dogs was Capellone, the "quasi Nazi" I spent my first day in Calcata with. He worked for the town as a sort of janitor, emptying village trash cans, picking up dog and cat dung, and doing other odd jobs around the medieval village and Calcata Nuova. As the story goes, every once in a while, perhaps under the influence of bad wine, he'd revert to a brilliant scheme of his: If there were fewer dogs and cats running around, he'd be able to spend less time cleaning and more time in his wine cellar. So meatballs would magically appear on the streets of both villages loaded with enough rat poison to topple a pachyderm. The last time a rash of magic meatballs had hit the streets, Pancho—the American who runs La Grotta dei Germogli—lost one of his beloved canines (about a dozen dogs were killed in all).

But on this morning, Abraham Lincoln securely on a leash, it was the cats who were threatening. The village was crammed with dozens of felines, no one really sure which were strays and which belonged to people. Abraham Lincoln and I walked down the steps of our apartment and toward the square. On the relatively wide Via Garibaldi (about ten feet across), cats came out of nowhere, lining up along each side, their noses sticking out to get a whiff of the newcomer. Some arched their backs. Others hissed. Abraham Lincoln walked tentatively through the all-feline gauntlet. Suddenly a black cat charged and Abraham Lincoln froze, looking straight ahead at impending doom. She gave him a quick sniff and then retreated down an alleyway. And the rest of the cats followed. After that morning, they never paid any mind to him again.

After a walk around the village, the midday summer heat bouncing off the cobblestones, Abraham Lincoln and I were almost back home when he encountered a black Pomeranian. I didn't think it was threatening, but I was doubly reassured when the dog's owner poked his head out of a café and called for him. "Kiss-Kiss," he yelled in a soft, wispy voice, pronouncing it like "kees-kees." The man, whose shoulder-length hair and colorful clothing belied his fifty-something age, stepped out of the café when he saw our dogs mingling. "She is in heat?" he asked.

I introduced myself, and—in near-perfect English—the Gianni Macchia show began. Act one was a tour of the café he owns, which was more like a temple to Macchia himself, bedecked with posters of movies he'd starred in. Gianni had been a movie star in the 1970s, playing the lead role in a dozen or so Italian films. From the look of the posters, it was immediately clear these weren't box office smashes. Gianni would probably prefer to describe them as art house hits, which is possible, but they would have also fit in nicely on Cinemax. As Gianni went on about the time he let Bianca Jagger stay at his Rome apartment after she'd split with Mick, I furtively glanced at the posters: There was young Gianni humping a lady; there he was in a postcoital moment; there he was with a machine gun darting through the streets.

For act two, he took me upstairs. He owned the entire building, which was called the Palazzo di Cristo because for centuries it was the sometime-home of the local archbishop. The walls and ceiling of the stairway leading up to the first floor were coated in colorful murals that Gianni had painted. Near the kitchen, a confessional remained in place. The top floor, which he sometimes rented out, boasted a dramatic antique four-poster bed. As in the rest of the palace, the walls were painted with grotesque figures.

On the way back down we passed by the dining room, which was centered by a large wooden table with an ornate and gaudy chandelier hanging above it that would have made Liberace proud. "Sometimes here, we entertain some personalities," he said.

Which brings us to act three of the Gianni Macchia show:

The "we" in his last statement, I'd soon find out, referred to his "assistant," Gianni (aka Little Gianni) who had "worked" with Gianni Macchia for a couple decades. Little Gianni was at least twenty years Big Gianni's junior. He was slightly more effeminate than Big Gianni, and cute and sweet and a little dumb. As I sat with Little and Big Gianni in front of the café sipping espresso, we were joined by an older woman whose large ruby jewelry and perfectly quaffed dyed red hair screamed aristocracy. And if I hadn't figured that out, I would have when she introduced herself as a *contessa*, a countess. Italians love titles, especially ones that imply a wealthy (i.e., upper-class) family history. Little Gianni bombarded me with questions about Chelsea clubs as the contessa and Big Gianni translated for me.

"What about the relic that was here?" I finally asked. "Do you know anything about it?"

"Oh, that *prepuzio*," the contessa said, "that's gone." She didn't appear to care too much about the relic, which surprised me when she began quizzing me about my own spiritual beliefs. I told her I was Catholic, which was partly true.

"Why don't you come to mass with me on Sunday?" the contessa asked. "You were probably going to go anyway, yes?"

"Uh . . . yes, I was thinking of going," I lied. But it was a great idea. I'd get my first look at Don Dario.

Before she could add any more, Gianni Macchia's soft voice interrupted. "You should talk to Patrizia," he said. "She knows a lot about the relic."

"Yes, I've heard," I said. "But I also heard she doesn't talk to many people about it. I'd pay her for it, though," I added. "After all, if she's done a bunch of research, it would be the same as paying a research assistant."

"She's a good friend of mine," Gianni added, before taking a sip of espresso. "I'll talk to her for you."

And with that, I sort of had my first lead. Well, it was more like a lead to a lead. But I was happy.

The next morning, there was a knock on my door. I was baffled at first, since few people really knew where we lived. When I swung open the door, there was Gianni Macchia, naked except for a pair of dark blue Speedos.

"Come to the café this afternoon around sixteen o'clock," he said. "And if we see Patrizia, you can ask her anything you want and I will translate for you."

As I thanked him profusely, he said he had a gift for me, handing me a small book and walking down the steps to the cobbled lane below. It was a book about his art, and as I leafed through it, I saw the book largely consisted of self-taken photos of a nude Gianni. Most were full-frontal angles, and in many he was fully erect.

Later that afternoon, I sat down outside Caffe Kafir, hoping to make a Patrizia spotting. Little Gianni and the contessa were still sitting there, gossiping about everyone who walked by. Gianni Macchia emerged from the café and, standing on the threshold of the building, announced, "Oh, look, here she is! Here is Patrizia!"

Approaching us, about forty feet away, was a woman with slicked-back gray hair, a round owlish face, and an advanced Buddha belly. She was wearing a purple sari-like gown and was walking a furry black cat on a leash. Was this a Holy Foreskin expert, I wondered, or someone who'd spent way too much time in the ashram? Still, because she held the information I so dearly desired, my stomach tightened up. Everyone I'd talked to so far had said, "Just ask Patrizia, just ask Patrizia," and now that I was about to ask her, I feared that a failure would be a permanent dead end to my quest.

Gianni ran over and introduced us. Patrizia threw a ruby red scarf over her shoulder and rotated between a smug smile and nervous giggles. The two made quick exchanges in Italian and then Gianni looked at me and asked what questions I had for the oracle.

I told him that I wanted to know about the history of Calcata and I'd heard that she was the one to talk to.

It depended, said Patrizia, on specifically what I wanted to know.

"Well, if I had to choose," I said, pausing for a second, as if I were really deliberating in my mind, "I'd have to choose the foreskin."

"That's what I thought," Patrizia said, and then let out one of her nervous giggles. She wanted to know what I was going to do with the information.

I shrugged. "I don't know. It's just something that interests me." And then she asked me if I was a journalist. I didn't lie.

"I'm writing a book about the foreskin," she said, "and I'm not going to talk about it until my book is done."

"When do you think it will be done?" I asked.

She shrugged and said she'd been working on it for years.

"That's a shame, because I was willing to pay," I said, finally pulling out my trump card in the form of cold, hard cash.

"Well, I *can* be bought," she said. "It just depends what you're going to do with the information and if I get credit for it."

Patrizia would later tell me that she hadn't just *wandered* over like it had seemed. Gianni had gone to her earlier that day and told her about me and that I'd be waiting there at four o'clock. "I can get some money out of him for you," he had apparently said to Patrizia.

"You'd get credit." I said. "Definitely. But I really don't know what I'm going to do with the information."

"I'm going to have to think about it," Patrizia said. "But because you're not being very specific with me, I'll say that I'm not likely to agree." And with that she and her leashed black cat walked away.

I looked at Gianni and he shrugged his shoulders—and then, perhaps not knowing what else to say, said, "Did you like the book I gave you this morning?"

In fact, I did like the book he'd given me. At the very least, it gave me something to read. One thing I found out quickly about Calcata was that if you didn't have a car, you were stuck. And if it was during the week, when many of the restaurants shut down, there was absolutely nothing happening. Having already exhausted my lead with Patrizia, I had nowhere else to go and nothing to do. So, I spent a lot of time sitting at the sole table in our apartment. I'd already read Gianni's penis book a few times and had moved on to trying to read a pile of Italian celebrity gossip magazines that Scot, one of the small handful of Americans in Caclata, had given me. On this particular evening, with Jessie visiting a friend in Rome, the door wide open, the thunder gurgling deep into the black sky, I was engrossed in an article about an Italian reality TV star's high school grades (she apparently was more interested in boys than history and math).

And so here I was sitting in a house atop this near-360-degree island of cliffs wondering if the months and months I was about to spend in Calcata were going to be just as uneventful as this night. Outside my open door, fog was wafting past. In sunlight, Calcata is a stunner. But in fog, it almost feels like time and space have imploded, turning the village into an atavistic medieval fortress, complete with thick walls and lookout towers. The opaque, dreamy atmosphere, the narrow lanes with their chunky cobblestones—originally brought up from the riverbed—really do seem like the perfect place for a mysterious relic like the Holy Foreskin. In fact, after the relic's discovery, climatic miracles occurred in the form of a very similar meteorological constipation.

I sighed and went back to the magazine article I'd been chugging through, when I heard a knock on the door. I looked up to find Stefania leaning against the frame of the doorway.

"Ciao," she said.

Stefania, who looks like a younger, curvier version of Susan

Sarandon, is half of the team (along with her ex, Alessandro) who rent out rooms and apartments in the village (in fact, it's the closest thing Calcata has to a hotel). The apartment I was in wasn't theirs, but they had helped me find it. And because of that, I suppose, they wanted to make sure we were happy here so far. Alessandro had installed a phone cable into our apartment from his place—which was about seventy-five feet away—just so we could have Internet access. And when Stefania asked me if the apartment was comfortable and I remarked that it would be nice to have something to sit on other than a wooden chair, she'd arranged to have an unused couch put in the apartment. Stefania and Alessandro had split up a couple years before, but were still living together for the sake of their two cute young daughters, Svetlana and Aman. Alessandro was at the beach with the girls all month and Stefania seemed to be enjoying her freedom.

I poured a glass of wine and was holding it out to Stefania, when I noticed she was staring at the stack of magazines that Scot had given me on the fireplace mantle.

"You read *Diva e Donna*?" she asked, cracking a smile and looking at me with a squinted, sideward glance.

"Yes, it's true," I said. "I'm a loyal *Diva e Donna* reader." I grabbed the magazine I'd been reading at the table and flipped back a few pages to the article on the pope's cats. "How could I really understand Italy without knowing about this?"

She laughed and took the glass of wine I'd put in front of her. "So, is everything okay? Do you need something?"

"No, not really. I'm okay," said, deciding not to admit that I had just been wondering what the hell I was doing here.

"David, can I ask you something?"

"Sure."

"Why are you here? In Calcata."

I was reluctant to just come straight out and say it. Whenever I'd brought up the relic so far, I'd orchestrated the conversation so that my question about it would seem like it was just in passing. But maybe it was the half bottle of wine I'd already imbibed. Or more like it was the desperation I'd already sunk to, but I decided to say it.

"I'm here to find the *prepuzio*," I said, using the Italian word for foreskin.

She stared at me for a long five seconds, probably trying to discern if there was as much sarcasm in my voice as a few seconds ago when we'd been talking about the pope's cats. "Really?"

"Yes, really," I said.

"This is why you come to Calcata?" she asked. "For the *prepuzio*?" The tone in her voice was as if I'd told her that I'd moved to Italy to learn how to become a safer, more responsible driver.

I pointed my eyes to the ground and felt my face get red.

"You know it's not here, right? It was taken more than twenty years ago."

"Yes, I know. But if I want to find it, isn't Calcata the best place to start?"

"Maybe. But I think better is that you go to Torino."

Turin, as it's called in English, is tucked away in the northwest corner of Italy and the only things I knew about it were that Fiat and the famous Shroud of Turin were based there. "Why would it be in Torino?"

"You don't know?" she asked, as if I were missing something obvious. "Torino is the capital of magic."

And with Stefania's big eyes staring back at me, I suddenly felt what I later would call a "Calcata Moment"; when an event or image or, in this case, someone's statement, would remind me that I was not in just any Italian hill town in central Italy. I was living in one of the most bizarre places on the planet. Yes, maybe there are stranger places, but relative to the culture Calcata largely eschews, the place was nuts. And you need only scratch the surface with your pipe cleaner to figure it out.

But despite all the hippy/new age jargon, people spoke with conviction and at times it kind of made sense. For example, as odd as it sounded to refer to a place as the "capital of magic," Turin, I'd later find out, really did have a reputation as having "strange vibes." According to occultists, Turin is part of the vortex of two mystical triangles: an axis of black magic, which it shares with London and San Francisco; and an axis of white magic, which it shares with Lyon and Prague.

Turin attracted the ultimate occult figure, Nostradamus, and is home to one of the Christian world's most famed (and controversial) relics, the Shroud of Turin, as well as a supposed piece of the True Cross. It's the place that finally drove Nietzsche mad. It had some serious occultist cred.

My mind began racing. When was the earliest I could go there? Who could I find in such a big city—a city in which I knew no one—to help me locate a tiny two-thousand-year-old foreskin? I pressed Stefania for more details.

She shrugged. "I don't know anything about it. It just seems that might be a place where it would be."

"So you don't have any solid evidence for this theory?"

"Not so much. But it is possible, no?"

I suddenly felt deflated again, but as outlandish as Stefania's theory sounded, at this point, anything was possible.

"Maybe," she added, "you should speak to Athon about this. If someone in Calcata knows something about the occult, it's Athon. You know her?"

I had just briefly met Athon, known to the children in the village as "*la Strega*" (the Witch), thanks to her long stringy red hair, wrinkled sexagenarian face, and the thick eyeliner she paints around her eyes. And the cave on the edge of one of Calcata's cliffs she shares with a dozen crows.

"Oh, yes," I said to Stefania. "I met Athon a few days ago and she invited me to meet her birds."

Stefania laughed, knowing what I was in for.

A couple days later, I woke up early, ready for my church date with the contessa. I wasn't exactly thrilled about the idea of sitting through a long mass (I'd be praying for brevity), and I was looking forward to finally getting an eyeful of Don Dario, the only person who really knows what happened to the relic. It was my ultimate goal to ask him about it, and I'd probably increase my chances of scoring an interview with him if he'd seen my face at a Sunday service or two.

For important religious holidays, masses were held in the old church in the medieval borgo, but all other masses were in the new village. Famed architect and Calcata resident Paolo Portoghesi had been commissioned to build a new church in Calcata Nuova, finally replacing the double-wide camper-like structure they'd been using for the last three decades, but Portoghesi's soaring crown-shaped structure was only half finished.

As the contessa and I approached the church in Calcata Nuova, the functionalist city hall at our backs, she told me about the difficult night's sleep she'd had, saying stomach pains and frequent trips to the bathroom kept her up all night. We sat down in the penultimate pew. About a dozen other people were sprinkled throughout the room, which was lined with metal siding and bedecked with terra cotta relief sculptures of the scenes of the Stations of the Cross that looked like they had just been purchased at a dollar store. I let my eyes wander around the church as the contessa held her stomach with one hand and fanned herself with a prayer book. People chatted in whispered tones until a short, round man entered the church behind us, wearing black slacks and a collared shirt, the kind you see middle-aged suburban golfers wearing in the United States. "That's Don Dario," the contessa whispered to me.

And so the village priest, onetime guardian of the Holy Foreskin, appeared, wearing a golf shirt to mass! He disappeared behind another door to the left of the altar and a few minutes later emerged wearing an off-white chasuble. Everyone stood and began to sing.

Before the hymm was over, something was amiss in my pew. An odor made an appearance, one that made my olfactory glands want to stand up and sprint out of the church. I glanced at the contessa, standing to my right; she was singing along. I tried holding my breath, but when I ran out of air, I had no choice but to breathe again and suck in the fumes. It smelled like someone had been eating the classic Roman dish pajata—veal intestines with the mother's milk (and literally all kinds of shit) still inside—and it was as if that veal intestine had been waiting until it had a captive audience to make a grand entrance. Those sitting behind the contessa and me, looking to cast blame, had to choose between a stately blue-blooded old lady and a lumpy blond foreigner. I was the easy target, the evildoer. The woman directly behind the contessa made eye contact with me and ruffled her nose.

Don Dario began a soliloquy about something, but I couldn't pay attention; as his sermon went on, the time between gas emissions grew shorter and shorter. After blessing the wine and host, he rang a bell and we all stood there as he lifted a wine-filled grail above his head and then put it to his lips. He lifted his head back and gulped the wine, wiping his mouth with a white cloth napkin. Finally, a few minutes later, it was time for the communion and everyone except for me lined up in front of Don Dario, including the contessa. I was left sitting in the unholy stench, and as the line processed past me, the communicants glared at me.

After mass, I asked the contessa if she knew Don Dario, hoping she'd be able to make an introduction for me. She said she didn't. In fact, she didn't really even like him much. "He is a country priest," she said dismissively, relegating him to holy hillbilly status. "The priests in Rome are better. Sometime when you are in Rome, we can go to my church."

It seemed natural that we'd wander over to Gianni Macchia's

café after mass—since it was at the café's one outside table where the contessa and I usually saw each other—but once we got back to the village she excused herself, saying she was going to stay inside for the day in the hope her stomach might recover.

Which, for obvious reasons, I thought was a great idea. After that day at church, I never saw the contessa again—not because of health problems or because of embarrassment, but because she spent the majority of her time in Rome. Which meant I could spend less of my time at mass and more time doing some less-than-holy tasks.

Chapter 7

ITALIAN FOR DUMMIES

T he woman who pulled up beside me on the rural road probably had me pegged as crazy, retarded, or both. She was screaming at me, but I understood nothing, so she resorted to bad English. "Money. For eating," she said, cupping her hand and making a shovel motion to her mouth. Driving around wasting gasoline seemed like a counterintuitive way to beg for money. So much so I could only stare back at her, saying nothing like some kind of useless imp. She drove away in frustration, but only got about five hundred feet before I saw her turn around. As she got closer, she swung her car over to me again. "You crazy walking this hour," she said, lowering her window. And then she tried handing me a ten-euro bill.

I suppose that walking a three-mile stretch of barren road between two isolated villages during hundred-degree heat while wearing blue jeans was not a fantastic advertisement for one's sanity. But it was a small price to pay for a can opener, which I desperately needed. I was on my way back from Faleria—a couple miles away—where I'd gone in search of one. But because I couldn't understand the directions to the can opener store, I was walking back to Calcata empty-handed. Maybe I should have taken that ten euros after all.

I've tried learning a handful of languages in my lifetime, and at least at the beginning, I always have the same problem: I can speak adequately well, posing questions like an intermediate speaker, but I can't comprehend anything spoken back to me, which means I can ask a lot of nice-sounding questions, and then it's like I'm deaf. Though I should have been used to this by now, I still verbally beat myself up the rest of the way to Calcata: How was I going to find a missing Holy Foreskin if I couldn't even understand directions to a appliance store?

There were several other things I still needed: a lamp to illuminate the loft at night so Jessie and I could read in bed, a tea kettle, and a rug for Abraham Lincoln (besides baths and the vet, he hates nothing more than bare floors). Given that there were so few shops around, I wasn't sure where I'd get them. More important, I wasn't sure how to understand directions to the places that sold them.

I had to learn how to speak Italian. Or rather, how to understand Italian. Desperately.

I have a long personal history of this type of learning (or, more appropriately, not learning). One day in the fourth grade I was yanked out of my class and given a series of tests. Afterward I was told I'd have to come to a class for three hours every day. I had, the teacher of this "special" class explained very slowly to me and my parents, a learning disability. Phrases like "slow learner" and "bad comprehension" were mentioned. My parents then relayed the information to my siblings, saying that from now on they'd have to talk to me slowly and give me just . . . one . . . command . . . at . . . a . . . time.

When my older brother would see me traipsing up to the front door after baseball practice, he'd tell me to go inside and get him a garbage bag. When I'd come out and extend the bag in his direction, he'd point to various piles of leaves he'd just raked, and say, "Now. Put. Leaves. In. Bag." I had suddenly become the village idiot in my house.

I went to the "retarded people's class," as everyone in the "normal" class called it, every day until I graduated high school. The teachers in the special education class didn't really teach as much as feed us the information we needed. In junior high, for example, I had the benefit of being able to take all my tests in the special education class. So, when there was a big exam in my history class, my teacher would hand me the test, and I'd leave for the special ed room. Once there, the teacher would hand me the "teacher's edition" of the history book, which had all the answers in the back, wish me good luck, and walk away. I'd copy down the answers, sometimes verbatim if I was feeling lazy, and head back to my class. A week later, I'd get the test back with an excellent grade, the teachers in my history and science and health-ed classes never questioning how I'd written the exact same answer that was in the teacher's edition of their books.

It didn't take a "special person" to figure out that the teachers and school administrators didn't really care if I or my peers overcame whatever learning disabilities we supposedly had; they wanted to get us through the system, so we could go out in the world and become productive underachievers. Even my best friend in high school told his girlfriend (which eventually got back to me) that I'd "never amount to anything in life."

Which is maybe why I sometimes fostered this image myself: In the seventh grade we had to take a survey about what occupation we thought we'd end up in when we grew up. I scanned the list of 150 different professions and then called out, "Where's 'Garbage Man'?" Everyone in the class—even the teacher—roared with laughter; not only because of the implied class issues in my joke, but because it was coming from the guy in class who seemed most likely to actually become a garbage man.

I knew that I learned differently, but I was never exactly sure what my supposed learning disability was. Especially after gradu-

ating from high school, when I had nothing else to do but to follow many of my friends to the local community college. I actually
excelled, earning great grades and, two years later, graduating with
honors. I then transferred to the University of California, Santa
Cruz, a four-year university with a respectable reputation. I also
graduated with honors there. Eventually, I went on to earn a master's degree in history. And I took the tests without looking at the
teacher's edition of the book. Really. I promise.

It gave me a confidence in intellectual abilities I'd never
thought I had. People could tell me two or more commands at
the same time and I'd actually understand. But then here I was in
Calcata, trying to learn Italian and feeling like I was back in the
fourth grade, not comprehending a thing. This time there was no
Classe dei Retardati in which to flee. No teacher's edition to filch
all the right answers from. There's not even a school in Calcata, of
course.

Then, after that pile of celebrity weeklies from Scot appeared
on my doorstep, I dove in, writing down every word I didn't
know. It took me about two full days to get through the first issue
of *Diva e Donna* (*Diva & Woman*), but by the next issue I could really see progress: I had to look up fewer and fewer words. I wasn't
sure how many times I'd actually say or hear "*tappeto rosso*" (red
carpet), "*seduzione*" (seduction), "*scandalo*" (scandal), and "*casa di ri-
abilitazione*" (rehab), but at least I was understanding something.

I tried talking to people again. And I set a goal that I'd have to
have at least one conversation a day. In time I even found a can
opener. So when I was walking to another one of the surrounding villages to find a reading lamp and another car slowed down
beside me, I decided I'd chat up whoever was in the car. It was
Costantino Morosin, a longtime resident of Calcata and one of
the most famous artists living there today. We had met the other
night at the Grotta when, sitting at the table next to me, he turned
and began asking me questions. Where was I from? Why was I
in Calcata? I understood the first few basic queries, but then

nothing after that. And we "talked" for about an hour. From what I could comprehend, as I stood there at his white pickup truck on the side of the road, he was asking me if I wanted to accompany him to nearby Lake Bracciano, where he was briefly meeting with someone. Costantino speaks no English whatsoever, which made having to spend an entire evening with him a challenge. I jumped in.

As we sat on the shores of the massive lake formed by a volcanic crater, I watched the plus-size sculptor with the gray Baby Huey ponytail scream at a Romanian mason who was doing some reconstruction work on his house in Calcata. I jotted down words I hadn't heard before to look up or ask someone to define later.

- *Fare cagare* (literally "to make one poop"), meaning something is very bad.
- *Non fare un cazzo* (literally "to not do a penis"): a slang term that could be translated as "to do absolutely fucking nothing."
- *Finisci il lavoro domani:* finish the job tomorrow.

I think I had a pretty good idea what the *disaccordo* (disagreement) was about. Later Costantino and I had dinner at a nearby restaurant in the town of Trevignano. We snacked on fried seafood and talked about . . . something. He showed me photos of his artwork on his Palm Pilot, which were computer-generated images of maps that, if you looked close enough, were made up of stick figures that seemed to be in a constant state of motion. The only work I'd previously seen of his were the bulbous stone Etruscan-styled thrones that sit in the square. I'd always admired them, but people here said the thrones were not even close to his best work.

As usual, when it came to talking about his art (or, really, anything), I understood little. I'd ask him questions and he'd give me long-winded answers. He'd occasionally ask if I understood, and occasionally, I'd admit that I didn't. He'd stop and, in Italian, try to explain to me what individual words meant. Costantino didn't seem to mind listening to himself talk, even when the person he was talking to couldn't understand a word, but I appreciated that he was giving me the chance. It takes a lot of energy to spend an entire evening with someone who can't understand anything you're saying.

The next day, while sitting on the doorstep at the top of the steps that lead up to my apartment, I saw Gemma, the Belgian woman who runs the teahouse. She was standing around looking somewhat bored. We'd exchanged a few words, almost always in English, but I was starting to feel more confident about speaking Italian. It was stupid of me, but without really thinking about it, I blurted out one of the phrases I'd learned from Costantino.

"*Non fai un cazzo?*" I asked.

"What?" she answered back in Italian. "Do you mean, 'Am I doing nothing?'"

"*Sì,*" I answered, somewhat cheerily because I understood what she had said in Italian.

She stormed away. Maybe, I thought, she'd heard her phone ringing and had to go answer it. But I saw her a few more times that afternoon around the village and she ignored me. People used the word *cazzo* so freely around Calcata, I wasn't expecting Gemma to react so strongly—which was as if I'd said something like, "Yo, wassup, bitch?"

Up at the bar in Calcata Nuova, Mario and Piero had spotted me walking by on my way to the food shop. They ushered me over and plopped a glass of prosecco in my hand. I mentioned the phrase I'd said to Gemma.

"Should I say this to a woman?" I asked.

The seven or eight men, who were sitting in a circle, wagged their fingers at me and erupted into a chorus of "No, no, no, no!"

"Never say this to a woman," one of the men said. Or at least I think he said. "This is talk for the bar—not for the ladies."

The next afternoon I went to the tearoom to see Gemma.

"I'd like to apologize for what I said to you yesterday," I said, this time in English.

"For me," she said, "this phrase is worse than cursing."

I explained to her that in trying to learn this language, I was still getting a feel for what was okay to say and what wasn't okay to say.

"I understand," she said. "It's just that this is not a phrase an educated person would say. It's for stupid and retarded people."

Chapter 8

THE ULTIMATE
CIRCUMCISION

Before going to Calcata, I hadn't thought much about circumcision. Sure, I'd heard about the recent movement among American men who were angry their genitals had been manipulated without their consent. On eBay, one can find several serious-looking devices that promise to somehow reverse circumcision. But for the foreskin-envious, eBay sellers offer another solution: prosthetic rubber foreskins. "Have you ever wondered what it would be like to have a foreskin?" the makers of the product ask. "Just put it on in the morning and keep it here all day long." I did ask my mom once why she'd had me circumcised at birth. "That's just what you did," she said in a defensive tone, the same tone she used when I asked her if she had smoked when she was pregnant with me.

The United States is the only developed country that practices circumcision in boys for nonreligious purposes. The practice in the United States became institutionalized in the Victorian era, when doctors such as P. C. Remondino, who in 1891 wrote a history of the procedure that included details about the Holy Foreskin, became convinced that the surgery could prevent nearly a hundred diseases, including epilepsy, asthma, gout, kidney disease, and even alcoholism. Keep in mind this was at the same time doctors were also treating women for hysteria by giving them a "vagina massage." The consensus among doctors of the Victorian age was that circumcision would lead to less masturbation—that, for them, was its main merit.

The circumcision of newborn boys in the United States went unquestioned until the mid–twentieth century, when a few doctors began wondering if it was necessary (or even harmful). Today, opinions on the procedure are more divided than ever, especially after a recent study concluded that circumcision can reduce the risk of HIV infection by 50 percent.

Despite all this, I didn't actually have a strong opinion on circumcision one way or the other. Pancho, the talented mosaic artist and chef/owner of the Grotta dei Germogli, did. He had strong opinions on a lot of things and loved expressing them. I'd spent enough time snuggled up to the bar in the Grotta to hear his views on a lot of stuff. And eventually, when I began going out to breakfast a few times a week with Pancho and his longtime friend Paul (the eighty-seven-year-old American choreographer), I was subjected to various (and often conflicting) opinions. Every morning about ten A.M. they'd drive over to one of the neighboring villages for a tramezzino (a half a sandwich with the crusts cut off and filled with various tasty ingredients) and a cappuccino. But there were rules. Don't talk to Pancho while he reads the paper. Don't talk to Pancho if we go food shopping afterward (because he would add up the items in his head, knowing how much money he wanted to spend). And last, as Pancho mentioned to me one day while we were walking to his car where we'd meet Paul: "Don't bring up circumcision with Paul."

Pancho and Paul had been friends for over thirty years. They'd traveled together, partied together, danced together, lived together, and gone into business together (the Grotta was owned by both of them). Pancho became a professional dancer only because of

Paul, who had, by the time Pancho was in his late twenties (he was now in his mid-fifties) achieved legendary status in Italy. Paul did something few choreographers had done before him: He eschewed ballet. For those not initiated into the history of modern dance, this would be like the general manager of the Yankees forgoing the organization's minor league teams and recruiting street players instead. It was maverick move by Paul that actually paid off, and it gave a lot of people a chance to become dancers who either started late (as in Pancho's case) or whose upbringing—for cultural or financial reasons—didn't expose them to ballet at an early age. He always had a unique way of looking at things. Quite randomly, I met an American woman in Rome who actually had taken one of Paul's dance classes decades earlier. She said there were a handful of Down syndrome and mentally challenged people in the class, who Paul encouraged. The woman told me Paul had said something during the class she'll never forget. Halfway into a dance routine he was leading them through, he said, "We're all mentally disabled. It's just that some of us are more than others."

For all the experiences Paul and Pancho shared together, they also have had their share of fights. A lot of them. I would become privy to many raucous arguments, almost always over lunch and always after a couple bottles of wine. Often, the arguments they had were provocative—they'd pick up on a blowout fight they'd had ten years earlier on the nature of reality, for example. Another famous fight had taken place a few years before I arrived in Calcata over the topic of circumcision. Paul was for the procedure and Pancho was against it. The argument became so heated that they didn't talk for a year after that day. Which is why, on the first day that I was going out to breakfast with them, Pancho set down the new rule for me. So, I didn't bring up circumcision with Paul. Which is a shame because I'd just read a fascinating book the night before and wanted to tell them about it:

It seemed like a normal morning for Lorenzo, the story's pro-

tagonist, who was weaving his Vespa through the usual heavy traffic in the center of Rome, when his cell phone rang. It was Sofia,
his ex-girlfriend; the girl he'd been pining for since she walked
out on him two years earlier. She needed to meet with him. As
soon as possible. She couldn't give him any details over the phone,
so they arranged to have dinner that night in a small village in
Maremma, the southern coastal section of Tuscany.

Over dinner in a classic southern Tuscan restaurant, Sofia told
Lorenzo why she needed to meet him. She was a on a mission—a
quest to find a painting by Renaissance master Caravaggio that
the Vatican had hidden away centuries ago. She wanted to find it
in order to include the masterpiece in an upcoming retrospective
of the hot-tempered Renaissance painter. "Will you help me?"
Sofia asked.

Lorenzo agreed, hoping the quest would bring them back together. And not long after beginning their search, popping into
churches in small sun-bleached towns along the Tuscan coast,
talking to priests and other locals about the painting, they noticed
a short, stocky man shadowing them. A Vatican agent, perhaps?
Such a claim might seem silly, until Lorenzo finally asked why the
Church would want to hide a painting by one of the all-time
greatest artists anyway?

Sofia's answer was an unexpected one: because the painting's
theme is the circumcision of Jesus.

"Circumcision?" Lorenzo said dubiously. "But isn't that for
the Jews?"

"Exactly," Sofia said. "The Catholic Church doesn't want to
remind the faithful that Jesus was a Jew. Because of this, they've
hidden away this Caravaggio for four hundred years."

The story of Lorenzo and Sofia's quest isn't exactly a conspiracy
of *Da Vinci Code* proportions, but it's shocking enough—especially
when it comes from a pamphlet-size Italian-for-beginners book
called *L'Ultimo Caravaggio* (in English *The Last Caravaggio*). Unaware of the plotline, but hoping it would help my Italian, Jessie

had handed to me the book just before I was heading off to the airport to begin my own quest. The couple's search for the lost Caravaggio—in which I could actually read the book's basic see-Spot-run sentences—and the possible reasons for its disappearance, made me wonder about how and why Jesus' foreskin had first come into existence as an artifact.

There wasn't much talk in the Bible about the circumcision of Jesus. Circumcision has been practiced by many different peoples for thousands of years, but the procedure's introduction to Jewish culture, as told in the Old Testament book of Genesis, began when God paid a visit to ninety-nine-year-old Abraham and told him that if he'd only take a stone knife to his penis as a sign of his commitment to him, he'd grant Abraham (and his ninety-year-old wife, Sarah) fertility. Abraham did as he was told and nine months or so later, Sarah gave birth to a baby. And Abraham didn't stop there with his newfound fertility. After Sarah's death, he remarried and quickly fathered a child with his new wife, Keturah. Then he moved on to Hayar, his wife's maid.

In Genesis 17:7, God says to Abraham that all his descendants shall also enter into this covenant. And thus it became obligatory that all Jews would be circumcised, and mass adult circumcisions began taking place. Circumcision became—as in Egypt, where it was also practiced—a premarriage ritual of initiation, preparing the man's organ for procreation, and therefore the circumcised penis was a perfect sign of the covenant between God and the chosen people, that thanks to the sexual use of this organ, a man became, in a sense, an ally with God. For a Jew, circumcision was a literal mark of tribal identity. And, as with many ritualistic and religious practices, there's a commonsense reason behind it, principally improved hygiene and a lower risk of infection. Whether or not such considerations were an inspiration for humans to begin circumcision a few millennia ago is still a matter of debate.

Centuries later, when Jesus was born, the process had become routine: Newborn babies were circumcised on their eighth day of life, at which time they would also be officially named. So customary was this that the New Testament dedicates just one passage to Jesus' circumcision: Luke 2:21 states: "And when eight days had passed, before His circumcision, His name was then called Jesus, the name given by the angel before he was conceived in the womb."

Jesus' circumcision, known as the Holy Circumcision, was given more attention in the so-called Apocryphal Gospels. Some scholars argue that these "lost books" of the Bible, mostly written from the second to the fifth centuries after Christ, were meant to be a part of the New Testament, but were edited out by early Church leaders who wanted the new church's doctrine to conform to their vision of Christ and Christianity. Other scholars say these "Apocrypha" (from the Greek for "those that are hidden away") aren't the real word of God and rightfully don't belong in the Bible, evidenced by the incongruous portraits of Jesus in the Gospel of the Infancy, for example, which reads like the script of a B-grade horror movie. In it an adolescent Jesus exacts revenge with his superhuman powers on those who have wronged him. For example, when one boy runs up and knocks the young Savior to the ground, Jesus wills the boy dead. Another time, having aroused suspicion in school because of his genius-like intellect, he's taken to the principal's office. And when the schoolmaster attempts to whip the prepubescent Redeemer, Jesus makes the man's hand wither until he falls dead on the floor. Apprized of what has happened, Joseph says to Mary, "We will not allow him out of the house; for everyone who disciplines him is killed." In the Gospel of the Infancy, even the son of God, apparently, goes through a rebellious phase.

Though the Infancy Gospel contains fantastical touches such as these, it's important for the historical record—especially when it comes to the Holy Foreskin. Like the Gospel of Luke, the second-century Infancy Gospel tells us that Jesus was circumcised on his eighth day of life. In the Infancy Gospel the ritual takes place in a cave—perhaps because, at various times during Roman rule, circumcision was banned—and Jesus' foreskin is given to an old Hebrew woman, who puts it in an alabaster jar filled with aromatic nard—an oil known for its preservative qualities. She then gives it to her son, a druggist, and says, "Take heed, do not sell this alabaster box of spikenard ointment, even should you be offered three hundred pence for it." The gospel then says that "Mary the Sinner" (Mary Magdalene) ended up with it, and during the crucifixion, she "poured forth the ointment out of it upon the head and feet of our Lord Jesus Christ and wiped them off with the hairs of her head."

What immediately happened to the Holy Foreskin after that and why it disappeared for hundreds of years, only to reemerge centuries later, is anyone's guess. But for now what is most significant is that—true or not—the reference to Jesus' foreskin in the Infancy Gospel is the earliest written evidence of the *idea* of keeping it as a relic.

And fittingly enough, Christ's circumcision would be—at least symbolically—the ultimate circumcision. After Christ's death, the apostle Paul, keen to convert the gentile world to the cult of Christ, quickly realized that the difficulty of getting adults to undergo the procedure in order to become Christians would seriously impede the spread of the faith.

So, he ingeniously reinterpreted the covenant God had made with Abraham centuries earlier by morphing physical and spiritual circumcision, writing in his letters to the Galatians that ". . . if you let yourself be circumcised Christ will be of no value to you at all. . . . For in Jesus Christ, neither circumcision nor uncircumcision has any value. The only thing that counts is faith expressing itself through love" (Galatians 5:2–6). Thus, in Paul's new reading of the doctrine, Christ's circumcision becomes the final circumcision, the last one necessary to fulfill the covenant.

The Holy Circumcision was given a feast day on the Church calendar; fittingly enough, on the first of January, the eighth full day after Jesus' arbitrary birthday on December 25. Through the centuries, and particularly in the late medieval period, sermons would spring up on January 1 about the meaning of the Holy Circumcision. In the time before Christ, circumcision was laden with obvious fertility overtones. But thanks to Paul's tweaking of doctrine and later theologians' waxing lyrical about the Holy Circumcision's significance, the slicing of the Savior's foreskin was seen as his first sacrifice, his first blood spilling, and a foreshadowing of his ultimate sacrifice for humanity.

It's no surprise, then, that if you look hard enough, many artistic depictions of Jesus' circumcision or paintings make this metaphor plain. In Francesco Bonsignori's "Virgin Adoring the Sleeping Child," painted in 1483, the Christ child is lying on a slab of stone, his lower half completely exposed, while his mother, hands steepled over him, prays. As scholar Leo Steinberg observes in his book *The Sexuality of Christ in Renaissance Art and in Modern Oblivion*, "And over his exposed genitalia, the Madonna's hands form a canopy, a ciborium. It is as though the very structure of such images of foreboding intimated a tragic, anatomically localized vulnerability."

In fact, Renaissance painters favored surprisingly detailed paintings of the nude infant Jesus. These had little to do with sexuality; instead, the exposed Jesus was meant to reinforce the church doctrine of incarnation. Christ was all too human and he suffered just like the rest of us.

Holy Foreskin aside, one topic the Church probably doesn't feel too comfortable talking about is the pagan fertility rites and phallic worship that snuck into the religion. Look closely enough at the architectural and design details of Romanesque churches around Europe and you may see the occasional stone penis—and in some cases, penises—affixed to the façade, tucked away in a side chapel, or disguised on a corbel (that is, if they haven't been spirited away by authorities). More specifically, the penises that often quietly sat in churches and on church façades were erect.

And for good reason. The erect penis was a symbol of fertility. It was, much like the justification for circumcision in the Old Testament, the tool (no pun intended) with which to do God's work: to procreate. One author on the subject of Christian phallic worship in the Middle Ages even goes so far as to suggest that church authorities intentionally promoted the veneration of Jesus' foreskin as an acceptable substitute to open phallic worship.

I never did bring up circumcision with Paul, but later that week, at a restaurant on Rome's Appia Antica, where Paul, Pancho, Jessie, and I were enjoying our lunch of fusilli pasta drizzled with a rich pistachio sauce and several bottles of wine, Paul asked what I was reading at the moment. "Anything about the foreskin?" he added.

"Actually, I'm reading an interesting Italian-for-beginners book about a lost Caravaggio painting." I was tempted to tell them the story—just so I could sit through another entertaining argument—but I needed to get back to Calcata so I could recommence my investigation into another circumcision-related mystery.

Chapter 9

CA' DANTE

T ime after time when someone in Calcata would ask where I lived, I'd tell them the address, Via Garibaldi 23. In return, I'd get a blank stare. "Where's that?" they'd eventually ask. Since Calcata has fewer than a dozen lanes, I was initially baffled by people's ignorance of my street—especially because Via Garibaldi forms part of the main promenade with the square.

But then I learned that there really are no street names in Calcata. Sure, there are signs with names etched into them—my street, for example, Via Garibaldi, met up with Via Cavour, which is around the corner from Via della Pietà; there's also the intriguing Via della Porta Segreta (Way of the Secret Door), as well as Via della Scuola and Via San Giovanni. The two squares—which are connected and form an L shape—are officially called Piazza Umberto I and Piazza Vittorio Emanuelle II; but usually everyone in Calcata just refers to them singularly as "*la piazza*."

Calcata's streets follow a medieval street plan—meaning there's no logic to the scheme, the opposite of the street grid plan the Romans gave us, the same plan modern city planners employ. Instead, a "straight" alleyway will have an ever-so-slight bend in it, the square will be irregularly shaped (in Calcata's case, one of the two connected squares is triangular), and some lanes will just dead-end. It looks and feels organic, a true relic of the Middle Ages when there was no central authority to impose its own civic planning. Perhaps that's why, walking around the tiny uneven-cobbled streets of Calcata, it's easier to let our imaginations sweep us away, like we're not just touching the past we've grown so far away from, but we're in an entirely new dimension altogether.

I'd often sit on the top step of the stairway leading up to our apartment, radiating with a sense of homecoming that I'd only felt when I lived in pedestrian-friendly and meandering places such as Prague. *I'm happy here,* I'd think to myself, even when my search for the relic wasn't going so well. *I'm genuinely happy.* Calcata felt like a fantasyland where you could walk out your door and traipse down a crooked cobblestone lane—one only big enough for two people to fit past each other—and, twenty seconds later, be sitting down at a restaurant. A restaurant where not only everyone knows your name, they know your nickname, your favorite dish, and your sexual preference; they know that when you're drunk (which is way too often, in their opinion), you say bad words in Italian just for shock value; they know that you have a strange fascination with bears—not the animals, but the fat hairy gay men; they know that you were a bed wetter until you were twelve years old. As Lorenzo, a grumpy but sweet old man who always hung out on the piazza once said to me, "Our houses are so close, I know when you fuck your wife." Everyone knows everything about everyone else here, which is the curse and beauty of living in a walled village with the population of a hundred. You can't remain anonymous and unknown if you're on this island known as Calcata for longer than a couple weeks. I loved it. There were times that I thought I could stay here forever. A village where people know where nothing is and where everything is.

"They just gave the streets names so the postman will know

where to deliver letters," someone in Calcata once told me. For that reason, I'm surprised the hippies who eventually took over the village several decades back didn't try to change the names of the streets to reflect their own sensibilities. Piazza Jimi Hendrix has a nice ring to it. So does Via Flower Power. Who needs an intersection of Via Cavour and Via Garibaldi when you could have Via Haight and Via Ashbury? Via del Hashish would be appropriate in more ways than the obvious: Generations of Calcatesi cultivated cannabis down in the valley to use for various materials.

After the tumultuous year of 1968, in which young idealistic liberals had seen (and participated in) riots in Paris, Chicago, Rome, and other cities around the globe, a Soviet stomp on Czechoslovakia's attempt at "Socialism with a human face," and an increasing disillusionment with America's involvement in Vietnam, finding a quasi-abandoned medieval village in the environs of Rome in which to isolate yourself from much of the outside world must have been appealing. And when these young people started asking if these abandoned homes were for sale, the people in Calcata Nuova were happy to sell. After all, the village was under a death sentence, so why not sell a house that was going to be destroyed sooner or later? Word got out and soon enough, young bohemian artist types were gravitating to this groovy village. Best of all, there was no police presence.

As a result of the village's hippie inhabitants, Calcata has garnered a few not-so-flattering nicknames by Romans, the most frequent visitors (in the form of day trips). *"Paese di fricchettoni,"* village of freaks, is perhaps the most valid. While many of the hippies and artists who gravitated here were from Rome or had been living in Rome, the village has a *relatively* large amount of people from all over Italy. Which, by Italian standards, is an anomaly; according to a recent survey, 70 percent of Italians between twenty and thirty still live at home. Even more shocking, 50 percent of Italian adults live less than a mile from the house they grew up in. Italy is a country of *bambocioni*, "big babies": Men who are grown adults but still look to their mothers for emotional support (as well as laundry, cooking, and cleaning help). Because (most of) the men in Calcata have cut the cord and moved to an isolated hippie island, they're "freaks," literally outsiders.

Of course, there's a historical explanation for why the phenomenon known as Calcata would seem so strange to the Italian mind: For centuries Italy was separated into autonomous provinces—ruled by princes and popes, magnates and monarchs—with each region's identity, language, food, and culture slightly different from those of the next. A Sicilian would be like an alien to someone from Turin (especially when they would try speaking to each other in their respective dialects). And, as was the case in various parts of Italy during the Middle Ages, when central authority broke down, families sprang up to protect themselves, building tall stand-alone towers (a few of these towers are still scattered around Rome's Monti neighborhood, and the Tuscan town of San Gimignano is famous for them). One of the results, besides the lack of desire to move away from one's family, is that Italians have a stronger attachment to the area in which they were raised and have an immediate kinship with their family first, followed by people from their hometown. Everyone else is a foreigner. In Italy, you get used to people looking right through you like you're invisible.

And those who support the rival of your hometown's soccer team are, of course, enemies, soccer being one of the main demarcations of Italian tribalism. When there are two teams representing one region—such as A.S. Roma and S.S. Lazio—it can divide a town or village. Calcata Nuova, for example, has two bars: Bar Sportivo, near city hall, is a Lazio bar, its walls bedecked with posters and scarves of the team that, in general, attracts a right-leaning fan base. Bar Amigos, on the other side of the village (and the bar where I'd sometimes drink prosecco with Mario and Capellone and the guys), didn't have an explicit allegiance to a soccer team, but when I'd ask a Bar Amigos regular why he never went to the "other" bar in town, the common response was that it was "*sporco*" (dirty)—a description that referred more to the bar's regulars (and, perhaps, their soccer and political allegiances) than to the actual cleanliness of the establishment.

But that was Calcata Nuova. In the medieval village, things were much different. After considering how strange a traditional Italian might find a village that's populated with people from Sicily and Milan, Puglia and Venice, factor in the relatively large amount of expatriates—a small handful of Americans, a couple Belgians, one Dutch, a few Spaniards, one Colombian, one Bulgarian—and you've got a village that just doesn't seem very "Italian." A village of freaks.

Then if you took a look around, you'd see Patrizia wandering around wearing a complicated maroon sari-like outfit with a furry black cat on a leash; the sculptor Costantino Morosin with his gray ponytail spraying out over his head; Paul Steffen, the octogenarian American choreographer, wearing an Indian headdress matched with a pink jumpsuit. Athon Veggi, with her flaming red hair and hilarious bird laugh. Massimo, the owner of a wood sculpture gallery, wearing a white terry-cloth outfit who, from a distance, resembles Gandhi; you'd probably see the past-middle-aged Gianni Macchia, with his bleach-blond hair, dancing by himself to Eurotrash club music in front of his café. You'd also most likely see Angelo, the proclaimed "village burglar" who was somehow tolerated in a town where he was widely known for stealing things from others. Jessie and I were always perplexed by his presence here: The village burglar squatted in a cave on the side of Calcata's cliffs, operated a shop that sold junk near the square, owned a car and a vicious dog, and actually had a cute girlfriend. Few Calcatesi ever talked to him.

The *parcheggio*, or parking lot, situated right in front of Calcata, was like a village unto its own. Lined with two-story houses made of tufo, Piazza Roma had all the charm of . . . well, a parking lot. Until recently, when the parking lot was repaved and made into a quasi pedestrian square, cars completely filled the space, crammed in together and arranged as if there was a convention in town for the Blind Drivers Society. The people who lived there rarely wandered up through the stone gate to the medieval village, preferring instead to hang out near their homes. Here you would have found Giorgio (known—at least to me—as Giorgio Iggy Pop because of his resemblance to the haggard seventies rock star) until he died of a heroin overdose recently that villagers say was really a suicide; you'd certainly see Giorgio il Matto (George the Crazy), nicknamed such because he really did seem insane, whose hobbies included stealing things and shuffling around the parking lot plastering homemade posters on walls that had some kind of esoteric political message few could figure out; an always-drunk old man that Jessie and I nicknamed the "Ciaoer of Pisa" because he would sit in front of his apartment in a lawn chair, glass of scotch in hand, and never fail to give a hearty "ciao" to anyone who'd look his way (unless you were Paul Steffen—then he'd say "Ciao . . . dirty Jew!"). Then there was the old Calcata family that ran the restaurant in the parking lot called Tre Monti who offset the village's typical Che Guevara flags and rainbow-striped antiwar signs with their own iconography: fascism. Adolfo worked the kitchen, while diners would eat among such decorations (particularly in the back room) as a bust of Mussolini, portraits of Il Duce, and even a calendar dedicated to the man.

The village had a Dante too. Sort of. The previous occupant of our apartment had made a habit of dressing up like the thirteenth-century Florentine scribe. He'd walk around the village, dressed shoulder to toes in red medieval garb, topped off with a saggy red hat that came to a point at the end, and recite passages from *The Divine Comedy*. He was overbearingly tall with a massive face and bushy eyebrows. He took great strides when he walked. An intimidating fellow, from what I'd heard.

Scot told me Dante had just moved out from the apartment I'd moved into. Which explains why so much of his stuff was still in the apartment: his bubble bath, his coffee, a bottle of low-grade prosecco, several cans of vegetables, and some plastic bottles filled with unidentifiable transparent liquid under the sink. It seemed he'd left in hurry.

"So that's *his* cologne-scented shampoo I've been using," I said to Scot jokingly.

Scot looked at me like I had just told him I'd been using Dante's suppositories. "If I were you," he said, "I wouldn't be using *anything* of his."

When I went back to my apartment that day, I filled up the trash can with Dante's leftover toiletries and food. I kept the prosecco.

Now the apartment was really Spartan. There was a back room, completely empty, which led to the bathroom (which always emitted a not-so-pleasant odor of sewage). The loft above the front room was big and dark and a great place for sleeping. Until Stefania found us that couch, the only place to sit was at the table in the front room or on the steep steps that led up to the front door. Which, by the way, didn't lock. There was a heavy sliding gate one could close and padlock shut. It was always disconcerting at night, when we were ready to go to bed, to have to slide the gate shut and lock ourselves in, as if we were imposing a short-term prison sentence on ourselves. And in my occasional periods of self-doubt in which I would wonder what the hell I was doing here, I'd start to see the apartment as a cell and Calcata as one giant prison: Calcatraz.

And for Dante, this might have been a foreshadowing of what was to come for him.

One day over a long, three-bottle-of-wine lunch at the Grotta, Pancho mentioned Dante. "What happened to him?" I asked, regretful that I hadn't gotten a chance to see Dante in action before he exiled himself from Calcata.

"He probably found a new girlfriend and is shacked up with her in some other town, I guess," Pancho said. As Pancho went back to the kitchen to cook our lunch, the others at the table started to fill in the story: Dante's girlfriend and live-in partner, "Beatrice," wandered into the police station one day and filed a report that Dante had been perpetually sexually and physically abusive with her. No one was sure what had happened, or if it was even true, but for a while Dante was going around the village asking locals if they'd testify on his behalf. To be fair, it had been said his girlfriend wasn't the most sane person in the world, either, and not everyone believed the accusations.

I lay in bed that night trying to remember if I'd cleaned the sheets when I first arrived. I hadn't. Maybe Gisa, my landlady had. I hoped.

After finally finding out that our actual address meant nothing to the locals in Calcata (except to the mailman), I began telling people I lived in Ca' Dante, short for Casa di Dante, and everyone knew exactly where that was. Unfortunately.

Chapter 10

FOR THE BIRDS

Het Sekhmet, read the sign on Athon's door. I peeked through the glass panes before knocking, wondering what I was getting myself into. Behind the door was a spacious room, carved out of the *tufo* with a high-arched ceiling, filled with an L-shaped couch and stacks of books. The walls were littered with intricate allegorical paintings reminiscent of Hieronymus Bosch. Two larger-than-life sculptures of pharaohs stared back at me.

Calcata is small enough that any house on the rock is reachable within sixty seconds. Athon's cave-cum-home, located in the farthest section from the main gate, is no different. But it's hidden enough that few nonlocals actually stumble upon it. Moments earlier I had made my way through an uninviting descending passageway twisting down the side of the cliff, passing by kittens meowing at me in desperation and abandoned caves that were littered with rotting junk. I stopped peeking through the windowed door and knocked again a few times.

Nearly every villager I met in the medieval village within the first few weeks of my arrival had said that I needed to meet Athon. "She lives with a bunch of crows in a cave," they'd say, as if it were some kind of virtue. "And when she laughs, she sounds just like her birds." Originally from Genoa, Athon had been living a hermetic life in India before she came to Calcata in the 1970s. She had never heard of Calcata, but while in India she had a vision of two angels who flew her across the world to show her Calcata. They pointed to the village and said, "Your house is there because there is the head of god." According to her, she moved to Calcata as soon as possible.

I was a little afraid to hang out with her. But when I finally did meet the red-haired Athon, I was surprised (and relieved) at how welcoming she was. I still wasn't sure how eager I was to meet her crows, but she might tell me something about the relic. And, having lived in Los Angeles when she was younger, she spoke English well, so I wouldn't have to rely on my faltering Italian.

Still peeking through the door, I suddenly heard a voice from behind me say, "You come to see the birds?" It was Athon, wearing a red shawl and red derby hat matching her hair. Her eyes, as usual, were framed with thick black eyeliner. "Let's go, I show you."

She led me to the adjacent cave and unlocked a metal grate door, which led to another door. I could hear birds whooping inside. "*Funfy!*" Athon screamed out to them, announcing her arrival. "*Funfy! Funfacchiotti!*" A cacophony of birds greeted her with squawks and chirps.

Inside, the cave was sectioned into the three rooms by floor-to-ceiling chicken wire. In the first section, there were nooks for a shower and a toilet, a table with a laptop on it, and a small kitchen area. The floors of the cave were covered in colorful mosaics. Athon continued calling the birds as she uncoiled a wire that kept the door locked to the next section, which the birds occupied. The air in the room was heavy with a faint scent of mildew (and, surprisingly, devoid of the smell of bird droppings).

Suddenly a football-size crow with a gray barreled chest landed on my head.

"You have met Uzer," she said, laughing. "She is greeting you. She likes you."

When Athon bent over to fill a bowl with bird feed, I took the opportunity to shoo Uzer, who was attempting to remove strands of hair from my head.

About a dozen crows, all smaller than Uzer, were cackling. Some sat on the heads and arms of large Egyptian statues that had been wrapped in thin Persian rugs (probably for protection against the bird dung). Others crouched on broomsticks that had been horizontally positioned around the room to give the birds perches. A part of the room had been sectioned off with more chicken wire and turned into a small cage for the thirteen parakeets and other small birds.

She gave the two dozen crows in the cage a moderate amount of attention. But she was always concerned for the whereabouts of Uzer. "Uzzzzzeeeeerr?" she'd call out, and then rattle off a slur of diminutives in Italian.

Uzer, who was now sitting on one of the broomsticks near my head, let out a rumbling warble.

"Uzer wants your caresses," she said.

"How do you know?"

"She told me."

"So, the birds talk to you?"

"Yes, of course they do."

With a deep sense of caution, I raised my hand up toward Uzer. As I slowly fanned my fingers out to a petting formation, Uzer snapped her beak at me, catching skin before I could quickly pull back. Athon let out a great guffaw, revealing that her Calcata compatriots were not exaggerating about her birdlike laugh.

"Do they ever go outside?" I asked.

"Oh, no," Athon said, shaking her head. "They couldn't survive now."

I wondered about the ethics of keeping a bunch of birds in a cave and not letting them out. But before I could ask, she added,

"They want to be here. We all have a karmic connection." Athon paused for a second, scanning the cave. "Help me move this," she said, pointing to a rectangular clump of sheets and blankets that were covered with a large swath of wax paper. Athon removed the paper and then bunched up a bundle of blankets in her arms. "We must put this outside the cage," she said, walking past me.

I was amazed to find that the object underneath the bundle of blankets was a bed.

"You sleep in here?" I asked.

"I tried to sleep in here, but it was too difficult," Athon said, picking up a pair of huge wraparound sunglasses that were on the mattress. "I had to wear these at night because I was afraid the birds would . . ." She didn't know the word, so she made a downward jabbing motion with her head.

"Peck your eyes out," I said.

"Yes," she said, stopping to laugh at the idea of such a thing. "Now, help me put this outside the cage and then we'll go to the cave next door and have some wine."

A few minutes later, we were sitting in her other cave. Athon was fumbling around her coffee table for a clean plastic cup in which to pour me some wine. This cave, the birdless one, was where she usually entertained guests. It was crammed with her artwork: foot-high sculptures of dog-headed Egyptian gods, allegorical paintings, and life-size Egyptian-themed sculptures.

With all her eccentricities, I was tempted to dismiss Athon. But I knew she was actually an accomplished artist, having published a book (in English) on Egyptian spirituality and magic, had a few fairly big exhibitions in Rome, and penned articles for conspiracy theory magazines in Italy. She had a Ph.D. in architecture. And she could also read and write hieroglyphics.

I'd almost forgotten that I wanted to ask Athon about Turin and the Holy Foreskin, and now that we were outside the reach of the pecking crows, I could hopefully find out the truth about Turin. First, however, Athon wanted to talk about her birds a bit more.

"Did you enjoy meeting the birds?" she asked.

"Yes. That Uzer sure is one charming bird," I said.

Athon nodded her head. "Very much."

"How did you find her?"

"She found me," said Athon. "We used to see each other down in the valley below Calcata. One time I was teaching a class on hieroglyphics here and the class wasn't going so well. So I took the students to the valley. I picked up a stick and gave it to a student. I asked her to draw a hieroglyphic in the dirt. She did, but I was not satisfied with it." Athon stopped to take a sip of wine. "But then Uzer came from the trees. She began to draw with her . . . what is this word for the bird's mouth?"

"Beak."

"Yes, beak. With her beak she made the Egyptian hieroglyph for the word 'peace' in the dirt. Then she flew to the student and took the stick and flew to me and put it in my hand."

I wasn't quite sure how to react, so I just said, "Wow, that's . . . amazing. You and Uzer must have a very strong connection."

Athon nodded her head as she refilled my glass with more wine.

"So," I added, "Uzer lived in the valley before she began living in your cave?"

"Yes, she lived in the valley and I would see her often," Athon said. "Then one day she just disappeared. I saw her a few months later in Mazzano," said Athon, referring to the village about three miles away, "And I told her that if she wanted to be with me she was going to have to come back to Calcata. About a week later, she was standing at my door and she said she was ready to be with me."

"So . . . ," I said, pausing for a minute to prepare her for a subject change. "Have you ever been to Torino?"

"Yes, of course, there is a great Egyptian museum there—the biggest outside of Cairo."

"What else do you know about Torino?" I asked, nudging her.

She didn't answer, opting instead to wipe up some cake crumbs on her coffee table.

"I—I heard that Torino is the capital of magic," I blurted out.

"Torino. I don't know nothing about Torino," Athon said in a dismissive tone. "I don't answer questions like that," she said, crumpling up her face.

I came out and asked her directly. "I heard that the Holy Foreskin might be there."

"The holy what?" she said.

"The *prepuzio*."

"Oh, the *prepuzio*. It's not in Torino," Athon said, and left me hanging. She moved on to straightening up pillows.

"Yeah, it's probably in New York or something," I said, all but begging her to correct me with her opinion about where it was.

"It's not in New York," she said, waving me off with her hand. "If you want to find the *prepuzio*, you only need to look in one place."

"So . . . the *prepuzio* is . . . ?"

"Everyone knows where it is," she said. "It's in the Vatican."

"The Vatican," I said, surprised. "Do you know that for a fact?"

"Yes, of course. Like I said, everyone knows where it is. They took the *prepuzio*."

I sat there, an empty plastic cup in my hands, mulling over this second mention of an ominous "they" who'd stolen the foreskin. And thinking how impossible the odds of getting a statement from the Vatican on the matter would be.

After I left Athon's I stopped by the Grotta to see what Pancho thought about all this. I breezed through the dining room and stepped down into the kitchen/countertop bar area where regulars watch Pancho in action; this time there was a familiar face cozied to the bar: Patrizia.

"Well, well, look who it is," Pancho said. "We were just talking about you."

I smiled, trying to hide my nerves in front of the one woman who could really help me but so far wouldn't, and sat down. Pancho poured me a glass of red.

"Patrizia wants to strike a deal with you," he said.

I looked at Patrizia and she nodded before rattling off a slur of sentences to Pancho in Italian. Pancho translated.

"She knows why you're here and what you want. She's willing to help you, if you help her."

"What does she want?"

Pancho translated back to Patrizia and she responded, taking about five minutes to answer the question.

Pancho finally cut her off. "Okay. She'll tell you where you can find a lot of historical information on the *prepuzio*. But there are a couple conditions. One is that you have to give her credit for what you find, meaning if you ever end up writing something about the relic, you have to at least say that she helped you."

I looked at Patrizia and nodded.

"The second is that you have to take the *prepuzio* seriously. She once cooperated with a journalist from Britain who then wrote a piece for a magazine totally making fun of the relic and making fun of her. She takes this *prepuzio* stuff seriously."

"Yes, of course. I'm serious about it too," I said.

Pancho translated and then relayed Patrizia's response. "So, here's the deal. Patrizia has done some research at the Vatican Library but she still needs some more stuff from there about the *prepuzio*. The problem is that, as a known Holy Foreskin expert, she's convinced she's being shadowed while she's there. She'll give you a list of what she needs—as well as a list of stuff that will be helpful to yourself—if you can just get yourself into the Vatican Library."

"Sure." I said. "But how do I do that?"

Pancho relayed my question to Patrizia and she went on for a few minutes. Finally, Pancho looked at me and chuckled before saying, "It doesn't sound like it's going to be easy."

Chapter 11

LOOKING FOR
THE KEYS TO ST. PETER'S

I had already tried getting myself into the Vatican, actually. Before leaving for Italy I'd called the Holy See Mission, the Vatican's outpost at the United Nations. The man who answered the phone had an abrupt tone, so I should have known better. But at that point in my search, I wasn't as aware of the church's reticence toward relics in general, and the Holy Foreskin in particular.

"You're interested in relics?" he asked, incredulity already melting into his tone.

"Yes," I said. "And I'd love to talk to a historian at the Vatican or maybe someone who is in charge of relics."

"Relics in general or something specific?"

This was when I should have lied, but I didn't know better back then. "The Holy Prepuce," I said, preferring to use the British term for foreskin, thinking that it sounded more serious.

"The holy what?" he asked.

"Prepuce. Holy Prepuce."

"What's a prepuce?"

"It's a foreskin."

"The Holy Foreskin? You want me to hook you up with

DAVID FARLEY

someone at the Vatican to talk about the Holy Foreskin?" His voice was now overcome with concern.

"Well, yes. I would."

"I don't think so. The Church does not want to talk to anyone about the Holy Foreskin. This is a ridiculous request. I'm sorry, I can't—"

"But it's a real relic. I mean, at one time this was a Church-approved relic. Pilgrims even received a plenary indulgence for coming to venerate it, and it was kept at one time in Rome, along with Christianity's greatest relics—"

He hung up on me, which I considered not exactly the most auspicious way to begin my journey. No more auspicious than my visit to the U.S. Embassy to the Holy See in Rome, a couple weeks after my arrival in Calcata. Still without a channel to the Vatican, I had read on the Vatican's Web site that the best way for freelance journalists to get press access to the Holy See was with a letter of introduction from your embassy.

This time, I decided, I should steer clear of direct references to anything foreskin-related, even when pressed. I'd be telling the truth without really telling the truth. That is, if I could enter the embassy without being shot. Commotion broke out as soon as I turned the corner and approached the black metal gates, a stone's throw from the Circus Maximus. And by the time I stopped at the buzzer in front of the gate, the guards stationed across the street suddenly had their guns pointed at me. I rang, knowing I was being watched through several gun scopes, and an officer from the palatial house approached the gate with a sideward glance and a what-the-fuck-do-you-want look on his face. In the post-9/11 era, a U.S. embassy visitor is a member of an Al Qaeda sleeper cell until proven otherwise. I flashed my American passport and told the surly guard who I was and what I wanted. He walked off, and after a three-minute delay, the back of my head still a potential bullet-depository, the gate creaked opened and I made my way into the building.

98

George Bush's smile and Dick Cheney's sneer greeted me in the form of eight-by-ten glossies as I entered the lobby, which had all the charm of a dentist's office. A few seconds later, a chipper blond woman named Amy Roth Turnley, the embassy's press agent, entered the room. I explained to her my project—cryptically, of course—mentioning the catacombs near the Appian Way, the history of relic theft, and relics in Rome's Santa Maria in Gerusalemme. We chatted amicably about Calcata, which she'd been to (she particularly loved Costantino's Etruscan-style thrones on the piazza), and about how great her life was because she got to live in Rome. She seemed eager to help and said she'd look into my request, whatever that meant, and get in touch with me. I left the compound, the guns from across the street back on me, feeling good.

That is, until I got back to Calcata that afternoon and found an e-mail from Ms. Roth Turnley in my in-box. Gone was her bright, helpful personality, replaced by a formal, distant tone. "I wanted to inform you as soon as possible that our Embassy will not be able to provide you with a letter of presentation for your work in Italy without a letter from a media organization with which you work in the USA." She went on to tell me that my problem would be further complicated by the fact that I'd officially need a journalist visa to work in the country. But if I wanted to stop by the embassy again sometime soon, she'd happily give me a tour of the compound and "discuss the nature of the work we do here."

And so the U.S. government would not be helping me find the foreskin of Jesus. The day after receiving her e-mail, I tried a more direct approach. This time I marched into the Sala Stampa, the Vatican press office, and asked about requesting interviews. A man whose face was nearly entirely forehead led me to a row of phone boxes inside the office and pointed to one of the phones. "Call this number," the lug grunted in Italian, and handed me a piece of paper with phone number on it and the words "Congregation for the Doctrine of the Faith."

The man who answered was polite enough, even after I told him I was interested in learning more about relics. In the end, I left with a fax number and a promise that my request would be seriously considered. After three requests via fax in as many weeks without getting a response, I let my breath out.

What I thought could be my last chance was a guy in Calcata who worked at the Vatican and was, apparently, very well connected. Sandro, the unassuming husband of Simona Weller (a writer and a painter and one of the most successful artists of the village), had taken a brief interest in me for some reason. Which was odd, considering he'd often walk by our stoop on the way to his palatial house, nicely dressed in slacks and a sweater and shoes that cost more than our monthly rent and see me sitting there, smoking a roll-up cigarette, trying to read an issue of *Diva e Donna*, dressed in sweats and a raggedy T-shirt or whatever I'd woken up in that morning. Eventually, we began chatting and one day I finally got the nerve to ask him if he could help me set up some interviews with Vatican officials to talk about relics. Sandro said he'd figure out who I could ask and get back to me.

From 1870 to 1929, popes never left the Vatican, claiming to be prisoners within their own house. The creation of a unified Italian state stripped the Church of the vast papal territories that had stretched from the region of Lazio all the way north to Umbria, Le Marche, and eastern Emilia-Romagna, some ten thousand square miles in all. And the new Italian state began a form of passive-aggressive urban planning in the neighborhoods around the Vatican in the late nineteenth and early twentieth centuries. The square just north of the border of the Vatican was named Piazza Risorgimento, the name for the fight for Italian nationalism, and new streets around the Vatican were tagged with Risorgimento-referencing names as well as those of historical figures, like the medieval Cola di Rienzo, who had challenged the papacy. In the historical center square, Campo de' Fiori, the place where the Church had enjoyed burning heretics in centuries past, a statue of sixteenth-century papal-critic-turned-papal-burn-victim Giordano Bruno was erected in the same place he had been immolated. No coincidence was the direction the somber sculpture faced: straight at the dome of St. Peter's.

Then, in 1929, with one swipe of a pen, the two sides reconciled; Pope Pius XI signed the Lateran Treaty, an accord with Benito Mussolini in which both parties essentially recognized the other's existence and which set the boundaries for the Church's new state. Vatican City, one of the world's smallest nations at 108 acres, was born.

And to celebrate, Mussolini gave a "gift" to the Holy See—something architects (including the Renaissance artist Leone Battista Alberti) had wanted to do for centuries: a dramatic approach to St. Peter's Basilica. Il Duce's stark five-hundred-yard-long Via della Conciliazione (Street of Conciliation) paved right through blocks of ancient buildings. Out were a handful of medieval-era burgher houses and palaces; in was one of the most dramatic approaches in the world.

I'd walked up this approach many times, transfixed by Michelangelo's dome in the distance, as if it were physically pulling me and everyone around me toward it. But this time was different. This time I wasn't a tourist, hoping to linger inside St. Peter's, gawking at Michelangelo's *Pietà* and Bernini's *Baldacchino*. No, I was approaching the Vatican with the intent of getting myself inside. I had to find the Vatican Library and talk my way in. If I could just get past the colorfully dressed Swiss Guards, who knows what I might find out about the foreskin's whereabouts.

The Vatican Library is open only to scholars from recognized and accredited universities. My ticket in, I'd hoped, was in my bag: a note from my director at New York University, affirming that I was affiliated with the university. My concern was that I teach in NYU's writing program, not in the history department.

I traipsed across St. Peter's Square to get myself to the library, where piles of historical documents about the relic were sure to be. I circumvented the mile-long line to get into the Vatican Museums, and as I approached the Porta Sant' Anna, the gate where employees enter and exit their offices, I tried to slip on a look of confidence. Scot, who runs a tour company that specializes in the Vatican, said that if I looked like I knew where I was going, the Swiss Guards wouldn't stop me.

"*Prego*," one of the guards said, stepping in my path. I stumbled through Italian before he switched the conversation to perfect English, pointing me to a guard shack. I went in and had to fill out a "*permesso*" to go any farther. After filling out the form and presenting it to a man behind a thick glass divider, I was ready for an interrogation about why I was there and what I wanted. Instead, he slammed a stamp down on my form, handed it back to me, and said "*Prego!*"

The Vatican City state has its own army—in the form of those Swiss Guards—as well as their own postal service, currency, bank, railway station, publishing house, commissary, pharmacy, electrical generating plant, and even a penal system (and two jail cells in which to hold lawbreakers).

And of course, it has its own library, one of the oldest working libraries in the world, founded in 1451. Its 75,000 manuscripts and 1.1 million printed books are held in thirty-seven miles of stacks, many of which are underground. The library is famously mistaken as having the largest collection of pornography in the world. And while some of the library's greatest treasures were lost to the booty-hungry invaders in the 1527 Sack of Rome and to Napoleon, it still has a few priceless manuscripts—including the Codex Vaticanus, the world's oldest copy of the Bible, written by hand during the reign of Roman emperor Constantine.

The twenty-person-thick line, starting at a closed frosted glass door with the word SEGRETARIA on it, was peppered with scholars in tweed jackets and Franciscan monks and priests, all waiting to get approval to undertake research in the library. I stood there, trying to convince myself that my interest in the Holy Foreskin would get me a library card and not land me in one of the Vatican's jail cells.

After all, technically, it was a punishable crime. Or at least excommunicable. The 1900 decree has been repeated in scholarly papers and Italian newspapers, and people like Patrizia who have done research on the relic speak about it as fact; I never did see the actual decree, but I figured it was legit, as Louise McDermott mentioned in an e-mail to me that she had a copy of the document. Don Dario, I'd been told, had a proclivity for citing the decree as the reason he couldn't speak about the relic and its disappearance. Excommunication doesn't sound too harsh these days—especially if you're not a Catholic—but the threat of spending an eternity in the fiery pits of hell still was hard to ignore.

Perhaps this is one reason many historians haven't wanted to touch the Holy Foreskin. In fact, since the Holy Foreskin fell out of favor with the Vatican, there hasn't been a whole lot of public talk about the relic. And many historians, even those whose focus is on the Church and relics, could hardly mention it in their tomes without scoffing. Eighteenth-century Benedictine monk and scholar Jean Mabillon said of the relic, "It is better to give over, to commend the entire matter to God, than to dare any explanation of it." And twentieth-century British historian G. G. Coulton called it "the most blasphemous relic of all." It appears in the index of his book under "Relics, strange." Coulton did write about the relic, but only in Latin, as if touching on such a heretical subject in the language of the Church might spare him from eternal damnation. The writer James Bentley dedicated five pages to the Holy Foreskin in his 1985 study on relics, *Restless Bones.* The segue into his brief discussion about the relic is, "None, however, ranks in absurdity with the cult of . . . [the] holy foreskin."

I didn't expect the person behind the frosted glass door at the Vatican Library to be any more enlightened—after all, if historians were too red-faced to write about the relic, the Church must have been very embarrassed about it. So I concocted a complex story about my need to find historical information about Calcata. Which wouldn't have been a lie. Calcata's history is part of the Holy Foreskin's history too. I began looking up words in my dictionary, forming sentences in Italian that I'd probably need to use during the interview. I heard someone speaking German next to me, but I didn't pay much attention until there was a tap on my shoulder and I found that the person who had been in line a few people behind me was a priest, and that it was me he'd been-speaking German to. The Italian-English dictionary in my hand was from a German publisher, which was probably why the thirty-something priest thought I was German.

I responded in Italian that though I had once learned German, I had forgotten most of it. I asked if he spoke English, but he said he *only* spoke Italian, German, Latin, and Czech.

"Czech?" I said. And then spat out some of the Czech I still remembered from living in Prague in the mid-nineties. The priest was impressed. We chatted for a few minutes in halting Czech and Italian, and then he asked me what I was planning to research at the library.

Perhaps it was our common bond of all things Czech, or my relief in having a casual conversation when I was so nervous, but I said it: "The Holy Foreskin."

He cocked his head. Maybe he hadn't understood *Prepuzio*. I said it in Latin, *Praeputium*, and he let out a soft "ahh," and nodded his head.

Then I explained to the best of my ability the story and that I was living in Calcata and had hoped to find some information here in the library about the relic. This time he said, "Oh," before bidding me good-bye and returning to the other priest toward the back of the line.

Shit! I thought. Why did I tell him that? I turned back to see him and his friends already deep in conversation. Perhaps I was just being paranoid, but I could have sworn they were stealing glances in my direction and talking about me. I tried to go back to looking up words and phrases in my dictionary, but I couldn't help but beat myself up over having spilled the beans to that Czech priest. Which is when I felt another tap on my shoulder. It was the priest again.

"I didn't get your name," he said.

Now entirely paranoid, I felt like I had to give him an alias. The night before, an actor who keeps a weekend apartment in Calcata had just told me that the 1980s sitcom *Diff'rent Strokes* had run on Italian TV and was, at one time, very popular. Everyone in Italy of a certain age group, he said, knew Arnold's catchphrase "Whatchu talkin' 'bout, Willis?" (in Italian, "*Che cosa stai dicendo, Willis?*").

The conversation now popped into my head, and I looked at the priest and said, "Gary Coleman. *Mi chiamo* Gary Coleman."

"Nice to meet you, Gary Coleman," the priest said, and then gave his name, which I didn't catch. He went back to his friends and their conversation about me continued.

With all this commotion, I hadn't realized how quickly the line had progressed; I looked up and there were no more scholars between me and the frosted glass door. A minute later it swung open and a man waved me in; I stepped forward, a nervous smile on my face. An older man, his arms behind his back as he paced, motioned for me to sit down in front of a desk, where a younger man was typing on a keyboard.

Before the interrogation began, I handed him my letter from NYU and then volunteered all my preplanned information, saying that I was an instructor at a university in New York and a writer and that I was looking for information about the village I was living in near Rome called Calcata. And amazingly, when I had finished my planned explanation, the younger man told me to look into the camera, took my photo, and about twenty seconds later, out popped a Vatican Library card with my photo on it.

I was in.

Chapter 12

ARMIES FOR JESUS

As summer began to wane, so did the day-trippers, making Calcata at midweek feel like the abandoned village it had once almost become. Sundays, however, were different. This was the one day when Calcata felt like a real lived-in place; it was the day when everyone in the village reserved a several-hour block to sit around the square to talk and catch up.

The day-trippers would arrive first, always before lunch. They'd stalk up and down every lane of the village, pouring into court-yards and down alleyways, trying to consume as much of the vil-lage as possible in just a couple hours. They'd flow back into the piazza around 12:45, and as if choreographed, they would, thirty minutes later, funnel themselves into the nearest restaurant—the Italian stomach apparently makes its complaints at exactly the same time in every person on the peninsula. After lunch, they'd wander back into the square for an hour or so, bathing in the late-afternoon sun, while all the artists who had been hibernating in their studios all week would begin to take back their public living room for themselves, lounging on the church steps, chain-smoking, and gossiping. Rotund Costantino, often wearing a bow tie and a wide-rimmed red hat, would be sitting next to the po-nytailed Giancarlo Croce, a painter whose gallery, Porta Segreta, houses his own magnificent renderings of Calcata. Patrizia would loom about, smug smile intact; just down from the square near Ca' Dante, Gianni Macchia, often dressed as extravagantly as pos-sible, would hold court in front of his café; the town burglar would be in front of his nearby junk shop, usually drinking with friends from the parking lot.

It was also the day the church doors would be open. I'd often wander in and gawk at the relief sculptures of the Holy Circum-cision above the altar and the rectangular niche above the altar about the size of a loaf of bread where the relic had been kept. The thick gold-plated door to the niche—to whose lock only the priest and the bishop formerly had keys—now sat slightly ajar, perhaps a reminder of what had once been there. Above it was a bust of a cherub, his eyes bulging out and teeth gritted tightly together.

One particular Sunday, I wandered in and, when the church was empty, quietly circumnavigated the altar, standing just below the niche. Through the crack in the door, I could see something inside, an unidentifiable object. I could see just enough of what-ever it was to imagine I was seeing the reliquary itself. There was no way to reach the door and swing it open. But behind the organ I found a duster, a three-foot plastic rod with furry bristles on the top half.

I approached the niche again, wielding the duster with both hands in front of me like a sword. Just as I was about to raise it, the sound of shuffling feet echoed throughout the church; as an older couple entered the spacious hall, I got nervous—after all, it's taboo for lay people to go behind the altar—so I thought quick and started dusting. I ran the bristly stick over the altar and then moved on to the chairs in the chancel, the place where the choir sits, pretending to be going about my business. I began humming something as I swept the duster over marble cherubs and church pews. The couple left a minute later and I resumed my mission.

Again, I stared up at the crack in the door and then raised the duster high above my head and wedged it into the crack. When I pushed outward, the plastic rod bent under the weight of the door, which wouldn't budge. So, feeling defeated, I turned around toward the front of the church, where Sveti and Aman, the two young girls of Alessandro and Stefania (the couple who found us our apartment in Calcata), stood staring at me, their mouths agape. "Um . . . I'm trying to open this door," I said in Italian.

One of them managed to emit a soft "oh" and then a few seconds later, Sveti lifted an umbrella above her head and said, "Here, use this." I had suddenly recruited a five- and a seven-year-old girl in my quest. Just like before with the duster, I wedged the umbrella inside the door and, with all my might, pulled. The door swung open, hitting the wall behind it and making an echoing bang as the girls sucked in their breath. We stood there for a few seconds, staring up at the open niche in silence before Aman uttered, "*Niente c'e*," there's nothing there. Just a small ruffled white towel lay inside—the place where two golden angels had once held up a green and red jeweled grail that contained the *carne vera sacra*.

In controversial French writer Roger Peyrefitte's 1955 novel, *The Keys of St. Peter,* the main characters, Father de Trennes and Abbé Victor Mas, journeyed to Calcata hoping to stand in front of that very same gold-plated door in the church. With Calcata's church campanile looming in the distance and looking "like a watchtower from which the sentries guarding the Holy Prepuce should be scanning the horizon," the two religious men approached the towering village. "I find it in no way strange that so prodigious a relic should have come here to rest," remarked Mas.

Once in the square, they met with the village priest, who ushered them into the church and then bolted the door behind them. As the priest unlocked the golden door to the niche and removed the reliquary, it started to rain; by the time he set it on the altar, it was violently thundering. He lifted the top off the reliquary—which was crowned by a diamond-encrusted cross—to reveal "two grayish membranes with an undertone of pink, curled into balls." Mas and de Trennes stood there in awe, as villagers began pounding the door of the church, yelling for the priest to put the relic away so the storm would stop.

Peyrefitte's account relied on historical legends, but in one of the last e-mails I received from Louise McDermott, she said, "Peyrefitte usually had his ear to the ground when it came to church gossip." When *The Keys of St. Peter* was published in 1955, it caused an immediate scandal due to uncomfortable Church-related issues woven into the novel, including the history of the Holy Foreskin. The book was an instant success, selling at least five hundred thousand copies in Italy before it was banned (due largely to lobbying from the Church, of course).

Peyrefitte got most of his information on Calcata from a couple days he spent in the village chatting with Don Mario Mastricola, who was the parish priest of Calcata from 1950 to 1961. I'd never even considered trying to track Mastricola down to get his views on the foreskin, because I figured he was long dead. But later that Sunday afternoon, while I was lounging on the square with my friend Elena and her friend Wilma, his name was mentioned. "Did you meet him before he died?" I asked.

"He's not dead," said Wilma. "He lives in Fabrica di Roma."

I looked at Elena, praying she'd take me there. I had to go see him. Elena was the perfect companion for stalking priests: She didn't have a job, which meant she was always available; she had a car; and she was beautiful and fearless. She spoke a broken English that relied partially on lyrics to Led Zeppelin, Coldplay, and Radiohead songs she knew by heart, but I always understood what she meant.

She could see the desire in my eyes and before I could ask, she said, "Okay. We go next week."

I was so happy I hugged her. In the meantime, it had been a few weeks since I acquired my Vatican Library card, and I decided to pay my first official researching visit there. The first morning I was headed to Rome, I opened our apartment door and found a note attached to our heavy green gate. It was a packet of about twenty business-card-size pieces of paper. Printed on each was a book or article title and a call number. Some of them had dates, 1679, 1728, 1802. Surely they had come from Patrizia. But I'd never told her I was going to the Vatican that day. In fact, I didn't remember if I'd even told her I had been given a library card.

Once I got there, I breezed by the Swiss Guards, flashing my library card with confidence, like I was meant to be there. And I was. But at the same time, my stomach tingled—both with excitement and nerves—as the lobby clerk at the front desk swiped my card. After putting my belongings in a locker and signing in—as "Gary Coleman," of course—I traipsed up the stairs and opened the library door. I could almost hear a chorus of angels belting out a long note somewhere from above. The long arched halls were highlighted by ceiling murals, and the two-story-high walls were flanked by ancient books.

Before getting down to my foreskin search, I wanted to see just how much of the library's contents were available for viewing. The Codex Vaticanus is apparently the oldest existing copy of the Bible in the world, said to have been made in the fourth century during the reign of Emperor Constantine. I walked over to one of the computer terminals, which looked like they'd been purchased during the Reagan Administration, and typed in "Codex Vaticanus." Several hits came up, but the original wasn't in the database. So, I approached the front desk and asked the predictably stern-faced man behind the counter.

"*L'Originale* . . . ?" I said, after stuttering out the name of the book.

The sweater-clad man didn't say anything; instead, he shook his head from side to side. I looked up at the ceiling hoping I'd find another way to ask. Instead, I just repeated the same thing and he responded with the same nonverbal answer.

Denied access to the world's oldest Bible, I'd have to find other ways to investigate the birth of Christianity. Ever since I'd begun reading about the formation of the early Church, I'd become fascinated with the evolution of Church doctrine, and specifically, how tenets such as the Virgin birth came about in the first few centuries after the death of Christ. The Christianity we've come to know wasn't exactly the same one that existed in the first few centuries after Christ's death. Because it was an underground faith for the first few centuries of its existence, there was no real central authority to keep doctrine in check or even, for that matter, agree on an orthodoxy. The Christian communities sprinkled around the Mediterranean, therefore, held vastly different beliefs about who Christ was, where he came from, and exactly what his message was.

That definition of Christ would eventually shape history; it would also help determine just how much power Jesus relics in general and the Holy Foreskin in particular would contain.

It was the disciples who made the first attempt to shape Jesus' legacy. And of those early followers, Paul, who never knew Jesus, was instrumental in inspiring what would become doctrine about Christ's resurrection and ascension into heaven. What's most important about Paul is that he largely rejected rational Greco-Roman schools of thought that had grown up around the Mediterranean, promoting faith instead. Plato, whose thought had pervaded the Mediterranean world, had specifically warned against using faith as a guide to the truth (ironically, Platonic thought would eventually be used to justify some aspects of Christian theology).

But soon people in the Greco-Roman world were being asked to reject chief aspects of their culture in the face of Christianity, a new cult that preached ritualized cannibalism and the veneration of parts of the deceased. Should they refuse, vis-à-vis the emerging Christian doctrine, they would face eternal damnation.

Everything changed in 313 when the Roman general Constantine was preparing for a huge battle just outside of Rome against his rival Maxentius. The winner would go on to become sole emperor. The problem for Constantine was that Maxentius's army was much bigger than his own. Defeat for Constantine seemed certain. That is, until he saw a massive flaming cross in the sky with the inscription IN HOC SIGNO VINCES ("By this sign, you will conquer"). In the ensuing battle, Maxentius's army was forced to use a makeshift bridge across the Tiber. When they did, the boats supporting the bridge planks came apart and a large part of the army, including Maxentius, drowned.

Constantine, now emperor, saw this as a miracle, and as a result, Christianity—once an isolated and often persecuted cult—became officially tolerated and eventually was made the state religion of the Roman Empire. This was a definitive moment for the Church and, on a larger scale, the world. Christianity would now be governed by the state; but more than that, the supposed circumstances of Constantine's conversion are significant. He did it as an act of war. According to most scholars, Constantine didn't know much about Christianity and mistakenly assumed Jesus was an acceptable god of war—much like the Roman gods he had often favored. Constantine's wartime conversion eclipsed Christ's message of peace and inserted in its place a bellicosity toward anything that existed outside of what would be defined as Church doctrine.

Most scholars view Constantine's conversion as politically motivated; it was expedient to control the fast-growing cult of Christ by incorporating it into the state. He then walked a fine line, paying lip service to both Christians and pagans. The emperor may have bowed to Christianity, but that didn't necessarily make him a saint. He still kept a lot of barbaric Roman laws on the books. Slaves who tried to seduce young women were punished by having molten metal poured down their throats. When he suspected his second wife was having an affair with his son from his first marriage, he had his son killed. And just for good measure, he then had his wife burned to death in scalding hot water. And Constantine wasn't alone. The fractured Christian communities were so at odds with one another over fundamental aspects of their belief that more Christians died for their faith at the hands of fellow Christians after Christianity was officially tolerated than had been killed in all of the pre-Constantine persecutions.

Under Constantine's statesmanship, the power of the state was used to hammer home a doctrine that left those on the wrong side of the argument branded heretics. In the fourth century, one bishop claimed there were 156 "heretical practices" within the Christian community. One such group was the Gnostics, an influential sect that believed they were privy to esoteric, divine knowledge (the word "gnosis" comes from the Greek word for knowledge). The Gnostic version of Jesus put the prophet from Galilee in the divine sphere, claiming Jesus was not human at all, but rather completely divine. At issue was the very nature of Christ. Was he a god, was he flesh and blood, or was he somehow both?

At the other end of the spectrum from the Gnostics was Arius, another thorn in Constantine's side. This charismatic preacher from Alexandria attracted such devoted followers (referred to as Arians and largely female) that he rankled Church leaders. But it wasn't until they caught wind that he was spreading the belief that Jesus was the "son of God" and not God himself that the Church clamped down. Arius argued he'd just been following the Bible, citing what is today the most widely quoted Bible verse (and favorite of sign-holding Christians at football games), John 3:16, which says: "For God so loved the world that he gave his only begotten son." Arius's contention that Jesus was more than a human but not quite a god—that in the Holy Trinity, Jesus and the Holy Spirit were not on the same level as God, but subservient to him—didn't sit well with factions that believed Jesus was part of the Godhead. They fired back with another verse from John—10:30, "The Father and I are one." But the Arians countered with John 14:28: "The Father is greater than I." And it wasn't just the Arians who believed this. Previously, early-Christian theologians Lucian of Antioch and Origen had promoted this belief (and they paid for it with eventual excommunication). Even churchmen who worked for Emperor Constantine sided with the Arian belief that Christ was the son of God, but not one with him.

Which is why Constantine called for a meeting in Nicaea, in modern-day Turkey, in 325. Constantine didn't care which way the "truth" swung, he just wanted an end to the controversy. The Council of Nicaea came down to one word: Was Christ "begotten" (i.e., born from), as the Arians and others had insisted, or was he not (i.e., was he one and the same as God?). They were arguing in Greek and the two words they were actually grappling over were *homoousion*, "made of the same material," and *homoiousion*, "made of similar material." The words are separated by literally an iota but philosophically were a universe away. And in terms of the Holy Foreskin, this decision would be important: Would this flesh just be the skin of the son of God or the flesh of God himself? In the end, all but two of the three hundred or so bishops voted against the Arian belief that Christ was of "similar stuff," giving way to the Nicene Creed, which declared that Christ was part of the Godhead (along with God the Father and the Holy Spirit).

Now that Christ relics had been imbued with the power of a god, Constantine's pious mother, Helena, became obsessed. Despite her fragile condition (she was eighty years old), in 327 she took off for a sanctified shopping spree in the Holy Land that some say was penance for the way in which her son had handled the alleged affair between his son and wife. As the mother of the emperor, she had all resources available to her and she could return to Rome with just about any Christ-related curio (even his foreskin). But she had her mind on one thing: the True Cross. Helena (soon to be St. Helena) realized that if Rome was going to be a Christian capital, it needed more relics—and not just the residuum of the holy humans we call saints and martyrs. She wanted relics of the Passion itself.

Most of the divine remnants she returned with are now behind glass in a stark Fascist-era chapel in Rome's Basilica of Santa Croce in Gerusalemme (which Helena founded in 320 when she converted her palatial villa into a sanctuary): a nail from the True Cross, thorns from Jesus' infamous crown, some shreds of marble from a pillar on which Jesus had been flagellated, and the very finger that the doubting apostle St. Thomas stuck in Christ's side. And, yes, she got what she'd come there for: The pièce de résistance of the collection was a large chunk of the True Cross. Along with this, she also obtained the Titulus Crucis, the placard supposedly put above Christ's head while he was on the cross that read, "Jesus of Nazareth, King of the Jews." It should be noted that Helena's True Cross didn't actually surface until 395, seventy-five years later, through Ambrose, bishop of Milan (but as with the most important relics, including the Holy Foreskin, a relic's founding myth was just as important as the object itself). What's most important, however, is that Constantine's version of Christianity promoted relic veneration while St. Helena's new collection of spiritual keepsakes would foster a relic yen in Rome for centuries to come.

Each morning I left for the Vatican I'd find more and more packets of paper attached to the front gate of Ca' Dante. This was the agreement: I'd fetch documents for Patrizia—in some cases, three-hundred-year-old Papal-approved short histories written about the Calcata foreskin, narrating the legendary account of Maddalena Strozzi and Clarice the seven-year-old virgin—and she'd keep me on a steady diet of historical information. I did other things to stay in her good graces: I paid her to give me the occasional Italian lesson (which improved my communication skills and also my knowledge of the relic), drove her to the supermarket when I had access to a car (and waited for what felt like hours as she laboriously worked her way through the store, reading the label on every item within arm's reach), insisted on carrying her stuff up to the village when I saw her in the parking lot, and, when I'd run into her at the Grotta, paid for her favorite dessert: brownies.

Because of the warnings I'd received about Patrizia when I first arrived—that she didn't just give out the information she had filched from historical documents—there was part of me that wondered what she wasn't telling me. And so I decided to further investigate the village for others who could reveal secrets of the foreskin.

Chapter 13

A HISTORY OF NOTHING

On June 1, 1828, the French writer Stendhal wrote in his Roman journal about the Holy Foreskin's rediscovery in Calcata, noting at the end of the entry, "The first time we have occasion to pass near Calcata, we shall go and see this relic which is unique in the world." The discovery of Jesus' foreskin is one of the few significant events in the village's history to lure wanderers into the hilly netherworlds north of Rome. A couple thousand years ago, the Faliscans—a pre-Roman, part-Etruscan people—lived in the environs of Calcata. Little is known about them today, as the Romans did a good job of destroying much of their culture (though thanks to the Roman taboo against disturbing graves, many Faliscan tombs still exist throughout the area, from which scholars have been able to glean a fair amount of information). Way before the Faliscans, the Tiber River—the legendary waterway that flows through Rome—ran a different course and it went right by Calcata, its source coming from Lake Bracciano; you can still see in the Valle del Treja deep ravines where the river once ran. But besides these footnotes, nothing else of significance has been recorded in extant histories of Calcata. The village seemed to have a history of nothing.

So one day, when I met the mayor—who seemed to have begrudgingly come down from Calcata Nuova to attend some kind of art event that was happening in the borgo—and he invited me to come take a look at Calcata's historical archives, I was excited. He whipped out his business card from the inside pocket of his designer suit jacket and told me to phone him when I wanted to come up to the city hall. And so the following Monday I rang and left a voice message for him. I waited a week and when I hadn't heard back, I called again. I sent a couple e-mails, but heard nothing. Finally, while running an errand with Pancho one day up in Calcata Nuova, we encountered the vice *sindaco*, or vice-mayor, Gianni Farauti, whose family is one of the oldest in the village (and which also owned the land that Calcata Nuova now sits on). Pancho explained to him my desire to take a look at the archives. Gianni agreed and told me to stop by next Tuesday afternoon.

When the day came, I shuffled up to the second floor of the boxy, functionalist city hall in Calcata Nuova and met Gianni in his office. I sat before his desk for a brief moment, focusing on a book called *Mystery of the Incas* that sat prominently atop it, hoping I could get through the afternoon only in Italian. Gianni moved some papers around and then said, "Okay, *andiamo*," let's go, and then whisked me into the coffer-filled room next door.

Like a magician pulling rabbits from a hat, Gianni began randomly extracting documents from the cardboard boxes. The earliest known document, he said, dated from the mid-seventeenth century. This Gianni removed from a coffer and tried to read. It was so faded he could only make out about every fifth word. "There were earlier documents, but sadly, many were lost in the move from the borgo to Calcata Nuova," he said in slow-motion Italian so I could understand.

One, from 1796, was a record of the arrest of a man who had stolen some grapes. It was signed by Giuseppe Farauti. Then, from another box, he pulled out a document from 1896 that was signed by the mayor: another Farauti. I asked him if there was anything here on the relic. He shook his head, telling me I should try the Vatican.

"Does that mean the Vatican has the relic?" I asked, raising my eyebrows and smirking at him. He smirked back.

And then he uttered one of the weirdest Italian expressions: "*Boh*." The word, which has the physical and aural characteristics of a light burp, is Roman dialect for "who knows?" and is always accompanied by a light shrug of the shoulders while extending the neck forward. The word protrudes from the mouth with a gentle determination, softly piercing its way out between the frowned lips. Besides sounding ugly, it's a conversation killer; there's really no way to respond to a burp. So I just stood there, waiting for Gianni to say something.

"No one knows," he finally added, going back to his smirk. "But why wouldn't the church want to get rid of it? It has an image to uphold and things like the Holy Foreskin and the idea that Jesus had a son or was married or whatever don't fit into that manufactured image. In fact," he said, "if these things were proven to be true, it could lead to the downfall of the Church itself. So, in my opinion, they're really just protecting themselves."

I was surprised Gianni should wax so much about the disappearance—especially for the vice-mayor of Calcata—but like most people in Calcata that I'd talked to so far about the relic, his knowledge about it was more speculative than factual. Instead I turned my attention to the archives. "So, when can I look at these documents?" I asked, tapping my fingertips across one of the boxes.

He looked confused, as if I'd just asked which one of these document-filled boxes would best double as a urinal. "Oh, these?" he said. "Well, not for a long time. Sometime next year maybe. They're a big mess, and there's no order to them at all. We have someone coming here a couple days a week trying to organize them, but we don't know when we'll open the archives again. So . . . maybe next year?"

"*Boh*," I said in response to yet another bureaucratic blockade. "*Boh*," Gianni responded.

In March 974 Calcata's castle was donated to St. Gregory's Abbey in Rome. It remained in the hands of the monastery until 1180 when the Sinibaldi family took over the village and the fertile land below it, calling the area Castrum Sinibaldorum. In 1291, there's a record from a papal tax assessor, Lanfranco di Scano, describing the village as derelict and in ruin. Perhaps plague or war had brought Calcata into decline. It was about this time that the adjacent hilltop about three hundred feet north of Calcata, Santa Maria di Calcata, became inhabited for approximately fifty years (visitors can stroll up the hill to climb on the ruins of a Romanesque church and lookout tower). In 1427, the village was sold (along with the nearby towns of Nepi and Monterosi), but returned to the Sinibaldi five years later. For the next four hundred years, Calcata ping-ponged between the Sinibaldi and the Anguillara families. Then in 1828 the Massimo family, supposedly the oldest aristocratic family in Europe, took control of it until the branch of the family that had owned the village died out in 1909. Fortunately, it wasn't difficult to find information about the Massimo family, as Prince Stefano Massimo lived in Calcata part-time. He was likely attracted to the beauty of the village and its surroundings, but it must have also been nice to stand in the middle of the village square and think: *My ancestors once owned this entire place.* One day I hung out with Stefano, who lived in London most of the time and spoke perfect Oxbridge English. We sat in the kitchen of his house sipping tea. His place was really five houses that ran along the side of one of the cliffs. He'd had Patrizia and Costantino (both trained architects) turn the five houses into one intriguing labyrinth of a residence. Stefano told me he had bought the houses from the head of the Farauti family, who hadn't intended on selling them, but because the Farautis had inherited the houses from the Massimo family in the nineteenth century, he felt it was fitting to turn the houses back over to them.

Stefano spent most of the day showing me photography books he'd done based on recent trips to Afghanistan and Palestine (he's a professional photographer), interspersed with intriguing tales about his family history (like how closely related he is to other historic royals like Maria Theresa or Marie-Antoinette). As nice as he was, the more I talked to him the more uncomfortable I grew. Soon I was nervously moving my hands to my lap and then back to the table and wondering if I was holding my teacup the right way. I'd set it down on the saucer oh-so-gently and wince when it clanged. In the presence of royalty, I even noticed a British lilt creeping into my voice. I was shocked at how I'd been intimated by a blue blood. By the way, we did talk about the relic, but his main advice was "Talk to Patrizia."

Instead, I did what any peasant would do: go talk to the lord. And by that, I mean Paolo Portoghesi. Living up on the cliff that overlooks Calcata (complete with a huge picture window so he could see the village from his bedroom), Mr. Portoghesi was among the most famous architects in Italy. His most prestigious projects to date were the mosque in Rome and a skyscraper in Shanghai. He'd written books, won awards, and designed structures all over world. He was also once the president of the architecture section of the Venice Biennale. When he'd stoop down and visit the medieval village (which was rare), the people treated him like he owned the place. And why not? In addition to being the best-known artist living in Calcata, he was a huge cheerleader for the village, boasting about it in editorials for the Roman press. Italian TV camera crews would show up in Calcata and he'd lead them around the village telling them why he loved the place so much.

Since he had such a passion for Calcata (and undoubtedly a profound knowledge of the village's history), I figured I'd pay him a visit. The pop-in—making an unannounced visit to someone's house—was de rigueur because cell phones don't work inside the village; but the only person in a ten-square-mile radius who wouldn't welcome such a random visit would be Portoghesi. So I called his studio, located in the hills around Calcata, introduced myself to his secretary, and set up an appointment. A week later, I began the trek to his studio and on my way out of the village everyone I passed kept telling me to give their regards to Portoghesi. It was odd: I hadn't really heard a good word about him since I'd arrived—most people in Calcata can't say they're fans of his work—but suddenly things were different (and how did anyone even know I was meeting up with Portoghesi, anyway?).

The people of Calcata had an ambivalent impression of him, which was shaped by both their reactions to his work as well as the great fame he'd achieved. He'd been hired to redesign the palace in Calcata, which had been neglected for decades (and looked it). His redesign prettied up the place (even though, according to Stefano, he had the Massimo family crest painted over in one of the rooms), but he also put in some installations that were wildly incongruent with the style of the palace. During the time I was in Calcata, architect Richard Meier's stark white structure surrounding the Ara Pacis had just opened in the center of Rome—the first major civic building in Rome's *centro storico* in half a century. Like everything in Italy, the building was politicized—the right hated it, the left defended it. *The New York Times* said Meier's structure was "a contemporary expression of what can happen when an architect fetishizes his own style out of a sense of self-aggrandizement." This just about sums up how some of the people in Calcata felt when they got their first look at the refurbished palace and saw the star-shaped light fixtures hanging from the ceiling and the white wood-

and-glass armoires done in Portoghesi's Islamic-meets-Gothic signature style.

The other reason for the enmity toward Portoghesi was his success. Some of the villagers, I suspected, were jealous toward anyone who stood above the rest as a representative of the village itself. People all had their own views about what Calcata was, and the more time I'd spent there, the more I saw unexpected resentment of this type. Even articles I later wrote about the village were met with disdain by some people. After one high-profile publication published a travel story I wrote about Calcata, Gianni Macchia e-mailed me to say I was a "stupid, stupid person" for referring to him as a B-movie actor in something I'd written (his agent sent a letter to the publication in protest, arguing that Mr. Macchia couldn't be a B-movie actor since Quentin Tarantino had recently mentioned him in an interview; Gianni and his agent, however, were the only people on the planet who didn't realize that if Tarantino speaks highly of you, you're most likely a B-movie actor). Patrizia was irate about several things I'd written, but from what I'd heard this was normal and to be expected from her. Romano Vitali, a painter I'd become friendly with, invited me to a man's house for dinner one night and, just as I was accepting the invitation, warned me, "This man only invites you because he wants to attack you for the last article you wrote about Calcata." I rescinded my acceptance and ate at the Grotta that night instead.

"What is it with this place?" I asked Romano, the next time I saw him sitting on the piazza.

He tried consoling me, saying that people in the village wanted to control everything that was related to Calcata. "This is what happens when they can't," he said. So, since Portoghesi received the most publicity (and because he was requested to speak on behalf of Calcata more than anyone else), he was also the most resented.

As I was walking up the hill toward Calcata Nuova, which I had to pass through to get to the architect's studio, I realized I was empty-handed. I couldn't just show up at the lord of Calcata's studio without a gift. I stopped into the Zio Avelio, the corner store just up the street from Portoghesi's house. I told Avelio and his brother Antonio that I was meeting with the Architect (as he was referred to) and asked what I should bring. "Johnnie Walker," Antonio immediately said. "He's bought it here before." I paid for the bottle and dashed out of the store. As I turned the corner by the bar, Mario and Piero and the other old men (whom I hadn't talked to in a while) were sitting out in their plastic chairs drinking prosecco. They raised their glasses to me and yelled, "Good luck with the Architect."

Portoghesi's studio, called Monte Menutello, is a tall, narrow keep-like building bedecked with Islamic-esque arches. I walked over the moat via the drawbridge and knocked on the door. His secretary ushered me in and sat me down on a couch upstairs. I waited, notepad and pen in hand. Then, a minute later, he arrived wearing a sport jacket over a sweater with a scarf thrown around his neck. His large shock of thick gray hair made him appear taller than he really was.

I handed him the bottle of whisky and we commenced bantering about what language we were going to speak. Much like Americans, Italians, in general (and at least from my experience), are not wont to speak another language, even when they know another tongue well. To my relief, we settled on English. He then suggested we go to his house, and as we drove back, we chatted about Calcata. Portoghesi recounted his first visit to the village in the mid-fifties. He had decided he wanted to know the Roman countryside, spending every Sunday exploring the back roads of Lazio (the region that encompasses Rome and its environs). Then he hit upon Calcata, which he said was "out of time." There were women carrying copper pots on their heads, men in flat caps and shabby clothes sitting about the square, empty wine bottles stacked up awaiting the harvest. The village was utterly poor and the condition of life was archaic.

The name Calcata, some say, comes from the Latin word for limestone. Others say it's a derivation from the Latin word for "hidden," which would apply to Calcata not simply on account of its isolation—anchored midway between the highways Via Cassia and the Via Flaminia—but because while it rises 450 feet from the valley, it's buried beneath higher hills that surround the valley. And until relatively recently, Calcata seemed nearly impossible to get to (or get away from). Timothy Potter, the archaeologist who did a series of excavations in the area in the 1970s for the British School at Rome, noted the area's inaccessibility in one of his studies, saying that, not unlike the Faliscans of millennia past, a majority of the population of Calcata had never been to the seaside or even to Rome.

A guide to the Roman countryside, published in 1894 by the Club Alpino Italiano, stated that the only way to get to Calcata from Rome was to go up the Via Cassia to the village of Campagnano. From there, one had to take a "mule road" for several miles until reaching the village (population 563), which was plopped on a rock amid deep ravines and a picturesque background. That "mule road" remained the main way to reach the village until the late 1930s, when a paved road linking Calcata to the Via Flaminia was finally built; it's likely this was the first act by the ruling Fascist government in its pact with Calcata to abandon the medieval village for what would become Calcata Nuova. It was a member of the Fascist party who tipped off the people of Calcata about the "Messina law," which would allow them to be forever freed from the cramped conditions of the medieval village where there was just one communal water pump and no modern sewage system (the cliffsides functioned as toilets).

The famous phrase about Mussolini making the trains run on time wasn't an exaggeration; in fact, it was an understatement. Italy almost didn't seem like Italy during the Fascist period (which lasted from 1921 to 1943). Things actually got done. Buildings soared. Towns rose from nothing. Highways were paved and repaved. In turn, the ruling government graffitied its Fascist slogans everywhere, including the buildings on the square in Calcata, which were scrawled with phrases about the greatness of the government.

The government was intent on remaking Italy to the Fascist ideal. Out were decrepit medieval villages; in was a stark neoclassical architecture that alluded to the greatness of ancient Rome. Today, the Roman neighborhood of EUR is a fascinating relic of this failed attempt by Mussolini to hijack the city's history for his own political gain. Calcata Nuova wasn't only an attempt to rid the Roman countryside of historic towns that weren't a part of the ancient Roman fold, but was also part of Mussolini's grand scheme to deurbanize the cities. Making new towns would encourage people to move back to the countryside.

A world war went by, the Fascist government was ousted, and the plan to build a new village had stagnated. But then in the 1950s a new priest showed up. Don Mario Mastricola, young and progressive, decided something needed to be done. He'd heard about the village coming under the Messina Law in 1935 and began lobbying the government to recommence the project to build Calcata Nuova. He was successful. Under the deal, each family, I was once told by Gianni Farauti, received a free plot of land. They had to buy the building materials themselves, but they were offered it at a discount. During the weekend, the men of Calcata would trek up the hill to their new plots and work on their houses. In the meantime, the postwar governments had inherited the road-building fever of the previous government. And in the early sixties, a road linking the village to the Via Cassia was complete. Calcata was officially out of isolation. And by the end of the decade, much of Calcata Nuova was constructed, allowing the old inhabitants to slowly gravitate up the hill to their new homes, about a quarter of a mile away. "At the time, we were more than happy to move, to have more space and better conditions," an ancient lady told me one afternoon in Calcata Nuova. "But as a result, we lost a sense of our humanity. In the old village we would sit on the church steps every day and chat and we'd eat together—our lives were interlaced. But now," she added, fanning her arm past a few of the detached three-story block buildings, "we're more isolated than ever."

As we sailed through Calcata Nuova in Portoghesi's boat-size BMW, he said, "This horrible new town . . ." and trailed off. We cruised in silence until we got to his place.

We began the tour of his vast estate in a grove of millennia-old olive trees, which he'd named after different architects—there was one named Michelangelo, one named Borromini—and then he took me up to a higher plateau, which overlooked a huge swath of northern Lazio, and unlocked a gate. Suddenly we were in a wild bird sanctuary. There were cages with colorful birds of all shapes and sizes. Other birds were free to stroll about the grounds. A five-foot-tall crane, bobbing up and down when it walked, like some kind of otherworldly character from a George Lucas movie, tagged along, shadowing us everywhere we went; it even followed us out of the bird sanctuary and into the part of the property where Portoghesi kept his llamas.

From there, he took me through his house, which, like the prince's, was several properties connected together. We walked through libraries designed like they'd been there for centuries, the walls bedecked by floor-to-ceiling bookshelves and the ceilings boasting intricate moldings. Occasionally, he'd say something (and while his English was quite good, he seemed to favor a low-pitching rumble when he spoke). Compared to the uncomfortable starkness of Ca' Dante, Portoghesi's dwelling was a palace fit for a king; I could partially understand why he never wandered into the medieval village now. As we strode from one room into another, he finally stopped in one of the libraries and pulled a manila folder from a bookshelf. "Here," he said, handing it to me. "This is a folder of photocopied articles written about Calcata.

Bring it back to me soon." And with that, he excused himself, saying that he'd invite my wife and me over for dinner in the near future. I saw Portoghesi a few times after that, but only speeding through Calcata Nuova to get to his Eden on the hill; I'd wave, and if he saw me, he'd give a tentative wave back, probably wondering who the hell I was.

Chapter 14

THE FORESKIN
PHENOMENON

O n the way to Fabrica di Roma to talk to Calcata's former priest, Don Mario, Elena chatted away to me about a "crash with the mouth" she'd had with a friend. I was listening and looking around at the surroundings as we made the thirty-minute drive northeast of Calcata. By the time we got to Don Mario's door, I'd forgotten that I wanted to prep her for the visit. I didn't want her to mention the foreskin right away out of fear of scaring the priest into silence before I could glean some information from him about the forbidden relic.

I pressed the buzzer, on which DON MARIO was written in thick black letters. The door slowly creaked open and there stood a bulbous man in his eighties with bulletproof glasses and a blank look on his face, his black cassock sprinkled with days-old food stains. In her best formal Italian, Elena told him who we were and the priest continued his expressionless stare, his light blue eyes wide and his mouth hanging open. But when he spoke he was lucid and he waved us into his book-strewn house. By the time we got past the entryway the priest heard Elena say the words "Calcata" and "*prepuzio*" and he froze.

"I can't talk about the foreskin," he said, shaking his head. "I won't talk about the foreskin."

"But were you surprised when it was stolen?" I asked in Italian.

"No, not at all," he said, swinging his chin from shoulder to shoulder. "But I don't want to talk about it."

Then Elena and Don Mario began to speak about something related to Calcata, but not the relic. The speed of their conversation was way too fast for me to understand, so I just sat back and hoped Elena was somehow easing him into a frame of mind where he'd be comfortable talking about the relic again. After a few minutes, still stuck in the place inside the door frame to his study where he'd stopped when he heard the word "*prepuzio*," Don Mario seemed to be loosening up while he was listening to (or perhaps looking at) Elena. She twirled her wavy dark hair and laughed a lot at his attempts at wit. He chuckled back a couple of times. Maybe she knew what she was doing after all.

"Ask him about Peyrefitte," I said to her in English.

"He was arrogant and a delinquent," Don Mario said in Italian, and Elena translated for me. And then he asked me what ever had happened to him.

"He died in the year 2000."

Don Mario smirked. "Well, God let him rest," he said.

"Why weren't you surprised when the relic was stolen?" I asked in Italian, hoping he'd open up more this time.

"Because the Church never believed in it. I didn't believe in it. Still, if I'd been the priest in Calcata in the nineteen eighties, the relic wouldn't have been taken away."

I understood every word he said and I wasn't sure what to make of it. I had specifically used the word "*rubato*" (stolen) and he'd answered back, changing the verb to "*portato via*" (taken away).

"So," I said, "was it the Vatican who took the relic away?" I asked, this time using "*portato via*."

Don Mario, an earnest look on his face, shook his head again and said, "I can't discuss this any further." And then he shuffled to the front door. "Thank you for the visit. And good luck with whatever it is you're doing," he said as we stepped outside. "Oh, yes," he added. "There's one more thing I want to say. Don't hang out with miscreants—especially priests." Then he laughed and shut the door.

I wasn't going take Don Mario's advice. If one wants to find a missing Holy Foreskin, miscreants and priests cannot be avoided. So, the following weekend, fresh from our visit to Fabrica di Roma, I thought it was time to try seeing if Don Dario would say anything about the relic.

Again, Elena would be my accomplice. And, just for good measure, I'd recruited Omar, a ginger-haired thirty-three-year-old, who, like Elena, didn't have a job, which meant he had all the time in the world to help me stalk priests. Omar had spent about a year in Los Angeles, where he learned English and a lot of American slang. And he used slang words whenever he could. Whenever I'd run into him, he'd drop some phrase on me he'd heard in a movie. "Hey, what's shakin', bacon?" "What's up, honkey?" Omar was one of the most charming people I'd met in Calcata. Whenever friends would come to visit, they'd eventually meet Omar and then start requesting that Omar tag along for every activity. So if he could charm all my friends, perhaps he could charm a priest into talking. He'd spent half of his life in Calcata and couldn't find a way to get out. So, instead, he'd sit in his apartment and play guitar and video games. I used to lecture him on such themes as motivation, but he'd tell me that Italy wasn't like America. You can't just decide you want to do something or be someone and then go do it, he'd say. In Italy, Omar told me, it was all about who you knew, how you knew them, and when you knew them.

Which, I suppose, was good for me at that very moment. Omar knew Don Dario. He'd been his altar boy. After each service, Don Dario would give him, as pay, paper bags full of Eucharist hosts that had been sprinkled with sugar. Having once served the priest, Omar was nervous about being my accomplice in this quest, but he was fresh off one of his most celebrated nights in years. The night before there had been a talent show of sorts at the Granarone, the large erstwhile granary owned by Marijcke, a Dutch marionette-maker. The high-ceilinged space acted as a café, exhibition hall, and performance space. After Mimmo, Marijcke's boyfriend, who served as MC, finally gave up the mic, Angela, a painter and sculptor, was announced. She sang Neapolitan folk songs on her guitar. Serena, an angelic-looking thirty-something who was the girlfriend of the heroin-addicted Giorgio Iggy Pop, went next, playing a couple Beethoven sonatas on the piano. Then Francchino, a parking lot guy who usually dressed in military fatigues, read his poetry. This village of artists, it turned out, was filled with hidden talent. Next it was Omar's turn. With his acoustic guitar, he played a couple cover songs by David Bowie. He sang with carefree emotion during his performance, and the sixty or so people packed into the Granarone watched and listened intently. After the third and final song, he stood up and walked down the middle aisle toward the door. With each set of chairs he passed, rows of people rose up to eventually form a full standing ovation. For this one night, Omar was a rock star in Calcata.

Elena was already at Omar's house on the day we planned to pay a visit to Don Dario. Wearing a hipster honky-tonk-type cowboy hat, a taut white silky shirt, and tight jeans, she appeared ready to provoke a priest. This time, I gave them instructions not to mention the relic right away. Tell him anything else you want, I said. Just don't say I want to talk about the foreskin. When we got to Don Dario's metal gate, nerves set in. No one wanted to ring the bell. Omar was having second thoughts. "Do you really want to do this?" he asked. Elena flashed Omar a what-the-fuck look and he put his hand forward and rang the bell. Nothing happened. "Maybe he's gone," Omar said, starting to walk away. I pressed it again.

Don Dario's house in Calcata Nuova resembled a compound. The house's thick stucco walls were surrounded by metal gates, and metal roll-down shutters covered the windows. I'd walk by it sometimes, hoping to see the priest out in his garden, and I'd wonder how someone could have broken into his house back in 1983 and stolen the relic, as he claimed.

"Look!" Elena said, pointing to a small window. "The curtain is moving." Omar stopped walking away. We all stared as the window opened up and the space filled with a fat round face. "Don Dario!" Omar said. "Do you remember me? It's Omar. I was your altar boy about twenty years ago. I live just down the street here."

Don Dario looked puzzled. Louise McDermott's statement that he wasn't the most lucid person in the world came into my head. "Oh, yes, *buon giorno,* Omar," the priest finally said.

"Listen," Omar said, "I have a friend here from New York who is interested in learning more about Calcata; he's going around and interviewing important people of the town—the mayor, some of the artists who live in the old village, et cetera—and it would be a great honor if we could sit down with you and chat about your thoughts on Calcata."

Don Dario, whose face was still taking up the entire window space, looked confused. "Not now. I'm—I'm sleeping," he said.

"No problem," Omar said. "Just tell us when is the most convenient time for you and we'll come back."

"Every Sunday morning I open the church and then close it in the late afternoon. Come find me there. But I hope you don't want to talk about the relic because I can't say anything about it."

"Okay," Omar said, keeping his cheery tone intact. "We'll see you later and we're sorry for disturbing you." Don Dario closed the window and we headed back down to Omar's house to listen to music and play video games.

Don Dario didn't want to talk about the relic, mostly because the Church told him (or anyone else subject to excommunication) that he couldn't. But long before 1900, the relic had begun to lose credibility with the Church. Thanks to competition to sell important relics to wealthy collectors, it's no surprise that within a few centuries after Charlemagne's death and, as some scholars have claimed, within a decade of the first mention of Rome's foreskin in the 1070s, Holy Prepuces began popping up just about everywhere in Europe. Relics of Christ were a cash cow. But "discovering" a Holy Foreskin in your town or monastery wasn't just a direct challenge to the legitimacy of Rome's prepuce; it was a challenge to Rome itself.

And it's no surprise to learn that most of the ten, twelve, or eighteen different foreskins (depending on what you read) could be traced—factually or fictionally—back to Charlemagne. It didn't matter if a town really had the true foreskin of Christ. If another village or monastery had a compelling link between their supposed Holy Foreskin and Charlemagne, they'd have a compelling case for relic-seeking penitents to visit their shrine.

Another theory for the existence of multiple claimants is that the relic may have had a brief stay in some of the towns, but its reputation lasted beyond its actual presence there. Aachen, Charlemagne's headquarters, for example, has been listed in documents as a home to a Holy Prepuce; centuries-old sources, however, also record that after Charlemagne supposedly received the relic in Jerusalem, he temporarily kept it in Aachen before deciding what to do with it.

Not all prepuce boosters were assiduous with connecting Charlemagne to their relic: The Holy Foreskin of Antwerp was an anomaly in that its arrival myth did not rely on a Carolingian connection. Instead, it was the famed knight Godfrey of Bouillon, the eleventh-century leader of the First Crusade, who obtained the relic in Jerusalem. He happened to be there with Henry Noese, his chaplain, who brought it back to Antwerp, where it was housed in the church of St. Maria Gloriosa. According to one story, retold in Alphons Victor Müller's *Die hochheilige Vorhaut Christi*, published in 1907 and the only book ever written solely about the Holy Foreskin, when the relic first arrived in Antwerp, the priest had it laid on the altar and watched as it miraculously emitted three drops of blood. The relic was then kept in a golden vessel in the Prepuce Chapel and even had a dedicated chaplain to look after it. Documents, however, don't record the prepuce's presence in the Belgian city until the fifteenth century. In 1426 a confraternity was founded in honor of the relic, "The Fellowship of the Holy Foreskin of Our Dear Lord Jesus Christ in Our Lady's Church in Antwerp." Reformation riots, however, swept through the city in 1566 and the relic went missing forever.

The Holy Foreskin of Conques, located on the Santiago de Compostela pilgrimage route in the mid-Pyrenees in southern France, used the reputation of Charlemagne to define and legitimize what they had in their chapel of relics. The Abbey of St. Foy's tenth-century compendium of relics listed generically "Christ's flesh" among its collection, which also consisted of curios of the Virgin and various saints. But because it would be impossible to have any piece of Christ's flesh besides his foreskin or his umbilical cord, over the centuries the monks, probably having heard the Charlemagne legend, revised their list of relics to include Jesus' foreskin and umbilical cord. And then they associated the relics' origins with Charlemagne, thus centering their Abbey of St. Foy and the village of Conques in the all-important Carolingian legend.

It's unclear if Henry V, fifteenth-century king of England, had heard of the venerated foreskin before he took over a large swath of France. Henry's French wife, Catherine of Valois, was pregnant and when word got back to Henry that the Holy Foreskin was known to give fertility and ease childbirth, he sent for the nearest copy, which was in the French village of Coulombs. After the relic was sent to London in 1421, Catherine reportedly touched it and then birthed the future Henry VI. True to the king's word that he'd return the miracle-inducing, baby-producing foreskin as soon as it had done its deed, he sent a cavalry back to France with the relic. But because of continued strife caused by the Hundred Years' War, the prized prepuce ended up in Paris's Sainte-Chapelle. The monks of Coulombs, fearing they'd never see their relic again (and likely lose out on a great number of pilgrims), requested that the prepuce be taken to the nearby monks of St. Magloire, the same fraternal order as theirs. Which eventually happened. But the relic was stuck in the City of Light because upon its arrival a law was quickly written claiming that it could not leave the city without the express permission of the grand counsel to the king. And then at last, twenty years later, on July 28, 1447, with peace restored in the area, the monks of Coulombs finally obtained a royal ordinance that authorized the return of the relic to their abbey. In April 1464, King Louis XI went to pray at Coulombs; and because he was the king, the monks granted him a special privilege by opening the reliquary so he could see the *Saint Prépuce.*

The abbey that put up the strongest fight in its bid for the "real" Charlemagne-connected Holy Foreskin was Charroux, located near Poitiers in southwestern France. According to one story, Charlemagne received the Holy Foreskin from Byzantine empress Irene as an engagement gift, which then made its way to Charroux. More popular, however, was the oft-repeated tale of Charlemagne's receiving the relic in Jerusalem from the Christ Child. The earliest source for the existence of the Charroux foreskin is 1082, placing it about a decade after the first mention of the Rome foreskin. "Holy Foreskin" wasn't actually used in the 1082 reference. Instead the term *Sancta Virtus,* the "Holy Virtue," was used, which could be translated as "all holy power" and suggested (at least to the monks at the time) that this "Virtue" was the flesh of Christ (of which only the foreskin would have been possible) and a piece of the True Cross. The words "Holy Foreskin" were not mentioned in relation to Charroux until a papal indulgence in 1380.

That the Charlemagne tale is almost certainly apocryphal, perhaps invented centuries after the king's death to try to lend legitimacy to the abbey, didn't really matter. After a series of fires in the late eleventh century, the abbey was rebuilt. The fires dealt a fatal blow to the monastery's collection of holy curios. Which didn't bode well for the relics race the monks had going with neighboring St. Jean d'Angély, who in 1010 announced they'd discovered the head of St. John the Baptist. So the monks of Charroux suddenly "discovered" several relics, including Christ's cradle, wheat that had been sown from the hands of Christ, leather straps that had bound Christ, thorns from Christ's crown, Christ's clothing, and, of course, something called the Holy Virtue. The fact that Rome had already claimed the exact same relics didn't stop the monks of Charroux, who created a series of false sources to justify the Holy Virtue's existence in their southwestern French town; these documents claimed the monastery was founded in 799 by Charlemagne (interestingly, one year before the great French king was supposedly to have given Pope Leo III the foreskin in Rome).

Even the architecture and structure of the abbey itself went out of its way to implicitly evoke Charles and the Holy Foreskin. The design of the new abbey was in the standard cruciform plan but boasted an unorthodox octagonal rotunda rising above a triple ambulatory. The rotunda and cross-like plan of the church had symbolic meaning, recalling and imitating the Church of the Holy Sepulcher in Jerusalem. Its very structure, therefore, alluded to both relics as well as the abbey's supposed patron, Charlemagne.

And as people began to build houses near the massive church and monastery, the village became known as Charroux. In French, *chair* means skin and *roux* means red: a reference to the incorruptible flesh of Jesus' foreskin that was housed in the abbey.

The Charroux foreskin was given a huge boost when Jacobus de Voragine, a thirteenth-century chronicler and archbishop of Genoa, recounted the Charlemagne-meets-the-Christ-Child tale in his account of miracles, saints, and Christian legends called *Golden Legend*, which was something of a medieval best-seller (in its first fifty years, there were seventy editions). After receiving the relic in the Holy Sepulcher, de Vorgine wrote, Charlemagne brought it to Aachen (or Aix-la-Chapelle) before emperor Charles the Bald (Charlemagne's grandson) transferred it to Charroux, where it would sit alongside a piece of the True Cross—perhaps the same piece Charlemagne supposedly had received from Jerusalem. Petrus Comestor (aka "Peter the Eater") also gave the Charroux foreskin credibility when he recounted the tale of Charlemagne praying in the Holy Sepulcher in 1170 in his *Scholastica Historia*.

And the problem with this, of course, was that the pope was in possession of the same relic in Rome. The Church had a theological dilemma on its hands. Pope Innocent III had a chance to decide on the "real" foreskin in the early twelfth century but took a pass, stating that it was better to let God decide the entire matter. St. Bonaventure mused about the theological existence of the foreskin later that century, and sided somewhat with Innocent III, leaving the door slightly ajar for the earthly existence of Jesus' foreskin.

With other copies of the foreskin now acknowledged, it was only a matter of time before Rome would harden its stance on the relic. But throughout the Middle Ages, the popes were occupied with other affairs. Medieval Rome was a mess, having never really recovered from the successive sacks that had helped topple the Roman Empire. In 897 the citizens of Rome were so frustrated with the shabby, disease-ridden state of their city that they exhumed the corpse of Pope Formosus and put him on trial.

Muslims attacked the city that same century. Normans burst through the gates in the eleventh century. The twelfth century saw the city in flames thanks to family rivalries. In the year 300 A.D., Rome had a million inhabitants, but by the thirteenth century there were only thirty thousand people living there. Eventually even the popes fled; from 1305 to 1378 the papal seat was relocated to Avignon, in the south of France.

Which is when St. Catherine of Siena comes in to the picture. Saint Catherine claimed she was the spiritual bride of Christ. And as proof, she was said to wear Jesus' foreskin on her ring finger. Catherine made an ambassadorial trip to Avignon in 1376 to try to broker a peace deal between Florence and the Papal States, which were at war. She also wanted to persuade the French pope Gregory XI to return to Rome, arguing it was the historic and spiritual home of the papacy. St. Bridget of Sweden, who died in 1373, also made a plea for the pope to come back to Rome, claiming the Virgin Mary had appeared to her. She wrote:

And Maria said: As my son was circumcised, I preserve the membrane with great reverence wherever I go. How I passed over the earth, with it testifying for me. As the time for my own calling approaches, I am giving it to St. John, my protector, along with the blessed blood, which remained in his wounds as we took him down from the cross. Then, as St. John and his successors took leave of this world, the evil and perfidy grew. So the believers who were then alive stored this object in a pure place under the earth and it remained there unknown for a long time, until finally an angel from God revealed it to the friends of God. Oh, Rome, oh, Rome! If you knew, you would be joyous. Instead if you could weep, would you weep without end, because you have a treasure so valuable to me, and you do not adore it.

And thanks to Catherine and Bridget, Gregory conceded and returned to Rome in 1378. But Saint Bridget's vision was more than a plea for the pope's homecoming; it also legitimized the Lateran foreskin with an implication straight from the Virgin's mouth to venerate Rome's relic.

But the reunion between the papacy and Rome would only last for a year. From 1379 to 1417, the period known as the Papal Schism, French-versus-Italian infighting caused two popes to be elected at the same time, an Italian pope in Rome and a French pope in Avignon. At one point, a third pope was elected to try to sort out the differences between them. The schism was played out between the Roman and French foreskins as well.

After the papal court was officially set up in Avignon in 1379, the French pope wasn't moved by St. Bridget's claim that the Virgin Mary had come to her and legitimized the foreskin in Rome. In fact, on April 15, 1379, one year into the Great Schism, Clement VII, a Gallic pontiff, granted an indulgence to those who came to venerate the Holy Foreskin. Not in Rome. In Charroux.

When the election of Pope Martin V at the Council of Constance in 1415 brought an end to the schism, anything the Avignon popes had done between the years 1379 and 1414 was considered illegitimate. The two popes who ruled from Avignon during this period were labeled antipopes. People whom they'd canonized (one of whom was Charlemagne) were discounted and indulgences for venerating certain relics (especially the Charroux foreskin) were dismissed.

Not that this meant the Holy Foreskin controversy had been buried for good. Within the Church, foreskin-inspired controversy would boil up through the ages. But huge historical events would nearly wipe out the relic's existence for good.

Chapter 15

SACRED CHOW

Meet Agnes Blannbekin. This early-fourteenth-century Austrian lived as a beguine—a single woman who resided in an all-women's home—and would spend her day going from church service to church service, having memorized the schedule of masses in every church in Vienna. We know this because a monk friend of hers wrote down a series of visions that Agnes claimed to have had. The writings were eventually published under the title *Life and Revelations,* and when it first hit the streets in 1731, it was an immediate scandal. Agnes's criticism of the pope wasn't too well received. Also, some of her daily devotional practices were strangely erotic. At the end of each mass, for example, she would partake in a practice that was apparently quite dear to her, making a beeline for the altar and showering it with an amount of amorous emotion and enthusiasm that would make modern Roman teenagers blush.

But that wasn't exactly what all the commotion was about when *Life and Revelations* hit the street. It was all about Chapter 37, titled "Regarding the Foreskin of Christ." The chapter describes how the young Agnes would always cry on the feast day of the Circumcision, saddened by the first spillage of Christ's blood. One particular year on January 1, Agnes, tearful and in mourning, began to wonder where the Holy Foreskin might have ended up. Suddenly, the inside of her mouth was overcome with a sweet sensation. She stuck out her tongue and there in the middle of it was "a little piece of skin alike the skin of an egg," which she promptly swallowed. And then the sweetness came again and there was another piece of skin. She swallowed. And again, it came back and she swallowed again. This happened about a hundred times, until she was tempted to touch the piece of skin with her finger. When she tried, the piece of flesh began going down her throat on its own. So amplified was the sweetness in her mouth, all of Agnes's limbs quivered and shook as they, too, were engulfed with the saccharine spirit of the Holy Foreskin.

Her confessor, the anonymous monk who scribbled down Agnes's visions, wrote that Agnes was reluctant to talk about this particular revelation. But she did anyway, which excited him to no end: "I . . . was really very comforted that the Lord deigned to show Himself to a human being in such a way, and greatly desired to hear [about it]."

Eating in Italy wasn't necessarily a spiritual (or orgasmic) experience for me, but—like sex or church—it was something I began planning my day around. And when the Grotta was open, there were extrasensory benefits to nursing a glass of wine and watching Pancho work. The first time, for example, I heard Pancho belittle one of his customers, I hardly batted an eye. He was standing on the kitchen side of the bar and a young Italian woman came up to pay her bill. Having heard Pancho speaking with me, the woman decided to have a go in English.

"It's a nice thing you have going here," she said. Or rather meant to say. Her English was good and her pronunciation was almost right on, except that she mangled the "th" sound in "thing," voicing it more like "ting." Pancho, having just helped me polish off a bottle of wine, pounced.

"Ting?" he said, setting the corkscrew down on the counter. Her face grew tight. "Ting? Is it really a good *ting*? Do you know what a '*ting*' is?" She briskly shook her head as her face shed its color. "*This* is a ting," Pancho said and then flicked the rim of his wineglass with his finger. "Ting. Ting. Ting. You want to say 'tttttthhhhhing.'"

Though the woman looked slightly rattled, I was sure she'd forget about the incident as quickly as she departed the Grotta. Volatility appears to be a characteristic Italians allow chefs and restaurateurs to exercise. When Jessie and I had previously lived in Rome, we would frequent Al Cardello, an ancient trattoria near our apartment. Owners Angelo and Lidia treated us like visiting family when we'd step down into the sunken dining room for dinner. As in many casual restaurants in Italy, menus were rarely produced. Instead, Lidia would recite what they had that day. Sometimes, however, she'd stop after one item. She never said it was the only dish Angelo felt like making that day, but there was something about the way Lidia would just show up at our tableside with two unordered steaming plates of the day's special, put them down in front of us, and walk away that made it clear we didn't have a choice in the matter. If Angelo was taking a newbie's order and there was a protest over the plate he was pushing, Angelo would cock his hand over the opposite shoulder as if he were about to deliver a nice backhand slap to the face.

Pancho wasn't one for physical violence, but he threw plenty of verbal jabs. I could intrinsically sense his mood go from placid to pugnacious in seconds. For a while, and for whatever reason, the presence of Scot would be greeted by Pancho's wagging finger. And Paul could send him off with the utterance of a single word. When American tourists would wander into the Grotta, I could see Pancho feeling them out for their political views. If there was even a hint that they were Republicans, Pancho would attack—even though they were about to part with their money at his restaurant. He didn't care, and I admired him for that. On a lunchtime excursion to Rome one day, Jessie and I accompanied Paul, Pancho, and his new boyfriend, Mario, to a wine bar near the Spanish Steps. When Jessie and I heard an American guy sitting behind us say that he thought George Bush was doing a great job as president, we looked at each other and then looked at Pancho, who was regaling his boyfriend Mario and Paul with a story. "Should we unleash the Pancho?" I said to Jessie, who smiled and nodded. She tapped Pancho on the wrist and, with her thumb, motioned behind her while mouthing "He likes Bush."

Pancho was like a dog whose ears had just gone up. "The Republicans have ruined the country," he said, talking to no one in particular. "The Bush Administration has led an illegal invasion for its own selfish reasons and has created more terrorists because of it." With the end of each sentence, he increased the volume of his voice. "The world is a worse place thanks to George W. Bush and I think he should suffer for it." Louder and louder he became. Our wineglasses began shaking as he pounded the table with each syllable of "George W. Bush." He got the Republican's attention and a five-minute argument ensued until the guy got up and left in a huff.

Despite Pancho's proclivity for occasional verbal skirmishes, he was one of the most charming and charismatic people I'd ever met. There was something very safe and protecting about Pancho. Like a big brother, if anyone wronged me, he'd go after them. When there was a misunderstanding over our Internet bill with Alessandro, Pancho went knocking on his door to try to figure out the problem. When Patrizia would get defensive about my Holy Foreskin–seeking presence in town, Pancho would stand on my side. And when we ran into any kind of trouble, somehow Pancho would always get us out of it. He'd handle the most knee-shaking situations with grace and tranquility, as if he'd been in that situation hundreds of times before. And from the tales he sometimes recounted—about growing up in Rome in the 1960s and '70s—he had a knack for attracting trouble and then finding a miraculous way out of it. When we were driving to Viterbo and his car broke down on a country road in the middle of nowhere Pancho just shrugged his shoulders and made a phone call. Within an hour, his mechanic drove out to tow us home. On a few occasions, the Carabinieri—the intimidating state police who set up roadblocks on the roads around Calcata, intermittently stopping cars for selective harassment and document checks—flagged us down and I didn't have my papers on me; instead of the police hauling me off, somehow Pancho would start talking, and two minutes later, we'd be driving away. When Pancho was out of town, he allowed me to use his car so that I could continue our tradition of taking Paul out to lunch on Tuesdays. The only problem was that Paul wouldn't drive with me. There was no way I'd be able to talk us out of a jam like Pancho would, Paul told me flat out. And he was right.

There was an implicit mantra that Pancho oozed: Everything was going to be all right. Like Paul, I often found myself depending on Pancho to cool my nerves. But Paul had a cool side to him too. He even had his own philosophy of life, which could be summed up (and practiced) in two words: We'll see. "We'll see" embodied years of wisdom and patience. It withheld judgment until either the situation in question sorted itself out or enough time had passed so that a better, more accurate assessment could be made.

Often "we'll see" would arise during our many weekend lunches at the Grotta. I ate lunch with Paul there every Saturday and Sunday and if I hadn't eaten dinner there, I was certain to stop in for a nightcap. In fact, I was in Pancho's cave so much, friends like Omar and Elena would just assume they'd find me there. "I'm not sure if I'm coming to the Grotta tonight," Elena would say to me before we'd even discussed future plans. I started washing dishes in the kitchen on busy evenings and no one did a double take when I'd help myself to wine or run into the kitchen to get a fork.

On nights when the Grotta was closed, we'd hit up other restaurants. Il Gato Nero, for example, was, run by Fabio, who rarely changed the menu and never changed the show-tunes soundtrack on the hi-fi. Fabio was a big, generous man and his cat-themed restaurant was a cozy place to tuck into a mountain of pasta and a carafe of vino. Often Jessie and I would go there and within a few minutes we'd be joined at the table by whoever else happened to have just walked in. Sometimes Costantino would show up; he'd eat a Pavarotti-size meal, washed down with several half-liter carafes of white wine. Other times, Athon would arrive and stay only a short time because she felt her birds calling her. About every other Sunday evening, we'd eat dinner there with the painter Giancarlo Croce and his wife, Deborah; they didn't speak much English, so we'd go the entire night speaking Italian, which was a great help for learning.

But when the weather was warm, there'd often be dinner parties. I'd be reading in Ca' Dante and hear, "Day-veed . . . Day-veed." Standing down on the cobbled alley below our front door would be Stefania, who'd come by to inform me that we were all eating together that night. Tables would be set up on the square, and around nine P.M., everyone would convene with a dish of something thrown together and a bottle of wine. Roberto would usually get all the Italians singing songs I'd never heard before. About an hour in, people would begin slowly changing seats so that everyone would get a chance to chat. Someone would eventually light up a joint and it would get passed around. The food—usually some variation on pasta and salad—was never spectacular, but that wasn't the point. Besides, everything tasted better after the joint went around the table a couple times.

No amount of hashish, however, could make the offerings from Palma digestible. Originally from Faleria—the neighboring village—Palma was an unlikely Calcata resident. Though generous and friendly, she wasn't artistic nor did she favor any trappings of bohemia that so many people here were partial to. She supported right-wing prime minister Silvio Berlusconi (she even once told me matter-of-factly that she was a fascist). Palma, who was in her late forties and had big black bushy hair, said her only experience in America had been a few weeks in Arizona, but by the look (and taste) of the food she'd bring to the dinner parties, it seemed like she'd been a high school exchange student somewhere in the deep South. No one would really touch her mini hot dogs in baked beans or macaroni baked with potato chips—at least not before a joint was produced.

On one memorable occasion, Palma did make something very Roman. She pushed a bowl toward us and, in her usual bossy manner, ordered us to eat. The crunchy, unidentifiable objects had that bitter, wrong-part-of-the-animal taste. I'm an adventurous eater, however, so I kept chewing. Finally, Jessie asked Scot, who was sitting across from us (and happened to be going out with Palma at the time) what we were eating. Scot had an annoying habit of staring back at you for a long five seconds before answering your question, but this time it seemed like he was really struggling to come up with adequate words. Finally he opened his mouth and cavalierly said, "Fried cow nerves." Jessie spit and I swallowed. "It's a typical Roman dish," he said, with just enough condescension to make us both feel like uncultured ignoramuses for not wanting to eat more. Of course, I didn't see him digging into the cow's nerves much.

But such is the irony of the Italian taste bud. In general, Italians will eat all manner of strange native food but won't touch anything that hails from outside Italy's borders. With the exception of Chinese restaurants and, thanks to Italy's failed conquest of Ethiopia, a couple African restaurants, the Italian capital is surprisingly devoid of ethnic cuisine. Instead, eating "ethnic" in Rome would be going to a Sicilian or Tuscan restaurant. I once interviewed a Michelin-starred Roman chef and asked him what he thought of fusion cuisine. He said he liked it: He used basil from Genoa and tomatoes from Campania. I'd heard stories about Italians who wouldn't eat anything but the cuisine of their own region.

Many Italians argue that they don't need to eat any other cuisines because they have the best in the world. Maybe. But for the country's small set of "exotic" food lovers, the Grotta was a popular place. Pancho used Italian cuisine as his base, but he deviated from there, using almonds to make pesto or adding curry to a tomato sauce. This was a man on a mission to broaden the Italian taste bud. It was always entertaining when someone would sit down at the Grotta and wrinkle their nose at the menu. That's when Pancho would begin the spiel. "You know what you are?" he'd begin. "You're just a slave to your mother. You're spoiled because you've got one of the best cuisines in the world, but you've also got to stop eating your mama's food and start thinking for yourself. That's the whole problem—we're living in a country of mama's boys." Then he'd offer to bring out a procession of plates—all on the house—until the nose-wrinkler got something he liked. Pancho claimed no one has ever gone past the first dish and that they were often grateful to him for forcing their minds (and their mouths) to open to something different.

One time when I lured Giancarlo Croce to have dinner with me at the Grotta, he was having a hard time deciding what to order. "I'm a traditional eater," he told Pancho. "I don't eat anything that's outside the canon of Italian cuisine. This," he said, fanning his hand at the menu, "looks very interesting, but it's not very traditional."

"Listen," Pancho began his gleeful retort, "what really is traditional? What you consider 'traditional cuisine' wasn't very traditional thirty or forty or fifty years ago. Some of the dishes you think are part of the canon hadn't even existed yet, or were even new and cutting-edge at one time. Tomatoes didn't even come to Italy until they were sent back from the New World. So, don't look at me and say that you like traditional food. What's considered traditional now might not even be around in decades to come."

Pancho's lecture, which made perfect sense to me, didn't open Giancarlo's mind (or taste buds) much. Another time, while walking up to Calcata Nuova, I got snared into Capellone's cantina. It turned out he was entertaining a few twenty-somethings from Rome. The four of them—they were two couples—all spoke English well and we hit it off. Eventually, we bid Capellone adieu and headed back to the old village for dinner. They asked for a recommendation, and naturally, I suggested the Grotta. When we got there, Pancho happened to be standing by the front door. After introductions, one of the guys said he wanted *cinghiale*, wild boar. "We don't have cinghiale here," Pancho said, handing him a menu. The young Roman lawyer scanned the menu, looking over the salads topped with sprouts and dishes infused with spices, and announced, "I want cinghiale," and then handed the menu back to Pancho and stormed up the steps with his male friend, leaving the two women and me standing in front of Pancho. "Fuck 'em," Pancho said to me and the guys' two girlfriends. "This is a special place and if they can't recognize that, it's best they don't even eat here." Eventually, we drifted up the steps and found the two guys at La Piazzetta, a more traditional Italian restaurant situated right above the Grotta. Cinghiale wasn't on the menu there, either, but they seemed more than content with a dinosaur-size pork chop.

I loved the Italian eating experience so much that, at times, I felt like my day was broken into two parts: the times I was eating and the times I was waiting until the next opportunity to eat. And with lunches and dinners so long and leisurely, the time in between meals grew increasingly short. Which is why I often tried to make time to eat lunch with Paul a few times per week. He'd often eat at Tre Monti, the fascist-themed restaurant in the parking lot. I'd often join him, trying to pry information about his noteworthy life. Jessie and I were both pining (and competing) to write a profile about him for a magazine, but when asked, he'd always decline, saying he wasn't in the mood.

Here was a man who had been trained as a dancer by the famed Lester Horton and danced in Hollywood films. He was best friends with Rita Hayworth and apparently had a relationship with her while she was married to Orson Welles ("But it was Welles who I really wanted," Paul once told me). During a few stints on Broadway, he became a part of Dorothy Parker's famed Round Table at the Algonquin Hotel. In the late forties, his friend Elia Kazan told him that this McCarthy guy in Washington didn't bode well for them. Paul wasn't a Communist, but he was gay and liberal, which for that time pretty much made him a Communist anyway. Kazan's advice to the young up-and-coming dancer: Get the hell out of this place.

So Paul fled, first to Paris, where he ended up with a steady gig at the famed Champs-Elysées-located Lido club. There he danced with Josephine Baker, helped bring Lena Horne's son out of the closet (at her request), had his photo taken by Man Ray, and was even given an apartment by Jean Cocteau.

As the eighty-seven-year-old Paul and I sat at Tre Monte inhaling wine, I briefly gave him a rundown on what I knew of his wonderful life, hoping that this would convince him it was worth writing about. "You used to hang out at the Café de Flore in Paris with Jean-Paul Sartre! And Simone de Beauvoir!" Paul nodded. We'd been over this before. Paul had said Sartre used to lament that Paul had come to Paris at the wrong time. Sartre preferred the Paris of the 1920s to the Paris of the 1950s. "It was only a decade or so later," Paul said, "when I'd tell people I was living in Paris in the fifties and dancing at the Lido that they'd swoon."

"And while you were living in Paris, is it true that you had some kind of sexual encounter with Marlon Brando?"

"I don't discuss my romantic endeavors," Paul said. "I never have and I never will."

In the 1960s, Paul was living in Rome and, again, found himself a part of the hippest scene on the planet, bouncing around the Via Veneto with Federico Fellini and Marcello Mastroianni. By this time, he'd become a famous dancer and choreographer. He'd bought an apartment around the corner from the Trevi Fountain and had his friend, designer Dan Johnson, go to work on it, laying a black-and-white mosaic floor and installing rich wood-paneling closets. Pieces of Roman relief sculptures tacked to the wall added to the theme of antiquity. In the end, his apartment, which he still owned, looked as if the Roman Empire and 1950s Rome had suddenly collided.

"So when you were in Rome," I continued my recounting of Paul's life to Paul, "you started a dance troupe"—the Paul Steffen Dancers—"and you became the resident choreographer for Italian TV."

Paul nodded and giggled.

"Then, in the nineteen seventies, you did shows in Las Vegas, opening for Judy Garland, and ended up spending time at the Eslean Institute in Big Sur, where you became good friends with Henry Miller. Right?"

Paul giggled again. "Yes, that's about right."

"And this is only what I know from the things you've told me during various lunches. It's remarkable, Paul."

Paul flashed a coy smile and took a sip of wine.

And for an octogenarian, it seemed he'd hardly slowed down. Just a few years before, he'd gotten his first tattoos. He had a spiderweb on one elbow and a Star of David on other, and on his wrist the tattooed replica of a thick Native-American bracelet he had bought in the 1960s. He was probably one of the most open-minded people I'd ever met. But, curiously, he was coy when it came to publicizing his eventful twentieth-century life.

"I don't know," Paul said, shrugging when I asked him again about the possibility of writing a profile about him for a newspaper or a magazine. "I just get embarrassed about it." Then he paused and grabbed the carafe of wine, filling his glass all the way to the rim, and said, "We'll see."

Chapter 16

"PRECIOUS RUBBISH"

In 1511, toward the end of a month-long stay in Rome, a young Augustinian monk from Germany walked up to the door of the Lateran Palace and stood at the bottom of a staircase. He eyed the twenty-eight steps for a long few seconds, made the sign of the cross, and knelt down on the first step. The marble stairway, known as the Scala Santa, or Holy Steps, had been brought back from the Holy Land in the fourth century by St. Helena, who was told the marble staircase had been taken from Pontius Pilate's palace in Jerusalem. Thus, it was on these steps that Jesus Christ may have taken his final strides before being condemned to death.

Since it had been installed in the Lateran Palace in Rome, the same building where the Holy Foreskin was housed, the Scala Santa had been a hugely poplar destination for pilgrims. According to tradition, ascending the steps on one's knees while reciting prayers along the way will release a soul from Purgatory. After finishing a short prayer for his departed grandfather, our young sixteenth-century German monk inched up to the second step on his way to the top of one of Christianity's most esteemed relics.

About halfway up the stairway, having recounted a prayer with each move, the monk began thinking about all the relics he'd seen during his month-long stay in Rome. His knees slightly ached from scaling the marble steps, as he likely realized, *Crawling up a staircase isn't going to help get me—or my grandfather—into heaven.* Neither, he would have agreed, would praying to Jesus' foreskin or a vial of the Virgin's breast milk. So he got up, walked down the stairs, and headed back to Germany. That monk's name was Martin Luther, and the Reformation had just been born.

Up until this time, there had been little criticism of the Church. And those who hazarded it usually paid the ultimate price. Prague-based Jan Hus, who voiced protestations about, among many other things, the cult of the Holy Foreskin, and whose reform movement came a century before Luther's, was burned at the Council of Constance in 1415 for speaking out against the pope and for preaching in the vernacular instead of Latin. But Luther was undeterred by threats of violence and after crossing back over the Alps, he nailed his famed Ninety-five Theses—a broadside against Church practices—to the door of Wittenberg Cathedral. This commenced the firestorm in Europe that would last more than a century and change the world forever.

And now, with Europe divided, criticism would rain down. The sale of indulgences, which were largely motivated to raise money for the building of the new St. Peter's Basilica, was a major target of reformers like Martin Luther and John Calvin. But it gave them a reason to look at all aspects of the Church. The nepotism within the papacy. The lavish lifestyle in which the popes lived. And, of course, the dubious nature of the cult of relics, particularly Christ relics.

And so, in 1527, sixteen years after Martin Luther stomped back down the Scala Santa, a massive army from the north led by Spanish king Charles V marched down the Via Cassia on its way to Rome. The reason for the attack on Rome was an intricate diplomatic mess between France, Spain, and the papacy. But what's important for us is that many of the soldiers were feared German mercenaries known as the Landsknecht. Indoctrinated with Lutheran thought back home, these soldiers were on a veritable crusade against the papacy, but their main concern was one thing: booty.

Once they penetrated the walls of Rome, the German soldiers (along with some of their Spanish counterparts) proceeded to ravage the city like barbarian hordes of previous centuries. They raped nuns. They dressed up a donkey in sacred vestments and paraded it through the streets of the city; when a priest refused to perform the most holy sacrament on the mule, they cut the priest into pieces. They chopped off the testicles of priests, roasted them in the fire, and then force-fed them to their erstwhile owners. They stumbled through the streets wearing valuable sacred garments and massive papal mitres and tiaras, their arms and necks festooned with a treasure trove of stolen sacred jewelry, imbibing voracious amounts of wine from silver chalices they'd swiped from altars. In the end, the streets of Rome were unusable due to mountains of rotting flesh and bone, which blocked passage.

Relics were tossed to the ground or mistreated. One Landsknecht took the Holy Lance—the spear that was used to pierce Christ's side while he was hanging from the cross—and attached it to his own lance while marauding through town. The Veronica, a cloth said to miraculously contain an image of the face of Jesus, was tossed around like a beach towel. The foot of Mary Magdalene also went astray, as did the bones of St. Blaise and thousands of other saintly body parts.

The soldiers had marched to Rome hungry and relatively penniless, their generals promising riches when they conquered the city. And much of the booty came in the form of reliquaries. Besides raiding the Vatican and churches throughout the Eternal City, soldiers hit the jackpot when they stumbled upon the Sancta

Sanctorum. The Holy of Holies was a literal treasure trove of holy relics (and reliquaries): the heads of Sts. Peter and Paul, the head of St. Lawrence, a chunk from the table that was used during the Last Supper, and a painting of Christ said to be "not painted by a human hand."

It didn't take long before saints' heads were being used in ball games on the street. Reliquaries had been ripped from the wall and swiped from the altar. One of those marauding Teutonic warriors was our soldier who ended up in Calcata. He apparently ran through the Sancta Sanctorum and grabbed a small silver reliquary and put it under his arm. Like a running back making a mad dash for the end zone, he sprinted for the Roman hinterlands, heading north back to Germany. The Landsknecht darted up the Via Cassia, the same road the massive army had taken into Rome, but fear of getting mobbed by angry pro-pope flocks and hoping to avoid the oveflowing rivers he had encountered in southern Tuscany on his way down, he took a small mule road that split from the Cassia in the town of Campagnano. He was tired, exhausted, and some say injured, and after about five or six miles on this road, he was captured by farmers who had probably never set eyes on a northerner before. Not sure what to do with the soldier (who was still hiding the silver case), they threw him in a jail cell in the nearest town, Calcata. It would be three decades before anyone would find that case, stashed under a pile of manure. The Holy Foreskin, brought to Calcata, by the forces of history, would be isolated and out of the spotlight. Which may have saved it from what was to come. The other foreskin relics were not so fortunate.

In other parts of Europe, which would be ravaged and ransacked in the succeeding wars of religion, a maelstrom against relic veneration occurred, spurred on by the writings of John Calvin. The Holy Foreskin, of course, did not escape criticism. "Let us begin then at Jesus Christ," wrote Calvin in *A Very Profitable Treatise*, "of whom because they could not say that they had the natural body (for concerning his miraculous body they have found such means to forge it, and such number and at all times, as often as seemed good to them) they have gathered in need thereof thousands of other trifles to supply this want. Although yet not withstanding they have not let the body of Jesus Christ escape without retaining some little piece."

In Calvin's other diatribe against relics, *Most useful advertisement of the great advantages that would come to Christendom if an inventory were made of all the holy bodies and relics, that are in Italy, France, Germany, Spain and other kingdoms and lands*, otherwise known as *Treatise on Relics*, first published in 1543, Calvin waxes sarcastic about the most ridiculous aspects of the cult of relics. Noting that there is no mention of relics in the Gospels, or in the writings of early Church fathers, he then goes on to describe several dubious relics and their locations. Of a piece of the broiled fish that Peter offered Jesus that was still prayed over in a church in Calvin's day, he wrote, "It must have been wondrous well salted, if it has kept for such a long series of ages." He cited examples of the adoration (and even kissing) of the arm of St. Anthony, which he says turned out to be a stag's bone. In a church in Geneva, he wrote, there was on the high altar the brain of St. Peter, no one ever doubting its genuineness, for it would have been blasphemy to do so; but after the Reformation administered a dose of skepticism with regard to relics, the brain was subjected to close inspection and it proved to be a piece of pumice stone. "I could quote many instances of this kind," he wrote, "but these will be sufficient to give an idea of the quantity of precious rubbish there would have been found if a thorough and universal investigation of all the relics of Europe had ever taken place."

The Church's hand was forced. Vatican officials and theologians were now taking stands on issues they had previously been able to ignore. The Counter-Reformation (or Catholic Reformation, as some call it) led to some internal reforms, but in some ways, the Church became more militant in its beliefs than before. The Jesuits emerged, a fraternity of militant monks, whose main mission was to re-Catholicize regions north of the Alps. Baroque art, eschewing the harmony, restraint, and classical themes of the Renaissance, developed as church interiors became billboards of pontifical propaganda, boasting dramatic glimpses of heaven complete with cherubs and statues of oversized saints beckoning the flock back to the faith.

The theological debate over the foreskin had actually been quietly continuing over the centuries. If Jesus was perfect, some theologians argued, wouldn't that mean his body would have to be perfect before he ascended into heaven? Wouldn't the "blemish of circumcision," as some theologians referred to it, be corrected upon his entry into paradise? And if so, didn't that mean the purported relic of Christ left here on earth was a fake? Or did it mean that he had ascended into heaven whole (i.e., with his foreskin) and that particular part was miraculously re-created so that the faithful could keep a piece of him on earth? Which begat more questions about other parts of Christ that could have remained on earth: his fingernail clippings, his hair, and as Calvin observed in his *Treatise on Relics*, his feces and urine. But the foreskin, because it was his flesh—the literal Eucharist—was the main point on which the debate centered.

Before Charlemagne—or the tales of Charlemagne—the prepuce was nowhere in sight, so the early church didn't have to grapple with such questions. Besides, Anastasius Sinaita, the seventh-century saint and abbot of the monastery on Mount Sinai, put the issue to bed when he commented, "And as Christ's immaculate blood, mixed with water, trickled on and purified the earth during the Passion, the cut and lost foreskin bestowed holiness on the same earth. In any case He, who let it be cut off freely, saved the foreskin, so that He could assume it again at his resurrection, and He, uncorrupted and whole, could possess every sin of every body. Because our bodies will be complete at the resurrection, and stand by his side."

Neither did the foreskin become much of an issue in 1150, when Theophylactus echoed his predecessor: "It is futile to ask where this snipped-off particle has remained. Because the writings are silent on the subject, we should not engage in any research, especially not if no use is to come of it. One could say, though, that as this particle was cut off, the earth was moved, it was sanctified, as with the water and blood as if flowed out of the Side. And it appears that this particle was stored intact and will be assumed again at the resurrection, without which he would not be whole. Just as we will assume a perfect body again at the resurrection."

But now in the sixteenth century, reputable theologians tried tackling the issue of whether Christ's foreskin was needed for his resurrection and even for the Second Coming. And instead of bending to the criticism of the Reformation, for the two centuries after the spiritual upheaval in Europe theologians would argue that there were loopholes for the existence of the Holy Foreskin.

The Jesuit Ferrandus argued that, like the blood Christ spilled when he was circumcised and on the cross or the hair and fingernail clippings he lost during his life, the foreskin was not an integral part of his being; it was only a fragment of flesh and therefore not necessary for him to assume again in heaven. Likewise, the Spanish Jesuit Francesco de Suárez came out in favor of the foreskin's existence, claiming that Jesus' risen body could easily have grown another foreskin and, quoting from an early English translation, the prepuce "belongs to the entireness of the Body formally and not materially: therefore some material part may remain on Earth, which was supplied to the Body of Christ in Heaven, from other matter that was sometimes of his Body, and had been resolved by continual Nutrition."

The opposition answered back. The seventeenth-century

Greek theologian Leo Allatius, a trained physician who, among other things, wrote the first medical treatise on vampires, penned *De Praeputio Domini Nostri Jesu Christi Diatriba* (*Discussion Concerning the Prepuce of Our Lord Jesus Christ*), in which he argued that the foreskin did ascend into heaven with Jesus, to become the rings of Saturn (which had just been discovered in Allatius's time).

Because the majority of claimed sacred foreskins were in lands (France, the Low Countries, Germany) where the Reformation (and the Church's sometimes violent reaction to it) caused especial destruction, by the end of the movement (in the mid-seventeenth century), there was only one surviving foreskin relic left. The foreskin that had been discovered in sleepy Calcata, far out of the reach of the Reformers, would quietly be venerated for centuries to come.

Chapter 17

"DOLCETTO O SCHERZETTO?"

"Well, well, well," Pancho said, "American priests in Rome." I had a feeling this wasn't going to end well. We were at a huge supermarket on the outskirts of Rome, buying hundreds of euros' worth of food in preparation for Calcata's annual Halloween party. This year was going to be the biggest one yet and Pancho was creating a special Halloween-themed menu for the Grotta. As I pushed the oversized cart through the wide aisles and Pancho studied his long shopping list while intermittently tossing items in the cart, we came upon two American priests, fittingly enough, in the wine section.

"Who would have thought we'd run into two American priests here?" Pancho added, waving his hand at the aisles of wine.

The two middle-aged clerics gave us welcoming smiles and asked where we were from. I decided to stand back and watch this car wreck occur from the curbside. "Calcata," Pancho said.

"Calcata . . . Calcata," one of the priests repeated, scratching his chin and looking toward the ceiling of the supermarket. "Don't we know someone who lives in Calcata, Jim?"

"Yeah, we do," said the other. "Oh, it's Sandro. Yes, we know Sandro. He works at the Vatican and lives in Calcata with his wife."

My heart suddenly sank with the mention of Sandro, the husband of Simona Weller, and my main link to the Vatican. I hadn't talked to him in a while, but I'd hoped he was still working on scoring me an interview with someone there. With Pancho about to start grilling these two priests, I feared the worst.

"You know what was in Calcata, don't you?" Pancho said.

The priests shook their heads from side to side.

"The Holy Foreskin. That's right, *Il Santissimo Prepuzio*. The foreskin of Jesus. And this guy," Pancho said, looking back at me where I had practically pinned myself up against the tall shelves of wine bottles, "is doing research on it. It was in Calcata since . . . what year?"

"Fifteen twenty-seven," I said, looking down at the ground.

"From 1527. While you guys were off slaughtering 'barbarians' in the name of your God in the New World, the Church was giving people an indulgence for worshipping the tip of Jesus' penis in Calcata."

I felt like begging these priests for an indulgence of my own.

The priests wore tight smiles as they waited for Pancho to finish. "Well, that's one way of looking at it," said Jim. "Another way is that the missionaries may have just been protecting the converted from the heathens."

Pancho scoffed. "You just want to make war," he said. "The world would be much better if you practiced peace." Then he accused them of supporting the U.S. invasion of Iraq, which they did not deny.

"Hey," one of the priests responded, "if we were against war, we'd all be speaking German right now."

"You guys," Pancho countered. "Going to war for peace is the same thing as fucking for chastity."

The priests winced again. I knew my hopes of Sandro getting

me an interview were fading fast. "Well," one of the priests said, "we'll certainly tell Sandro we met you."

Once we were outside, Pancho asked, "Do you think I was too rough with those priests?" (The answer came a few days later when I was standing in the square in Calcata and Sandro walked by. Even though we were five feet from each other, he didn't say anything to me; he didn't even look at me. In fact, except for the occasional "ciao," he never talked to me again.)

But at the moment, I had no time to reflect on the damage that had been done. We had to get back to Calcata for a Halloween planning meeting. Halloween becomes more and more popular every year in Italy, although it's more of an adult excuse to party than a holiday for children. For the past decade or so, revelers had been turning up in Calcata on October 31, ready for a raucous evening; the village's bewitching beauty and mystique made it a natural place to congregate on such a day. But there was never much planning put into Halloween by the Calcatesi because no one had the money to do much. Asking the city to help pay for materials to deck out the village with Halloween decorations or to help facilitate a party was out of the question—most of Calcata's mayors rarely strayed from the high plain where Calcata Nuova sits, their contempt for the old village and its residents never wavering. This year, however, was different. For the first time Calcata's civic government was cooperating with the hippies and bohemians of the old village. In a sign that tensions between the two villages were finally thawing, the new mayor—whose party, Forza Italia, was headed by former prime minister Silvio Berlusconi—was officially lending a hand in the planning of the Halloween festivities. I sat in on some meetings in the mayor's office with Pancho, who was the official delegate of old Calcata. They'd go back and forth about small technicalities, but in general the mayor was fully on board, supplying police and porta-potties and even giving money from his own pocket to help pay for stuff.

At the Grotta that night, Jessie, Pancho, and I sat around with a dozen Italians who were, in essence, trying to plan a holiday they'd never really celebrated. Stefania, the unofficial head of the planning committee, farmed out the assignments: Gabrielle would be in charge of hanging effigies with nooses around their necks from lampposts around the village, Ilaria and her husband, Adoo, would make a giant spiderweb out of used plastic shopping bags and then affix it over the piazza, and Marijcke and her wild-gray-haired Sicilian boyfriend, Mimmo, would be in charge of the costume contest. Jessie and I, as the resident Americans, were named as judges, along with Mimmo and Marijcke and part-time resident, full-time Italian celebrity, Victor Alfieri, whose fame was mostly due to his starring role on the American soap opera *The Bold and the Beautiful*.

As Stefania finished up going over the various assignments, Mimmo raised his hand, sticking his index finger in the air. "We're going to have all these kids walking around Calcata in costumes going door to door," he said. "They'll be saying *dolcetto o scherzetto*"—trick or treat—"and we give them a sweet. But what about a trick? What kind of tricks can we play on the kids?" He shot glances at everyone around the table, his broad smile reflecting how impressed he was with his idea. His question was met with silence until Pancho jumped in. "Uh . . . Mimmo. You always just give them candy. No tricks."

Then someone else had another great idea: "We have all these pumpkins lying around, right? Why don't we carve scary faces in them?"

"Yes," someone else jumped in, "and we can put a candle in them and they'll glow!"

Everyone agreed, offering a loud "*si!*" or "*d'accordo*." Pancho, the best Italian speaker (by far) among us Americans, schooled everyone on the rituals of Halloween. We would carve up the pumpkins and the task would be done at the house of the young couple Daniela and Enzo, who own and run a shop in the village that sells fair trade food products like coffee and chocolate.

During the run-up to Halloween, I was so busy carving pumpkins, cutting up sheets to make ghosts, and helping Pancho get the Grotta ready for a fully reserved night of eating and partying that I didn't even think about a costume. Then, a light-bulb moment occurred: Why not go as the Holy Foreskin?

But what does a foreskin even look like? And what does it look like when it's two thousand years old? From the excruciating YouTube videos I'd watched of circumcisions being performed on infants, the thin piece of flesh is only a few centimeters long and lightly curled. There's no way I could replicate that without looking like I had dressed up as a piece of calamari for Halloween. Which meant I had one option: The next morning I took the bus into Rome and went shopping. I bought some paint at a craft store, a long piece of purple fabric, some gold wire, a brown ski cap, and a brown turtleneck sweater. When Halloween evening arrived, I put it all together, asking Jessie to pin on my homemade cape, on which I had written SANTO PREPUZIO with a large Superman-style "SP" underneath. Finally, I put on the brown ski cap, the color of which perfectly matched my brown turtleneck, rolled up the edges of the cap, and affixed a gold circle with the wire over my head.

With the sun having just set behind the hills of the valley, the village lanes buzzing, I emerged dressed as a brown, halo-topped penis wearing a purple cape. Lorenzo, the sometimes grumpy man who one could always find lingering in the square, dressed in black and holding a skull-topped walking stick, led a group of two dozen children—not unlike Virgil leading Dante through the depths of hell—so they could get the hang of what it meant to go trick-or-treating.

"*Ciao Santo Prepuzio*," people called out to me, as Jessie and I strolled around the village. I'd tried convincing her to dress up as the Virgin Mary, but in the end she couldn't find the right materials, so she went as a generic ghoul instead. Lifelike effigies hung from lamps, eight-foot grim reapers stood in the corners, and white-sheet-clad ghosts lurked around corners. The costumes mostly leaned to the traditional: The narrow lanes were crawling with vampires, demons, and ghouls. A group of a dozen nuns and priests were congregating in the square.

"Hey, do you know who I am?" I said. They looked at me up and down and shook their heads. "I'm the Holy Foreskin!" They gave a collective shrug and walked on.

Scot walked by dressed in a mishmash of Halloween minutiae: His face was painted white and he was wearing a top hat and a cape. Luca, Roberto, Davide, and Gabrielle followed, all dressed the same as Scot. A band from Puglia was playing in a courtyard. People danced, clapped along, and drank wine straight from the bottle. A bonfire was raging near the corner of the square and some drunks dressed as demons danced around it.

As midnight neared, Jessie and I took our place at the top of the church steps. We stood facing out onto the piazza, which was packed with revelers. Mimmo, the master of ceremonies of the costume contest, of course, introduced the judges. I'd been walking around all night, looking for a creative costume that I wanted to vote for. Amid all the fake blood and black capes was Palma (who fortunately did not cook anything for the night's festivities). She was wearing a white dress, reminiscent of a wedding dress, and white face makeup. On paper, her costume wasn't very original, but it was well done, like she was a professional ghost. Jessie and I had both intended to vote for her, while Victor had his sights set on a Bela Lugosi–like Dracula. Which left Mimmo and Marijcke to choose their favorites. They both liked a couple— two weekend Calcata residents—who were dressed like S & M vampires. I have to admit, the black goth wings were impressive, especially on the guy whose bald head, big black mustache, and rotund body made him look a flying walrus. Still, Jessie and I liked Palma's outfit better. The voting came down to two votes for Palma, one vote from Victor for a vampire, and two votes for the S & M vampires. How, I wondered out loud to Jessie, were we going to fix this stalemate? But no sooner did Jessie answer than Mimmo suddenly announced, "We have a winner!" He took the S & M vampires' hands and thrust them heavenward. I later found out they were good friends of his and Marijcke's.

The next morning, I helped take down the effigies, remove the grim reapers, and get Calcata back to normal. And for me, that also meant resuming my search for the relic. So far, I had some intriguing comments from Calcata's old priest, Don Mario, but that was about it. I was still, however, digging up historical documents about the relic at the Vatican Library.

And one day, soon after Halloween, while slowly transcribing a centuries-old text about the Sancta Sanctorum, I received a piece of the puzzle—just not the piece I'd been expecting.

Chapter 18

MISSING PIECES

In 1559, two years after the foreskin's discovery in Calcata, two papal agents showed up in the village with orders from Pope Paul IV to inspect the object the Anguillara family was claiming to be the Holy Foreskin. When the two men, Pipinello and Attilio Cenci, canons of San Giovanni in Laterano—the official church of the pope and the place from where the foreskin had been stolen—arrived, they were immediately whisked in to see the relic. Their intention wasn't just to confirm the authenticity of the long-lost relic, but to take it back with them to Rome. During their investigation, Pipinello decided to start stretching and bending the relic, saying he needed to test out its flexibility and elasticity. It's unclear why this was necessary, but it was a definitive moment: The small piece of flesh broke in two pieces.

Within seconds, Pipinello's hands became icy and as hard as wood. A violent thunderstorm erupted. They feared that God was going to strike down not just him, but anyone who had witnessed the snapping of the foreskin. The local priest suggested they return the relic to the silk sack, which Pipenello did immediately, and he placed it back behind the altar. The thunderstorm stopped.

When Pipinello and Attilio Cenci reported back to Pope Paul IV about the freak thunderstorm caused by the tearing of the relic, he made a wise decision: Paul reasoned that considering the number of miracles in Calcata since the rediscovery of the Holy Foreskin there, the relic obviously had a predilection for the place where the chances of war had deposited it. Therefore, Calcata was the place it would remain.

Afterward, a series of popes put their seals of approval on the Holy Foreskin of Calcata. Pope Sixtus V, at the insistence of Emilia Orsini (the sister-in-law of Maddalena Strozzi), granted a plenary (ten-year) indulgence in 1584 to anyone who came to Calcata to pay his or her respects to the relic. Urban XIII cut it down to seven years in 1640. His successor, Innocent X, upheld the seven-year indulgence. So did Alexander VII in 1661. And to officially honor the memory of Lucrezia and Clarice Orsini, Pope Benedict XIII (also an Orsini) renewed the indulgence in 1724, making it *in perpetuo*. During this same time, the Vatican had the church in Calcata reconstructed and extended out into the square (and had a relief sculpture of the Holy Circumcision put above the church's altar) to befit the home of such a precious relic.

But the Vatican still wanted its piece of the prepuce, and in the first part of the eighteenth century, Pope Benedict XIII finally got the Vatican's way—at least according to one document I found dating some decades later. Through the local bishop's office in nearby Civita Castellana, the pope arranged for a slice of the foreskin to be returned to Rome. And even though my main goal was to find out the location of the piece of the foreskin that was stolen from Calcata in 1983, I thought an excellent consolation prize would be to find this sliver. And if you were a Holy Foreskin and were back in Rome, where would you go? There could be only one place.

Like Martin Luther five hundred years earlier, I slowly creaked open the large wooden doors to the Lateran Palace and saw before me the Scala Santa. About a dozen pilgrims, all on their knees, all reciting prayers with each step, were making the slow crawl to the top. Unlike Luther, however, I walked around the staircase, choosing to ascend the less holy steps that run on both sides of the Scala Santa.

At the top, a window looked into a small room; I peeked in. The room was dominated by a huge altar. Inscribed above it: NON EST IN TOTO SANCTIOR ORBE LOCUS ("There is no holier place on earth").

The entrance to the Sancta Sanctorum was around the corner, and as I stepped in that direction, I remembered I was carrying Abraham Lincoln in a black shoulder bag. Sometimes he could be so still and calm, I'd forget he was with me. Though he was mostly hidden by the bag, I was certain dogs would never be allowed in a place called the Holy of Holies. I tried pushing his head down so it would look like I was just carrying a purse. This might seem odd to the guard standing in front of the Sancta Sanctorum's entrance—women hadn't been allowed inside until the last century—but wouldn't necessarily be grounds for denying me entrance. But every time I pushed his head into the bag, it popped back up. He insisted on seeing what was going on. So I tucked his tiny head (and huge bat-like ears) into my armpit and approached the guard.

The entry ticket was three euros. With my left arm still covering Abraham Lincoln's head, I reached for my wallet with my right hand. The problem was that my wallet was actually in my back left pocket, which meant I had to reach all the way around behind me, making my chest bulge out at the guard, like I was doing some kind of strange body contortion in front of him. He squinted his eyes at me in either confusion or suspicion, as I finally pulled my wallet out. I flipped open the change holder and picked out three one-euro coins and plopped them in his waiting palm. He ripped off a ticket from the stack he was holding and said, "*Prego*," stepping clear of the door for me to enter.

Inside, intricate and colorful mosaics—a technique common

in Roman church floors called Cosmatesque—made up the floor, which had been worn dull and smooth by the hordes of pilgrims who have visited the shrine over the centuries. An altar, home to some of Christendom's most famous relics in history, dominated the room. On a side wall, a plaque announced that the loaf-size chunk of wood encased in glass was a piece of the table used for the Last Supper.

Abraham Lincoln began growling as a man next to me suddenly knelt to pray, and I turned and headed toward the door. The guard smiled and nodded at me. I stopped and asked him what relics had been kept here in the past. He began reciting a litany in a bored monotone voice, but concluded without mentioning the Holy Foreskin.

"What about the Holy Foreskin?" I asked.

"The Holy what?"

"The Holy Foreskin. The foreskin of Jesus."

"Oh, yes, of course," said the guard, as if it had simply slipped his mind.

"It's here?" I said, starting to get excited.

"No, it's not here."

"I heard it was," I said. "What happened to it?"

He shrugged.

"It was in Calcata," I said, sort of answering my own question. "But I also heard that centuries ago, Pope Clement VIII took a piece"—I actually used the word *pezzino*, little tiny piece—"and brought it here to the Sancta Sanctorum."

He shrugged again. And then asked, "Where is this town?"

I could suddenly feel my heart pounding. For a few weeks now I'd been quietly searching the stacks in the Vatican Library, locating centuries-old documents that told the history of the Holy Foreskin, mostly focusing on the one that had been here in the Sancta Sanctorum and ended up in Calcata. Having a conversation about the Holy Foreskin with a guard/ticket salesman at the entrance of the Sancta Sanctorum was, for some reason, extremely exhilarating. Then I spit out as fast as my Italian would let me, "It was the Sack of Rome in 1527 and a soldier stole the relic from here and also the jewel box in which it was contained."

The guard pushed out his lower lip, raised his eyebrows, and slowly nodded his head, as if I'd just recited the name of every pope in chronological order. Maybe, I wondered, he'd be impressed enough with me to give me a clue about the foreskin.

"And then," I continued, "the soldier arrived in a village that's called Calcata. It's forty-five kilometers from Rome. And he was put into a jail. Thirty years later, they found the relic and put it in the church." I paused, waiting for the guard's reaction. He was still nodding his head.

"How do you know all this information?" he asked.

"I live there," I said. He squinted his eyes and cocked his head, and then I added, "It's that village with all the artists and hippies north of Rome . . . ?"

"Ah, yes, I have heard about this place," said the guard.

"Anyway," I continued, "the relic existed there until about twenty years ago. Then it disappeared. In fact, many people in the village believe it was stolen. But some people say—"

"Okay, enough," the guard said to me, using the word *basta*, his voice suddenly stern. He turned away, craning his neck into the Sancta Sanctorum, pretending to check the place out, and then stood there, ignoring me and nervously thumbing the pack of tickets in his hand.

"What?" I asked. "Why *basta*? Why *basta*?"

He ignored me.

"Hey, what about the Holy Umbilical Cord? That was here, too, at one time," I said, hoping he might regain interest. "Want to hear what happened to that?"

Nothing. Finally, I turned and walked away. Abraham Lincoln, who I'd forgotten about, let out a soft growl.

It's possible the guard didn't want to hear the history of the Holy Foreskin because he knew of the 1900 decree threatening excommunication to anyone who speaks or writes about it. There was a tiny chance that the pope—or some higher authority within the Church—had told him that if anyone asked about Holy Foreskin, he should shut them down as soon as possible. But most likely, as I'd slowly realized after months of asking people about the relic, he'd simply concluded that he didn't want to be conversing with a lunatic. When I walked past the Scala Santa and out of the thick wooden doors, the robust Roman sun splashing me in the face, I realized that the guard was simply the latest to see me as just that: a crazy person.

That said, I couldn't stop now. While I hadn't gotten very far at the Sancta Sanctorum, there was still one additional *pezzino*, little piece, out there. And it belonged to an eighteenth-century relic fanatic in Rome.

Cardinal Camillo Cybo's relic collection was said to be legendary. No one knows exactly how the devout cardinal gained thousands of precious relics. But the best guess had to do with a black market relics dealer.

Even though the catacombs around Rome had been declared "clean," new ones kept popping up, even in the sixteenth century (in fact, since the Middle Ages they've uncovered a few dozen catacombs and there are probably still a lot more undiscovered ones on the outskirts of the Italian capital). One person who took quite an interest in the newly discovered catacombs was Signor Boldetti, the canon of the church of Santa Maria in Trastevere. Along with his partner Giovanni Marangoni, he helped "preserve" many of the newly found relics, taking many to his church or elsewhere. It has also been suggested—by the very church Web site that houses Cybo's relics—that many of the curios in Cardinal Cybo's collection came from Boldetti and Marangoni.

Cybo, whose name is sometimes written "Cibo" (which translates to "food," by the way), would go to great lengths to get his hands on the most prized relics. His private collection, housed until 1742 in the Basilica di S.S. XII Apostoli in Rome, consisted of, among others, the breast milk of the Virgin Mary, a piece of the True Cross, the Virgin's dress and cloth, hair of the Virgin, bones of the Virgin's father and mother, the column that St. Paul was decapitated on, a bone of St. Peter, a piece of the cross St. Peter was crucified on, and body fragments from just about every apostle. And when he learned about the Holy Foreskin of Calcata, he was determined to have it. Or at least a piece. At least that's what was written in a short history from 1747 that I found at the Vatican, exhaustively titled "*Istoria dell' Antichissimo Oratorio, o Capella di San Lorenzo nel Patriarchio Lateranese Comunente Appellato Sancta Sanctorum e della Celebre Immagine del S.S. Salvatore Detta Notizie del Culto, e Vari Riti Practicati Anticamente Verso la Medisima: Raccolte da Momumenti Antichi, e Specialmente dall' Archivie della Nobile Compagnia, che ne Ha la Custodia,*" written by none other than relic hunter Giovanni Marangoni.

According to this account, Cybo took a trip out to Calcata to view the relic in 1723. He was astonished to see the humble silver-plated dish that the relic was kept in. He made the case to Bishop Francesco Tenderini, whose office was in Civita Castellana and whose diocese included Calcata, that such a rare holy relic needed a grander reliquary. Then he offered to pay for the new reliquary, and in return, all he wanted was a small piece of the foreskin for his private collection. Bishop Tenderini agreed and, not long after, traveled to Calcata down the old Via Narcese that runs between the village and Civita Castellana and nipped off a speck of flesh from the relic and placed it in a silver container. Then he boxed it, securing the package with his seal made of Spanish wax.

Cybo held up his end of the bargain and had the reliquary made for Calcata's foreskin: two six-inch-tall golden angels, in a gentle contrapposto pose, holding a small grail encrusted with red and green jewels topped by a cross made of diamonds.

When Cardinal Cybo received the box from Bishop Tenderini, he opened it immediately and withdrew the silver container. He removed the lid and lifted out the relic, which was wrapped in silk. According to Marangoni, a subtle perfumed scent emerged from the jar, which Cybo took to be a sign of the relic's authenticity as well as divine approval that he now had it in his possession. He stood for a long time in front of the relic, taking in the sweet scent, feeling touched and blessed. He then took the little sliver of flesh out of the container and placed it in a golden, jewel-encrusted cup and set it at the center of his relic collection.

On March 24, 1742, Cardinal Cybo moved his relic collection to the Church of Santa Maria degli Angeli up the street in Rome from the church that had housed his collection. The Michelangelo-designed church was built over the Baths of Diocletian, where the Roman emperor (and his predecessors) had spilled the blood of many Christian martyrs; Cybo thought this a more fitting home for the Holy Foreskin.

A chapel was built next to the sacristy to contain Cybo's relic collection as well as a sarcophagus to serve as the eternal resting place for Cybo and his family. On one side of the chapel was a compendium of the relics that the chapel housed. In all there were 134. Cybo donated the relics to the church and paid for the upkeep of the chapel, but only under the condition that the collection would remain there as a whole forever and that votive candles would always be lit. In January of the following year, 1743, Cardinal Camillo Cybo passed away, perhaps fittingly, a few days after the Feast Day of the Holy Circumcision. After his funeral in the Basilica di S.S. XII Apostoli, he was interned in his eponymous chapel in Santa Maria degli Angeli where, along with his relics, he now rests.

So, naturally, I had to pay the relic-collecting cardinal a visit. Or at least his tomb. I wandered into Santa Maria degli Angeli, which is hidden behind the ruins of the baths. Once through a tight entryway, the space opens up to form one of Rome's most majestic rooms. I walked around the circumference of the church, peeping into the small chapels, hoping to locate the Cybo family chapel. But I couldn't find it. I approached three old ladies who were anchored behind a table full of guidebooks to the church and asked them to direct me to it. They looked at each other and chattered away about something until one of them finally looked at me and, a sheepish grin on her face, said, "*Non lo conosciamo*," we don't know. Did I have the wrong church? I asked if I could look in their guide, and on the map of the church, there it was: just to the left of the altar, beyond a rope that prohibits visitors from getting too close to the altar. I set the book down and headed for the chapel, stepping over the rope and waiting to hear someone yelling "*Prego!*" in my direction. It never came. I got to the Cybo chapel and could see nothing. It was darkened, despite the cardinal's stipulation that votive candles be forever lit. I stuck my face through the black metal bars that separated the nave from the chapel, but I still could see none of the cardinal's 134 relics.

So, remembering that on the map there was a church office somewhere in the back, I walked through the sacristy (today filled with posters detailing the church's history), past the toilets, and found a flimsy glass door with a sign, written in English, saying not to knock, not to come in. But I had no choice, so I went in.

The old lady behind the desk was just as staid as the dusty wood-paneled room she inhabited. Despite the note on the door, she didn't seem at all alarmed that I'd just walked into the room. I introduced myself as a scholar from a university in New York (which I considered a forgivable fabrication) and that I was studying the relics of Cardinal Cybo. I asked if it were possible to see a list of the relics that were in the Cybo family chapel. She excused herself and, two minutes later, reemerged with a priest. I reintroduced myself.

"We haven't opened that chapel in years and we don't intend to anytime soon," he told me in Italian.

I tried to pressure him by saying that I'd come all the way

from New York, which, again, wasn't exactly an outright lie. "Do you know much about the relics that are in the chapel?" I asked.

"Yes, more or less," said the priest, bobbing his head around.

"I know this is a strange question," I said, using a preface I'd developed when talking about the foreskin, "but do you happen to know if the foreskin of Jesus is among the relics in the Cybo family chapel?"

The priest didn't blush or look at me like I was crazed, which I hoped also meant I was conversing with him in a comprehensible fashion. He paused for a minute, looking up at the ceiling, and then said, "I don't think so."

"I heard it was here," I said, and then launched into the history of Cardinal Cybo's obsession with the foreskin and how he paid for the reliquary in Calcata in exchange for a small piece of it.

"No," the priest said, shaking his head. "I don't recall that relic being here. But even if it had been, the Church may have taken it away. Relics like the foreskin and the Virgin's breast milk and so on. They're too uncomfortable. And products of a past age."

"So you don't think the foreskin is on the list inside the chapel?"

"I don't know," he said, and then handed me a piece of paper with a Web site on it. "Have a look at our Web site. The compendium should be there."

I ran to the nearest Internet café I could find and went to the church's Web site. After digging through pages and pages of material, I found it about twenty minutes later. I carefully scrolled through all the relics, going past various secondary relics of the Virgin and bones of apostles and early martyrs, and got to the end. There was no mention of the Holy Foreskin. Maybe, if the theory was correct that the Vatican had taken the foreskin of Calcata, they hadn't stopped just there. Perhaps they'd taken all the pieces of the Holy Foreskin they could find.

Chapter 19

ENERGY BOOSTERS

I rarely remember my dreams, but on this particular morning I woke up and Bruce Willis was fresh in my mind. Mr. Willis was being chased by four or five tinted-windowed black sedans through a gray, apocalyptic landscape where mattresses were on fire and turned-over jeeps were smoldering. Willis made a sudden left and leapt over a brick wall, then leaned against it, catching his breath. But just then, the black cars skidded to a stop in front of him. A black-suit-wearing man with slicked-back hair, aviator sunglasses, and an earpiece opened the door and crouched behind it.

He yelled over to Willis, "Give it back to us and we'll spare your life."

"No," Bruce Willis screamed in response, "you'll never get it as long as I'm alive!"

And with that, the men opened fire. With each bullet that pelted Bruce Willis, the action star was thrown up against the brick wall. His gun dropped on the ground, and with the little energy he had left, he pulled from his pocket a small silver box, held it above his head, then collapsed with a thump to the concrete, the silver box skidding across the pavement, jarring open, as he took his final breath. There, in the middle of the palm-size container, was a wrinkled-up piece of flesh. The Holy Foreskin.

When I suddenly awoke, I wasn't so surprised I was having dreams about the relic—it had been on my mind since the day I stepped foot in Calcata. What really shocked me, however, was the following weekend: As I was sitting on the piazza, I noticed a few people on the other side filming something. More important, they were peppering their conversation with *prepuzio*. I had to find out what was going on.

It turned out Dario (or Bacco, as everyone called him, thanks in part to his wine-drinking habits) was making a movie about none other than the Holy Foreskin. I'd never seen Bacco around, but I introduced myself and within a few minutes we were at the Grotta, beers in front of us, talking about why he'd decided to make a movie about the relic.

"My friends and I were just sitting around one day trying to think of a good movie topic and someone suggested the *prepuzio*," Dario said in near perfect English. "There's so much mystery surrounding its disappearance I thought it would be perfect."

"So, the movie is a documentary about the disappearance of the relic?"

"No, it's more like a mockumentary—a movie meant to look like a documentary, but it's really not."

Bacco then explained the plot to me, which used real-life Calcatesi. The overly complicated story revolved around a guy named Hemingway, a local guy who actually died halfway through the shooting of the movie. They'd continued filming anyway, not changing the plot much, but just shooting around Hemingway's absence. "Calcata is really the protagonist," Bacco said. There was also an alien—in the form of a pretty forty-year-old woman— who had come to earth to find the Holy Foreskin. She claimed that since the moment the relic had gone astray from Calcata, the earth had been out of whack; that both Calcata's energy and the energy of the Holy Foreskin had basically kept the seams of the planet in place and now that they'd become unstitched, Armageddon could be afoot.

Bacco finished off his beer at the Grotta and said he had to get back to filming. But before he left, he invited me to play a part in the movie. The very next weekend, I found myself in the Porta Segreta gallery, owned by Giancarlo Croce. All the established artists of Calcata were there—Athon, Romano Vitali, Costantino, Giancarlo, and a few others—to film a scene in which the alien stumbles upon a party of Calcata's famed artists. Which was easy enough, since the presence of wine and cigarettes and food made it seem like we really were having a party. Everyone was in a festive mood except for Giancarlo, who was treating the gallery space like it was his brand-new Ferrari, putting cups on coasters or napkins, sweeping up crumbs, and practically diving to the ground, cupped hands in front of him, to catch a falling ash from a cigarette. In the 1970s and 1980s, this space had been the scene of frequent parties and, from what I'd heard, much debauchery. But now it was unlocked only when Giancarlo felt like showing it off. Which was a shame, considering it housed Giancarlo's striking paintings and etchings of Calcata as well as a few sculptures that Costantino had made.

"Okay, everybody in their places," Bacco screamed. No one really moved since we were already in place, sitting around the room smoking and drinking and eating. "And . . . action!"

The sexy alien, a woman I'd never seen before, clad in an elegant gown, strolled through the door and feigned surprise when she saw us sitting there. "Are you the famed artists of Calcata?" she asked, as the camera panned around the room. Everyone nodded and mumbled in agreement, and then, one by one, we began to introduce ourselves and say a little about Calcata. My line— "*Me chiamo* David Farley *e sono un scrittore di* New York"—didn't strain my Italian very much and I nailed it in one take.

"Is it true," the alien asked, "that the Holy Foreskin was here? And if so, what's its connection to Calcata?"

"*Sì*," Costantino said, volunteering to recite the story about how the relic arrived in Calcata.

Then the camera swung toward me, my mug smack in the center of the frame. Bacco nodded at me, having just fed me a second (and final) line, but I couldn't spit it out. Finally, I said it. "The moment I arrived, I could immediately feel a very particular energy."

And suddenly, everyone was talking about an energy in Calcata. Athon gave a long soliloquy about Calcata being a spring of energy that's released from the center of the earth. Costantino jumped in, disagreeing with some point Athon was making. This wasn't in the script, but Bacco kept filming anyway. At the same time, the most intoxicated person there, a woman from the parking lot who was apparently in attendance just to watch, knocked over her glass of wine during an inexplicable fit of laughter. Giancarlo looked like he was about to lose it. Athon and Costantino's voices grew louder. Suddenly Patrizia emerged from outside and jumped into the argument as well. Finally, after about ten minutes, Bacco intervened, to get the shooting back to the script. Filming resumed.

"What do you think makes the energy so particular?" the alien asked, and following the script, Romano then launched into a dream he'd had about the pope being a fish.

I began questioning the Calcatesi about this energy, but few could give me a solid answer, most people referring to it as *"particolare,"* meaning special or distinctive. But then, a couple weeks later, I met Paolo D'Arpini. I was putting the finishing touches on a travel article about Calcata I'd been assigned to write for an American newspaper and I'd mentioned that there was a painting of Jimi Hendrix on one of the buildings in the square. My editor wanted to know what century the building was from. So, I darted out of my apartment and into the square. As always on late afternoons during the week, there was a short, late-fifty-something man sitting there. He had closely cropped gray hair and a warm smile like a Buddhist monk's. I stumbled my way through Italian, asking about the building.

"Sometimes," he began his reply in very good English, "dates and years and centuries are not important. Sometimes you can understand just by being here, concentrating on it, and feeling how old it is."

I looked at him and nodded. I just needed a century. A number. I was on deadline and didn't really have the time to ponder on the building until a date of construction manifested itself to me.

"It's the energy," he added. "Feel the energy and you will learn a lot here." As Paolo went on to tell me, we've lost our ability to feel earth energies, but thousands of years ago, it was a large part of the human experience. And even though most of us don't feel the energy, we're still very much susceptible to it. I started to feel myself sink into the concrete, ready to finally learn about the energy everyone had been talking about.

"People are not meant to live a normal kind of life here," Athon had told me when the topic came up during an evening of wine-drinking and bird-watching in her cave. She certainly seemed to be a shining example of that. "We have to live as spiritual people, to be connected to the higher energy. If you want a place to connect with higher energy, this is it."

I asked her if she could feel the force all the time. "Yes, of course. It's not easy living here, though—the negative deeds of the past are still active and they interfere with the sacrality of the place. It's like a battlefield between the sacred and the profane." It seemed to depend on who you asked, but various places in the world—particularly those that had a reputation as sacred—were energy centers. Athon went on to tell me about the global grid.

Apparently, the planet is made up of a matrix of energy lines and certain points on those lines make up energy centers, like the pressure points in our bodies familiar to acupuncturists. Subscribers to this theory say the energy comes in the form of radiation, which can be harmful or beneficial, depending on flow direction. Earth energy proponents point out that thousands of years ago, humans had the ability to feel energy and could recognize places in the earth where energy would flow. As a result, they built structures marking the energy spots: the Great Pyramids at Giza, Stonehenge, and some say even Mecca, are but a few examples. The massive esoteric lines and images carved into rural landscapes and mountainsides in South America are said to be an acknowledgment of energy lines.

And from the people who had opinions on it, such as Pancho, it didn't seem like the energy in Calcata was very benevolent. When I asked him about it, he said he'd seen it control people in a negative way and that he'd witnessed several people show up in Calcata to live for a while only to turn into drug addicts or raging alcoholics or, in a few cases, have mental breakdowns on the square. He told me about a woman who had bought a house there—a woman I eventually met who would corroborate the story—and brought her spiritual guru from Indonesia to Calcata. They were doing a meditation retreat and, she told me, they could feel so much negative energy (a "large demon," as she put it) inside the very rock Calcata sits on that she decided she couldn't live there anymore.

For Athon (and a lot of the hippie types who moved to Calcata), it was this energy that gravitated them here. "It's definitely the reason I came here," Athon told me. "I was in India and had a vision of two angels guiding me to Calcata." Part of Calcata's appeal is its structure—not just its bewitching beauty, but in New Age terms, Calcata is a "power spot," boasting the perfect balance of yin and yang. A power spot can be any location with a higher energy intensity than its surroundings. So, as the theory goes,

Calcata sits on a tall rock (yin), sticking out in the middle of a valley (yang). The river running around the rock amplifies the yang.

Mauro, a journalist who came to Calcata on the weekends, was making a show for Italian TV about the weird vibes in Calcata and one day at the Grotta we got to talking about it. He seconded the yin/yang theory of Calcata. "The energy comes from the rock," he said. "Calcata is in the shape of the Shiva linga. You know what that is, right?"

I did, only because he wasn't the first person who had told me this. Everyone from Lorenzo, the guy who worked in the Indian-style clothes shop and was always pacing around the square, to Athon to Paolo had mentioned it. In short, the Shiva linga is a sacred phallus-shaped image found in temples and homes throughout India. The veneration of the Shiva linga—a symbol of the Hindu god—actually precedes Indian civilization. The linga, some say, is shaped to induce concentration in the mind. And because of its phallic form, the linga has been known for its fertility powers (among many other powers granted to it). The linga is always surrounded by a yoni, which has been translated as "divine passage," "place of birth," and "womb," and is often thought of as the vagina to the linga's phallus, the ying and the yang. The yoni, which has ridges around its circumference, traps water that is poured over the linga.

There are several natural lingas in India that have been sacred places for centuries, huge phallic rock formations in the middle of a valley. Many of the hippies who came to Calcata in the 1960s and '70s had spent a significant amount of time in India on spiritual quests. And when they first came to Calcata, fresh from the subcontinent, I can imagine what they thought when they got their first glance: a rock, rising straight up (with a rickety village plopped on top) smack in the center of a verdant valley with a river running around it. Certainly they saw it as a natural linga. Then, factor in the existence there of the Holy Foreskin (which has been associated with fertility), take a few hits from a joint, put on an old Ravi Shankar record, and you can see how the newcomers might have believed they'd just discovered a very special place.

But, as Paolo told me on the square that day, the new inhabitants of Calcata were only carrying on a tradition that had been going on from time immemorial. Because the ancient inhabitants of Calcata had been isolated for so long, they continued a way of living that had disappeared in industrial societies. "The Faliscans could feel an energy here," he said. "This is the reason they used Calcata as their sacred place. They lived on Narce, the hill near here, and they built temples on Caclata and used it for worshipping."

"How can I find out more about the energy of Calcata? Has anything been written about it?" I asked.

"No. But that doesn't matter. Because you should feel it. It's all about something called 'psycho storia,' which means that just being here in Calcata, you will subconsciously pick up the past energy here and then you will understand the history. Also, I will tell you more about it in the future."

"That would be great," I said. "Do you mind if I record our conversation about it?"

"No. You cannot record it or even write anything down. That will defy the point of the psycho storia. You have to *feel* it."

"So what about this building?" I asked, getting back to the whole reason I had come out on the square in the first place. "Do you know when it was built?"

Paolo made a long blink and then opened his eyes again. "It was built in the eighteenth century."

"Wow," I said. "You just learned that from your psyscho storia technique?"

"No," Paolo said, "I read it somewhere." And then he burst out laughing.

I eventually went back to writing my article, but was intrigued by the Faliscans and their supposed connection to the energy. And despite Paolo's disapproval of research with books and written materials, I did a bit of reading about the Faliscans at the Vatican Library and the library at the British School at Rome, the latter of which had conducted a fair amount of archaeological research in the area from the 1960s to the 1980s.

A few millennia before the hippies discovered Calcata, the area was occupied by the Faliscans, a pre-Roman tribe of people who spoke an Italic language akin to Latin. They were closely associated with the Etruscans, who had been settled throughout central Italy (and where the name Tuscany comes from). The Etruscans have been the object of study for centuries, but much less is known about the Faliscans, whose main territories included the modern-day towns of Nepi, Sutri, Civita Castellana, and Calcata. Narce, the armchair-shaped hill adjacent to Calcata, was a major Faliscan settlement. During the 1960s and '70s, archaeologists and students from the British School at Rome conducted excavations at Narce. The researchers found tombs, caves, pottery, and even sculptures of fertility goddesses. Because Calcata has been continually inhabited for centuries (no one knows exactly how long), there has never been archaeological research done.

Narce was one of the earliest inhabited Faliscan sites from about 1500 B.C. Road networks were eventually created (the footpath Via Narcese, which goes between Narce/Calcata and Civita Castellana, can still be walked). Settlements around the area, called South Etruria, began increasing in the fifth and fourth centuries B.C. But as Rome grew in political and military importance, the Faliscans of South Etruria (and eventually the Etruscans farther north) were doomed. Faliscan settlements slowly began to fall to Roman troops: Fidenae in 434 B.C., Veii in 396 B.C., and Nepi and Sutri around 383 B.C.

A battle in 241 B.C. put the final nail in the Faliscan coffin. Led by Roman general Furio Camillo (who has a subway station in Rome named after him), Roman troops marched into the large Faliscan hilltop town of Falerii Veteres and obliterated most of the population (fifteen thousand Faliscans died in six days of battle). Then they moved the surviving population to a flat, indefensible plain about five miles away. Falerii Novi, as the town was called, is still partially standing today; it's a ghost town, surrounded by high ancient walls. The people lived there until about the eighth century A.D. before crawling up to their old hilltop again and reestablishing their town, naming it Civita Castellana.

After the troops from Rome had conquered the Faliscans at nearby Falerii Veteres, they marched down the Via Narcese and finished off the people at Narce. This was one of the "negative deeds of the past" that Athon claimed had caused a bad energy in Calcata. It also didn't help, Athon and others had told me, that the Romans forced the surviving Faliscans to live in Calcata, which had allegedly been used before that only as a sacred place of worship.

It was the Faliscan/Etruscan road system that the Romans used for conquering the Faliscans. Soon after, the Romans would build the still-existing trunk roads, the Via Flaminia and the Via Cassia, which would keep the area pacified. (Ironically, just as the Romans had used the Faliscan roads to conquer, it would be the Roman roads that, centuries later, the barbarians from the north would take to eventually bring down that empire; and over a thousand years later, in 1527, the soldiers of Charles V's army took the same roads when they sacked the city.)

There's no documentation about what happened to Calcata after 241 B.C. (or even, for that matter, if the Faliscans living on Narce really used Calcata as their place of worship). Some of the inhabitants today, like Paolo, are convinced it was used as a sacred site. I was eager to learn more.

The next day when I saw him sitting on the church steps, he invited me to a meeting he'd organized. Paolo was the president of the Vegetarian Club of Calcata, one of a series of partner vegetarian clubs around the area. "We are going on a walk down in the valley where we'll give some food back to the wild animals."

It wasn't really something I'd normally volunteer to do, but because I liked Paolo and because I was intrigued by what he had to say, the following Sunday I showed up at his house, just outside of the door to the borgo, and met with a dozen or so ladies. They were sipping tea while Paolo scurried around his yard, preparing things for the walk. Several of the women had daypacks strapped across their backs and were sporting hiking shoes.

"Okay, let's go," Paolo announced, and we began our descent down into the wooded valley. There are a few trails below Calcata, some of which had existed as part of the medieval network that stretched between villages, but it wasn't until 1982 that the Valle del Treja, Valley of the Treja River, became an official regional park with a group of park rangers to keep the trails in good shape. On our way down the steep path from Calcata we passed by ancient Faliscan tombs, set into the rock Calcata sits on, and then crossed the river via a fallen tree. Paolo, hands clasped behind his back, and the rest of us behind him, mused about the vegetarian diet.

We eventually stopped at a long picnic table next to the trail and sat down. Paolo began talking, giving a long soliloquy on, I suppose, vegetarianism; my Italian had become noticeably better in the months I'd been in Calcata and now I could at least understand the essence of what someone was trying to say to me, but during Paolo's speech I tuned out, thinking about my search for the relic and wondering why I was wasting my time down in the valley when I should be stalking the priest or pounding the pavement at the Vatican. I was sitting near the head of the table, close to Paolo, when the guy next to me took up where Paolo had left off. About five minutes later, still thinking about the relic, I noticed it was completely silent and everyone was looking at me.

"What do you want to say?" Paolo asked me.

"About what?"

"About vegetarianism," he said.

I was baffled. I hadn't known I was going to be a keynote speaker; that is, until I realized that everyone had to speak. I was going to be held prisoner here while more than a dozen people sang to the chorus.

"I—I really don't know what to say," I said in English.

"Just say anything you want about vegetarianism—what it means to you, why you like to eat the vegetables or your feelings on the animals. If it's easier for you, say it in English and I will translate for you."

I sat there for a second, still frozen. Paolo nodded at me in encouragement. I thought back to my brief vegetarian phase in college but could come up with little in the way of profound things to say about it. Eventually, I took a cue from a Smiths album and muttered, "Meat is . . . murder."

Paolo translated and everyone in unison nodded their heads in agreement, some mumbling "Sì . . . sì."

"That's all for now," I said.

Paolo looked pleased. "That reminds me. Come to me next week and we will continue our talk."

"Sure. In the piazza?"

"Wherever you find me, that's where I'll be," he said. "And if that doesn't happen, focus on the energy and sooner or later our paths will cross."

Then Paolo nodded at the woman to my left to begin her soliloquy. She spoke for about ten minutes. And so did the next person and the next person and the next person. Finally, literally hours later, the conversation got back around to Paolo again.

"And now we shall give back some precious food to the animals of the valley."

He nodded at a middle-aged woman, who unzipped her backpack. We all got up and stood around the table as she handed

Paolo a plastic bag. He then slowly pulled something out and set it on the table. And there was the grand offering to the wild boar, birds, foxes, and other animals of the valley: one small open-faced feta cheese and grilled veggie sandwich. He smiled contentedly and steepled his hands; the rest of us followed, giving a slight bow, before drifting back up to Calcata.

Chapter 20

CURSED!

If one needed any more evidence that Calcata is not your typical Italian town, here's a list of some of the names of the offspring of the old village's new inhabitants: Felix, Adé, Gioese (a boy, whose name is pronounced Joyce), Gaia, Commancia, Morgan, Joanas, Lores, Sava, Ravi, Sati, Svetlana, Aman, Terrian, Tyi, Ramón, Jana, Jura, Bart, Omar, Crystal Jewel, and Nkruma.

One name you'll never hear a mother calling after her child in the old or new village is Clarice (pronounced: Clar-ee-chay)—this goes back to the seven-year-old daughter of Maddalena Strozzi, the virgin named Clarice who successfully opened the silk sack that contained the Holy Foreskin in 1557. As the legend goes, after the miracle in which Clarice's hands didn't freeze from trying to untie the sack, she mysteriously died a couple weeks later. While death was very much a part of daily life, sixteenth-century Europe was a world of unexplained forces against which men and women could do nothing except attribute all to God and take refuge in acts of piety. Even the dark was a common cause of serious apprehension: Guibert of Nogent, the medieval French theologian, is said to have kept a lamp near his bedside, to better his chances of keeping the demons at bay. Dreams, depending on the context, were either divine messages or evidence that the devil was trying to seep into your soul. A huge wind gust was sometimes viewed as the breath of Satan. Natural disasters were defined as divine punishment. It's safe to assume the Anguillara family suspected Clarice's sudden demise might have had something to do with the relic.

As the generations went on, the case of Clarice grew. According to common belief all girls named Clarice in Calcata would die before they hit their teens. By the nineteenth century, it was common wisdom that if you lived in Calcata and named your daughter Clarice, she'd live a very short life. In fact, Patrizia once told me the curse of Clarice was so cemented in Calcata's cultural belief system that before abortion was legalized in Italy in 1978, women in Calcata with unwanted pregnancies would tell themselves that the baby's name was going to be Clarice. Not long after that, they'd miscarry.

Calcata is, in fact, pregnant with curses. Ask anyone about it in the village and they'll rattle off all the *maledizioni* that have been attributed to the place. They'll tell you that Don Dario Magnoni, the priest who was responsible for the foreskin when it went missing, has been stricken with a curse ever since the relic was stolen in 1983: half of his face became paralyzed not long after the relic disappeared, giving him an unfortunate sneer when he talks.

"It's a good thing you and your wife aren't planning to stay in Calcata for a longer time," Gemma, the Belgian woman who runs the teahouse, told me. "Couples don't stay together here. There's a curse on couples." She herself was a living example of that. She'd had four children from three different men. One of the men—who happened to be the lovable (and apparently very fertile) Paolo—had even fathered a child with Gemma's sister (who also lived in Calcata), creating a mind-boggling matrix of incongruent family relations rarely seen outside of Appalachia. I'd sometimes sit on the steps that led up to our apartment trying to figure it out: *So, if Paolo is the father of Gemma's first son and also the father of Gemma's sister's daughter, that makes them siblings and cousins, which makes Gemma and her sister aunts and/or mothers to all the children. Felix, the son of Paolo and Gemma, now has a son of his own, Sava, thus making the newborn boy the . . .*

Likewise, the web of former relationships people had in Calcata could be equally confusing. Two people would see each other on the square and not say a word to each other as they passed, leaving me to conclude that they probably didn't know each other. Later I'd learn those two people had a long and deep history together—that they had produced a child, traveled around the world together, had blow-up fights in the square on a regular basis, and/or had been in a ten-year relationship—and had since stopped talking. In fact, it seemed that nearly everyone in Calcata had at least one person they'd stopped talking to. As far as the couples curse, it was too confusing to keep track of, but I could hardly find any couples in the village who had been together for longer than ten years. I immediately told Jessie that we would be in Calcata only for nine years or less. She was relieved.

But, of course, even if I had wanted to stay in Calcata for that long, I'd sometimes convince myself that I'd never survive. Because I'd arrived in Calcata to find out what had happened to the Holy Foreskin, which seemed to be the origin of many of the village's curses, I'd often wonder if I'd make it out of the village alive. Or at least without a limp. I'd mention to Jessie what Pancho had said about people coming to Calcata and turning into alcoholics or drug addicts (because of some kind of curse or the energy) and then remind her of the gout-inducing amount of wine we'd been imbibing since we arrived, and she'd dismiss it, reminding me that there was absolutely nothing to do in Calcata *except* to sit around drinking good wine and gossiping about people (the latter was a village pastime). I knew she was right, but there was still something in the back of my mind that made me wonder.

And then one day I heard about a Clarice who had survived. In fact, she was still living in a neighboring village and was quite proud of the fact that she had made it. *Had she broken the curse?* I wondered. Is there hope for me? Will I actually live to tell my tale of hunting the Holy Foreskin? I had to find her. I recruited Elena for the mission. I told her that I thought I remembered hearing Clarice lived in nearby Mazzano. She put out the word to her friends there and nothing came back. No one knew of a Clarice who lived there.

So one morning we went there ourselves. Our first stop was the village priest, Don Italo. I'd met Don Italo a month earlier when Elena took me to see if he knew anything about the Holy Foreskin. He asked me a lot questions about my religious background (yes, I was raised Catholic), my family (my parents are still alive and still married, I have two older sisters and an older brother), if I was married and for how long (yes, for six years), whether or not my wife and I were going to have kids (probably not), if I voted for Bush (no), and if I thought the Catholic Church in America would ever recover from the pedophile scandal (if the Catholic Church recovered from the Reformation, why not?). Don Italo didn't have much information about the relic, but he did reveal yet another curse of the Holy Foreskin. "He who searches for the Holy Foreskin will produce a child within one year," he said. It seemed to make sense to me, since both Calcata and the Holy Foreskin had a legendary knack for giving fertility. I rotated glances between him and Elena, and finally he burst out laughing and slapped me on the back. "I'm joking with you," he said, "only because you said you and your wife might not have children."

On our next visit, the day we were searching for Clarice, Don Italo opened his door and smiled warmly when he saw Elena and me. "Is your wife pregnant yet?" he joked with me.

"Not yet," I said. "Maybe I haven't been searching for it long enough."

Elena explained to him the nature of our latest quest. Don Italo shrugged, saying there hasn't been a Clarice in Mazzano for a few decades and he didn't think she was born in Calcata. He pointed us in the direction of Clarice's daughter-in-law's house. An old lady now herself, the daughter-in-law invited us into her home. She was wearing all black. As is the case in Italy—though much more common in southern Italy—women who have recently been widowed wear black for an entire year. This woman had lost her husband six months ago and when she spoke about it, she picked up a framed eight-by-ten photo of him that was resting on the coffee table and began to caress his cheek. Her mother-in-law, she said, had died in 1971 and was born in Mazzano. She'd had absolutely no connection to Calcata.

Which left me wondering how I'd been misinformed. Was this another case of Calcata gossip gone awry? After Elena dropped me off in Calcata, I happened to run into Pancho. When I told him that I'd just been on an unfruitful quest to find the last Clarice, he told me I was looking in the wrong place. The last Clarice was in Rignano, a village about five miles away. In fact, he reminded me, she ran an appliance shop with her son and a few weeks earlier I'd even been there with him. I ran to the nearest spot where I could get a signal on my cell phone and sent a text message to Elena, who by now was back at her home in Faleria. "Clarice is in Rignano! We had the wrong village!" She wrote back a minute later, "I'm on my way."

We pulled up to the appliance shop in Rignano and darted in, excited and anxious to meet the Clarice we'd been searching for. There she was, short and frumpy with bleach blond hair that belied her age, standing behind the counter helping someone with a toaster. Her son asked if we needed help and Elena explained in only the vaguest terms that I was a journalist from New York and I wanted to speak to his mother. I could see a look of horror come over Clarice's face as her son relayed the information to her. Then she disappeared into a back room. Her son told us that she'd be out in a little while. So Elena and I waited, gawking at all the fancy blenders and kitchen gadgets, until finally Clarice emerged. But she didn't approach us. In fact, she seemed to be ignoring us, pretending we weren't there. Elena went over to explain and this time she said the reason for our visit. Clarice suddenly smiled brightly and let out a sigh of relief. Rignano was being rocked by a huge pedophile scandal that involved teachers and bar owners and video cameras. The national news in Italy was covering it nightly. Journalists from the biggest dailies in the country were sniffing around Rignano looking to uncover information. Clarice, when she heard I was a journalist from New York, feared I'd come to get her opinion about the scandal and didn't want any part of it. But once she found out I was there to talk about how she'd outlived the curse of the Holy Foreskin, she was relieved and thrilled to talk about it.

Clarice began recounting her story with an almost automated but gently enthusiastic tone, like she'd told it hundreds of times. Her parents were both from Calcata and when Clarice was born, the father—a realist, if there ever was one—wanted to call their new baby daughter Clarice. "My father insisted on it," Clarice told us, "perhaps to prove that the curse didn't exist." Her mother thought this was insane. A death wish. But her father was so adamant, her mother nervously and reluctantly gave in.

As Clarice got older, she became riddled with health problems. She was sickly and weak. And she wouldn't eat. She hated food. Her mother was convinced young Clarice was going to succumb before she became a woman and she couldn't help thinking it was all because of the name she'd regretfully agreed to give her. Her mother would have to force-feed her, grabbing a handful of pasta, shoving it into her mouth and down her throat.

Then World War II broke out. Italy fell out of the axis with Germany and now the Nazis were advancing down the Italian peninsula. Clarice's family wanted to flee, and together with her uncle's family and her aunt's family, they planned to take refuge in Australia. The uncle took care of all the preparations, getting tickets for the six-week boat journey, putting passports in order, and dealing with the family homes.

But the day before they were scheduled to leave, Clarice fell deathly ill. She hadn't eaten anything for days and her mother could not get her to take any food. The mother thought about the long boat journey, telling a friend that given Clarice's health as well as this stupid curse, she feared the worst. The friend, however, was nonchalant, saying that if Clarice passed away on the journey, they'd just put her body in a potato sack and throw her overboard. That's when her mother decided: She and Clarice were not going to Australia—they'd stay right there in Rignano, and brave the encroaching Nazi soldiers. As a result, no one from the three families went to Australia the next day.

Elena and I were rendered near speechless by Clarice's story. I reflected that those three families would have had completely different lives if they'd made it to Australia. And, quite possibly, Clarice might not have survived the boat journey.

"If I'd had a different name," Clarice added, "perhaps my mother would have made the journey with me. But she had the curse in the back of her mind, knowing it was against us—and that's why she didn't take the chance."

A week later, I was sifting through documents at the Vatican Library. There, in a long-vaulted room adorned with Renaissance-era frescoes and flanked with towering bookshelves, I came across the name Clarice again in a nineteenth-century document that retold the story of how the relic had come to Calcata. In this document, however, there was a little more info—just a couple of lines. It turns out the Clarice who opened the silk sack that contained the Holy Foreskin didn't really die as a prepubescent girl after all. She grew up, married, and lived a long, happy life in a town on the outskirts of Rome called Castelnuovo di Porto. As with many things related to the foreskin, legend and reality were a contradiction. Not that this stopped people from genuflecting before it. Nor did the increasing forces of modernization keep devotees from the cult of the Holy Foreskin.

Chapter 21

RED SKIN

In 1856, about nine hundred miles north of Calcata, a worker was breaking down a wall in the old abbey of Charroux and discovered some stashed-away reliquaries, perhaps hidden by a monk during the Reformation or French Revolution. The local bishop, Louis-Édouard-François-Désiré Pie, was alerted and had them brought to his residence in Poitiers. Three years later, on January 14, 1859, Bishop Pie made a grand announcement: The *Saint Prepuce*, the piece of the Savior's flesh that had made Charroux so famous in the Middle Ages, had been found. It was, he said, the same "piece of desiccated flesh" and "coagulated blood" that Clement VII had written about in his fourteenth-century bull granting a plenary indulgence to pilgrims who came to venerate the French foreskin. In a June 1862 pageant pregnant with pomp, the bishop and town officials handed back the relic and reliquary to the Ursuline nuns who were now in control of the abbey and reestablished the fourteenth-century indulgence. The faithful were encouraged to come every day to pray in front of the Holy Foreskin and even to kiss the reliquary. A short time later, the mayor of Charroux, moved by patriotic sentiment and by local opinion, made a request to the minister of the interior to authorize a lottery to pay for the construction of a shrine "for this relic unique to the world."

Then, four years after the Holy Prepuce of Charroux re-emerged, officials in the village of Coulombs announced that their long-lost foreskin of Christ had been miraculously rediscovered, too, apparently stashed inside a dusty armoire in the church sacristy. The local priest garnered attention when he made the relic available to pregnant women and those looking for improved fertility. Wearing his surplice and stole, he would have the women kneel in front of him and kiss the reliquary. This practice was noted as late as 1872. Until these rediscoveries in France, Calcata's sacred foreskin had been the only extant foreskin to fawn over.

The reason for this relic resurgence lies partly in the larger social and political forces of the mid- and late nineteenth century. Ideologies like liberalism, nationalism, and socialism, which partly were opposed to the spirituality that the Church put forth, coincided with another ism: secularism. In Italy these forces would change the political shape of the peninsula forever. Italy had long been separated into autonomous duchies and kingdoms and regions, which made foreign domination a simple matter of just sending troops. Pan-Italian nationalism in the mid-nineteenth century became the cause célèbre for the Savoy family, rulers of the Kingdom of Sardinia (and actually headquartered in Turin, today's capital of the region of Piedmont) who wanted to spread the liberal ideals that sprang from the Europe-wide 1848 revolutions. Which wasn't a good sign for the Church's temporal power in Italy. The Savoys booted the Jesuits from Piedmont and the rest of the lands they ruled over. They ended Church-controlled schools. And they promoted freedom of religion (the first Italian translation of the Book of Mormon, for example, was published in Turin). They also gave protection to Protestants and Jews.

In December 1864, Pope Pius IX issued one of the most controversial encyclicals of the modern age: *Quanta Cura*. An annex to the encyclical was the infamous Syllabus of Errors, which even for the 1860s reads like an anachronistic throwback to a time when the sun still revolved around the earth. This list, consisting of earlier papal proclamations that should not be carried out, wasn't necessarily a direct response to the Savoy threat to papal power, but more a rejection of emerging rationalism, liberalism, and modernity. In 1879, Pius's successor, Leo XIII, issued a decree calling for the flock to embrace their medieval theological heritage in order to combat the spread of modernity and secularization. The culmination of which was a 1907 pontifical condemnation against Modernism.

Which wasn't as absurd as it would seem. The nineteenth century saw a great spiritual awakening, as a reaction to both a quickly changing, industrializing world and to Enlightenment thinking, which generated an intellectual response to the dogma and orthodoxy of the Church. The Romantic movement inspired Europeans to dig deep into their collective memories, focusing on European popular culture. The Grimm Brothers began recording folk traditions; historians focused on the Middle Ages; and cathedrals rose in a style called Neo-Gothic, with an exaggerated use of gargoyles, flying buttresses, pointed arches, and ribbed vaults that outdid genuine Gothic architecture of the Middle Ages.

Given the yen for all things medieval, it's no surprise the Holy Foreskin, that most medieval of relics, reemerged. And it was immediately criticized. The rediscovery of Charroux's Holy Foreskin set off a blaze of criticism in Europe's Protestant press, many of the journalists noting the existence of the foreskin of Calcata. It didn't help that a Church-sanctioned booklet called *Narrazione Critico-Storico della Reliquia Preziosissima del Santissimo Prepuzio di N.S. Gesù Cristo*, recounting the tale of the prepuce and its journey to Calcata, had been published earlier that century.

In response to the criticism, Bishop Pie organized a conference in Poitiers. In front of the invited guests, Pie tried to justify the existence of the Charroux foreskin. "The Sovereign Pontiffs in their bulls of indulgence about the exposition and the cult of relics in this monastery," said the bishop, "mention the tradition that concerns this particular devotion with the parenthetical *ut fertur, ut pie creditur* [as it is presented to us, so it is piously believed]. It's thanks to this disclaimer, which brackets the question of fact, that the popes could so often offer spiritual favors to different places using the same relic and authorize its usage in specific churches according to legend without needing to reconcile [the conflicting claims]."

In the end, Pie managed to say something without saying anything about the relic: "None of these things allow, nor absolutely deny, nor in any way point out, the existence of the particular relic indicated by the inscription and by secular tradition."

This caused French writer Pierre Saintyves to quip, "This ecclesiastical pragmatism does nothing less than legitimize by a sort of sacred prescription an infinite number of deceits, inventions of counterfeit relics, and fabrications of phony legends."

Curiously, after much hubbub in Charroux over the relic, the celebrations (and the controversy) quietly went away. Was there still a Holy Foreskin in Charroux? Did the same thing happen there as happened in Calcata, that the relic was quietly venerated but otherwise not mentioned? I needed to find out.

The problem was that I dreaded the idea of going to France. For weeks before my flight to Charles de Gaulle International Airport, my stomach churned every time I thought about spending any time there. I had baggage. Serious French baggage. Allow me to explain: I can no longer count the times stereotypes have been completely shattered when I go to a new country. When the light in my hotel room in Krakow burned out, only one Polish guy showed up with a ladder. Likewise, the Mexicans aren't shiftless sombrero-wearers who use donkeys to get from one bar to the next. Other times, however, a stereotype can confirm a preconceived idea or image we had before going to a country: Many Italians really do speak with their hands. And it's a fact that Germans drink a lot of beer. Similarly, the first time I was in Paris, in the early nineties, I remember seeing couture-clad women walking down the Champs-Elysées holding perfectly groomed toy poodles. I left France, having spent only twenty-four hours there, this image etched in my mind.

Ten years later, I found myself in Paris again. This time I'd be living there for a few months. I'd spend my days writing travel stories for a weekly arts-and-entertainment paper in San Francisco and my evenings sitting on the banks of the Seine imbibing wine. It was great. And despite the reputation that Parisians were rude, I was being treated gently. I was even writing an article for the magazine about the myth of Parisian impoliteness.

I had arrived in the City of Light, a one-month intensive French class under my belt, feeling confident that the Parisians would like me because I could conjugate a few of their more difficult irregular verbs. But when you're trying your hardest to speak French to, say, a shoe salesman and he stops you midsentence and says in bad English, "What you speaking no is zee French—now we going speaking zee English," it's impossible not to take it personally. Especially after the fifth time in as many days by as many shoe salesmen. As the summer went on and more vacation-bound Parisians were replaced by tourists, it wasn't just shoe salesmen in the City of Light who gave me eye rolls, head shakes, and clicks of the tongue. Cultural misunderstanding? Maybe. To me, the stereotype of rude Parisians had reared its ugly head. I abandoned my story about Parisian politeness and fled Paris thinking that no matter how eager you are to try to speak their language, the French will always hate you.

So, after a few long hours of sitting on the motorway in Paris, and then four hours speeding in the direction of southwestern France, at ten-thirty P.M., seven hours after I got off my flight and three hours after I was scheduled to arrive in Charroux, I finally pulled up to the Romanesque gate of the village. I checked into my B & B, a cozy house run by a woman named Claudine, and promptly fell asleep.

DAVID FARLEY

The next morning, I traipsed downstairs ready to see the village and, more important, find out about the relic. Claudine was
a jolly, rotund woman in her late sixties. She didn't speak English,
but made it known she wanted me to watch a DVD of Charroux
before I went outside. Any kind of verbal misunderstanding
would have certainly been quashed when she put her hand on my
shoulder and pulled me into her living room, pointed to a comfy
armchair, and popped in the DVD. The short feature on Charroux was in French, of which I understood little. But every time
Claudine's house or her street or the intersection down the street
from her house was on TV, she began bouncing up and down in
her plush chair, which she'd positioned next to the television,
screaming, "Do you see it? Do you see it? Do you see it?" If the
national evening news were doing a story that took place in my
neighborhood, and by chance they happened to catch my apartment building on film, I admit, I'd be a little excited too (not
jump-up-and-down-in-your-chair excited, but excited). This,
however, was a DVD—a short documentary on a village few people visit—that she could pop into her DVD player anytime she
wanted. Even so, by the last time the camera caught the façade of
her house, I, too, started to get excited.

Claudine's enthusiasm was disarming. I liked her. And she
liked me. She didn't tell me that I wasn't speaking French (not
that she knew how to tell me in English that I wasn't speaking
French). Nor did she make me eat foie gras and then scoff when
I didn't eat it properly. I felt a sense of relief. And she eventually
allowed me to leave her house when the DVD ended.

I next met Yvette, a local tour guide who was going to show
me the foreskin sights, which mostly consist of the now-ruined
monastery. The Reformation, the succeeding wars of religion
that followed, and the French Revolution, had taken their toll
(and a good deal of precious marble and other material) from the
once towering abbey.

Yvette, a pleasant middle-aged woman who lived in one of

the surrounding villages, led me around the grounds of the abbey. She knew why I was there, but she still insisted on giving me every single detail of the abbey's history first. I was tired and with my mind mostly focused on the Holy Foreskin, I was, at times, only half listening to Yvette.

"This is not so interesting for you?" she asked, interrupting one of my daydreams.

"Yes, yes, of course it is," I said.

"I tell you about the local duke who maybe founded the abbey with Charlemagne, but you write nothing—you stand with your notepad and pen in your hands, but write nothing when I speak."

"Um . . . I'm memorizing a lot of it. Please continue."

She gave me a sidewise glance. And instead of continuing, she walked me over to the wall of the abbey.

At first I thought she was going to punish me by giving a detailed history of every wall in the building. This wall, however, was the one behind which in 1856 the Holy Foreskin was discovered by the worker. I found myself, all of a sudden, ferociously scribbling in my notebook.

Then she waved me forward and stepped out of the arcaded courtyard and into an open doorway. She pointed to a glass case. "There it is," she said. "There's your Holy Foreskin reliquary."

I approached the glass case. In it stood a foot-tall silver reliquary of two angels holding an egg-size glass box. Next to the reliquary were two silver containers.

"This one here," she said, pointing to the smaller of the two cases, "held a piece of the True Cross and when it was retrieved from the worker, it was found inside the bigger one, which once held the Holy Foreskin. They both were inside the glass box that the angels are holding in the reliquary."

The round two-inch box that held the Holy Foreskin had a Byzantine Christ etched on it. The Christ on the front of the box was crudely rendered by the Medieval artisan, all scrunched up, his knees at his chest—in an attempt, perhaps, to fit on the relic holder. A sentence, in Latin, etched into the side read: Hɪc Caro et Sanguis Christi Continetur. "Here is contained the flesh and blood of Christ."

Goose bumps popped up on my upper arms when I saw it. Just a sheet of glass separated me from the box that held the Holy Foreskin.

"Can I see it?" I asked.

"See what?"

"The relic. The Holy Prepuce."

"But it isn't there," she said.

"It's not? Where is it?"

Yvette shrugged.

"Did someone steal it again?"

"We don't know," said Yvette, shaking her head. "We don't know what happened to it. It hasn't been here for a long, long time."

"Was the relic even in the reliquary when the worker found it in the wall?" I asked.

Yvette shrugged again and then told me that the worker, who lived in Poitiers (about thirty miles away), apparently took the reliquaries home and sold some of them before getting caught by the authorities. The church retrieved some of the relics and reliquaries—including the one we were standing in front of.

"So, you don't know if the Holy Foreskin was in the reliquary or not when it was recovered? Didn't the local church and town authorities make a big deal about it when the Holy Foreskin was supposedly rediscovered?"

"Yes, they did," Yvette said.

"So do you think the worker sold it? Or that it somehow went on the relics black market?"

She shrugged again. "We don't know."

"Or do you think there never was a relic in the reliquary when the worker found it?"

"It's possible," she said. "We really don't know." She had a sly smirk on her face, one that perhaps suggested I'd cracked the code.

Yvette and I retreated back to the café, and over a couple glasses of wine, she asked me questions in an incredulous tone about the search I was undertaking. And I, in an incredulous tone, continued probing her on the whereabouts of the Charroux foreskin. I didn't get anywhere. Still, it was enough for me to speculate, with some confidence, that the rediscovered foreskin of Charroux had been a hoax, an attempt to raise money, to get attention, maybe even to reestablish the medieval competition that had been going on between France and Italy over foreskin relics.

My work was cut out for me: there was only one foreskin remaining, the one that had been in Calcata. So the next morning I said au revoir to Claudine and hopped back in my rental car for Paris. I got on the overnight Paris-to-Rome train that night and recommenced my search in Calcata. Soon enough, I found myself standing in front of Don Dario, finally, asking him the same questions I had been asking Yvette—"What happened to the Holy Foreskin?"—but this time, I'd get back more than a shrug.

Chapter 22

IL GIALLO

The day the relic disappeared, Don Dario arrived back in Calcata from Rome around three-thirty in the afternoon, but he didn't go directly into his house, which was connected to the new church in Calcata Nuova. Instead, he met someone in the church who wanted to arrange a dedication mass. Don Dario needed to look at his agenda, so he excused himself for a minute and went into his house to fetch it. That's when he noticed the curtains to his living room window billowing in the late-afternoon breeze. He never left his window open, especially since, months earlier, he had taken the relic and its eighteenth-century bejeweled reliquary from the church in the medieval village to his house in Calcata Nuova and stored it in a shoe box in his wardrobe. *Someone was in here*, he thought. He could just feel it. He dashed over to his dresser, where he'd stashed a bundle of cash, and brushed away his socks to get to the bottom of the drawer. The rubber-band-bound lump of money was still there, which stumped him for a minute. *Why would someone break into my house if they didn't want money?* Then it hit him. The relic. He darted to the wardrobe and swung open the doors. There, on the bottom of the armoire, was an empty space where the shoe box had once sat.

For months after the theft—and even weeks after Don Dario told his congregation—few people in Calcata knew the relic had disappeared. One Calcata native told me that he didn't know about the theft until he read an article about it—wittily titled "*Santo Imbarazzo*"—in the January 16, 1984, issue of the popular weekly magazine *Panorama*. And he worked at Calcata Nuova's city hall.

But Calcata's muted reaction to the slow-spreading news might be more than typical Italian indifference. For there had been signs the relic might disappear one day.

The priest who preceded Don Dario, Don Antonio, had closed the church to the public, only opening it for Sunday mass. Parishioners began to notice that items in the church were quietly disappearing: The precious jewelry that adorned a life-size statue of the Virgin—and then the statue itself. A centuries-old triptych. And the diamond-encrusted cross that formed the top of the reliquary that held the Holy Foreskin. Because the church became off-limits (except for an hour on Sunday) and because the relic could only be seen one time per year, no one was exactly sure when some of these valuables went missing. The church was constantly locked, so it was unlikely the objects were victims of a smash-and-grab burglar. Calcata residents had to ask themselves: Were the priests slowly selling off the church's property?

Or was the Church quietly taking back its own precious possessions? Perhaps in the knowledge that Calcata had been abandoned to the "*fricchettoni*," they wanted their valuables back before pagans draped the statue of the Virgin with a tie-dyed shirt. Or perhaps the Church was removing the objects in accordance with its longstanding disapproval of the veneration of the Holy Foreskin.

In 1954, the Church convened a conference at the Vatican to discuss the Holy Foreskin. The meeting's events were preserved for posterity thanks to Roger Peyrefitte, who reprinted the transcripts from the meeting in his book *The Keys of St. Peter*. The meeting's attendees were all real people and, according to Patrizia, the reason for the meeting was also real. On May 15, several cardinals and bishops convened to discuss a proposal to resurrect the Holy Foreskin. A French monk, says the text, wanted to include Calcata (and its relic) in a guidebook on pilgrimage. Or, as the announcement at the beginning of the congregation went; "He petitions that revocatory letters be granted, relative to the decree of February 3, 1900, No. 37A, whereby the Supreme Sacred Congregation prohibits all speaking and writing concerning this relic, kept in the Church of SS. Cornelius and Cyprian of Calcata."

Before making the decision, the bishops and cardinals were treated to a detailed history of the relic; they often interrupted, asking questions. When it was said that the prepuce had been mentioned in the Book of Luke and also the apocryphal Infancy Gospel, Monsignor Graneris objected, saying that you couldn't consider the relic real if it were based on a Gospel that wasn't included in the Bible. His suggestion was shot down by Cardinal Canali, who reminded the monsignor that "since the existence of the Holy Prepuce can be deduced from the canonical writings of St. Luke, the details given by the Gospel of the Childhood are secondary, and that the relic in question has always and deservedly received attention from the Church and the doctors of the Church."

At one point, the discussion touched on the questions of which body parts were "of consequence"; a decree from the year 1281 was cited, asserting that only the body parts of martyred saints were important relics. Of those saints who died in other ways, the head, heart, tongue, hand, arm, leg, and—decided in 1899—the knee were worthy parts of veneration. The congregation then got caught up discussing whether or not the ear would be included in such a compendium of relics, before Cardinal Pizzardo finally steered the group back to the relic in question, the prepuce. There was an argument as to whether the foreskin should be classified as a "major" relic, a "minor" relic, or a "notable" relic, but they moved on before deciding.

St. Bridget's vision of the Virgin, in which the Madonna gave her nod of approval to the veneration of her son's foreskin in Rome, was brought up, the congregation agreeing that because Bridget had been canonized (and her visions therefore would have been severely scrutinized), the Roman (or Lateran) relic— the one in Calcata—must be the most authentic. Cardinal Ottaviani interjected, "St. Bridget sent her *Revelations* to Innocent IV as a means of persuading him to leave Avignon in order to join the Holy Prepuce in Rome. Thus, the relic played a part in bringing the papacy back to the fold." He added, "Some consider this to be one of the great secrets of the Church."

The discussion on the history of the relic led all the way up to the 1900 excommunication decree before circling back to the monk who had wanted to include Calcata and the Holy Foreskin in guidebooks in order to raise money. The cardinals and bishops proceeded to a vote. One person abstained, five voted for, and four voted against. Which meant the Holy Foreskin was about to be resuscitated. That is, until some of the cardinals retired in private to debate. They returned one hour later with the verdict: Even though the vote had been in favor of bringing back the Holy Prepuce, the petition was rejected, and an announcement was read aloud: "The Apostolic See reserves the right to excommunicate whoever shall write or speak of the Holy Prepuce without permission." Moreover, they upped the excommunication level from "tolerated infamous person" to "infamous persons to be avoided," the most severe level of excommunication. Instructions to practice "increased vigilance" were sent on to the bishop in Civita Castellana (to be passed on to the parish priest of Calcata).

Why did a select few bishops and cardinals overturn the vote? One answer could be the most obvious: that, as it had been stated, the relic was attracting "irreverent curiosity." Today people associated with the Church like to say the relic was just a "medieval fantasy," but Patrizia once mentioned to me that they outlawed (and then re-outlawed) the relic because they knew it was the genuine foreskin of Christ and they were protecting it. Real or not real, reverent or irreverent curiosity, the Church was quite serious when it came to the Holy Foreskin.

Which was why no one wanted to talk about it. Especially Don Dario. Still, I had to confront him and ask what had happened to the relic. I'd even heard that, sometime in the early 1980s, a man came to his house and complained of severe depression, and in an attempt to make him feel better, Don Dario had snipped off a flake of the foreskin and given it to him. If this was true, I wanted to know who had been the lucky recipient of a flake of Jesus' foreskin.

And since Don Dario had said that he'd talk if we happened to find him opening or closing the church in the borgo sometime, I decided one Sunday to sit on the square all afternoon, hoping he'd be around. I'd just had my usual Sunday lunch with Paul at the Grotta. Omar was waiting tables at Il Gato Nero, located just off the square, and told me to come get him if I spotted the priest. It was a typical Sunday afternoon. The day-trippers were fading out of sight and the local artists were emerging from their houses and planting themselves around the piazza. I sat on the church steps, rotating between conversations with Elena and Costantino and Giancarlo Croce and a talented Bulgarian painter named Sofia Minkova and others. The weak autumn sun was slowly descending behind the buildings in the square and the first hickory scent of burning chimneys had begun to envelop the village.

I can't remember what Elena and I were talking about when I saw him, but my attention froze on the lumpy priest as he marched up the four steps and into the church. Elena stopped talking to see what I was looking at and then said, "Go! Go get Omar!" I sprang up and began a brisk walk across the square toward Il Gato Nero. "Run!" Elena yelled. "Run!" So I did.

Don Dario wasn't anywhere to be found when Omar and I scampered into the church. Breathing heavily, we whipped our heads around in every direction trying to find him. "The side door outside," Omar said. "Let's try the side door." When we re-emerged on the square, everyone on the church steps was looking at us expectantly. We darted up a cobblestone ramp to a decrepit wooden door that led into a back room of the church. Omar gave it a nudge but it was bolted shut. We walked back to the church steps, both of us feeling slightly defeated, when we heard a clang come from inside the building. Without saying a word or even looking at each other, Omar and I dashed toward the door and just inside, blowing out a couple of votive candles, was Don Dario.

Omar, his voice rattling with nervousness, reintroduced us and reminded him that he'd said we could talk to him if we ever saw him opening or closing the church. I interrupted and, in my improving Italian, said that I was trying to interview all the important people in Calcata about the village's history.

"I'm no authority on the history of the village," Don Dario said. "I could talk a little about this church, but if it's the relic you're interested in, forget it." The priest paused for about three seconds, perhaps assessing our interest in the topic and hoping we'd ask him about something else. Instead we kept our mouths shut and Don Dario continued, "I'm under strict instructions not to talk about the relic. Besides, I could be excommunicated, you know?"

I asked Omar to ask him if it's true that he'd given a piece of the relic to a sorrowful man who came to his house one time looking for consolation.

"I can't ask him that!" Omar said. Don Dario was staring at us, unable to follow our conversation. "I mean, c'mon, honky," Omar continued. "We're talking about the foreskin of Jesus here. I really can't ask him that."

Suddenly Don Dario interrupted. "Like I said, I'll talk to you about the history of this church, but I'm too frightened to talk about the relic—especially since its disappearance in 1986."

Suddenly, somewhere in the sky, a needle scratched across a record. *Had he just said 1986?* "Did you say the relic disappeared in 1986?" I asked.

"Yes," said the priest, still holding a smoldering votive candle. "It was 1986."

"Wasn't it 1983?"

"No," he said with conviction in his voice. "It was 1986."

Don Dario scurried us out of the church, saying he was going to be closing, and I sat there on the church steps telling everyone about our encounter. But I couldn't shake the idea that he thought the relic had disappeared in 1986. Perhaps he was advanced in age, but it would seem that if someone broke into your house and stole your foreskin of Jesus (not to mention the valuable gem-studded reliquary), you'd at least remember what year it was.

The priest had always claimed he went to the Carabinieri, the state police, in Faleria to file a report of the theft. I had never doubted this, but after his ambiguity over the date of the disappearance, I was suspicious. Something just didn't seem right. So one day Elena and I stopped by the Carabinieri office in Faleria to see the police report Don Dario had filed after the theft of the relic.

The Carabinieri compound looked fit for Baghdad. An imposing thick metal fence surrounded the central stone building, serrated at the top with points sharp enough to stop anyone foolish enough to try to scale the fence. They didn't keep prisoners there, so I wondered why they were protecting themselves from the outside. Maybe it was because they were such power-loving numbskulls.

After my first few encounters with Carabinieri, I'd assumed they were a remnant of Italy's interwar fascist government, but they had actually been created in 1814 by Vittorio Emanuele I of Sardinia, Duke of Savoy, Piedmont, and Aosta, following the French occupation of Turin. After the unification of Italy in 1871, the Carabinieri became Italy's national police force as well as the country's military police (they've fought in every war Italy has been in since their founding). It wasn't necessarily the Carabinieri's smart dark military-like outfits and their steel-faced demeanor that sometimes made me feel I was living in a police state; it was their modus operandi that baffled me.

The Carabinieri would set up checkpoints on the road that winds its way through Mazzano, Calcata, and Faleria. You'd be driving along and then turn a bend, and there they were. They might wave you by or, as was always the case whenever I encountered them, they would hold up a little red circle on a stick indicating that I should pull over. They'd scrutinize my passport, taking it back to their car to make (I suspected) faux-deliberations about what they were going to do about me. A minute later, one of them would walk over, hand it back to me, and say I was free to leave. They didn't seem to care about traffic violations—only that one's papers were in order. Nearby Mazzano was filled with Romanians, many of whom were in Italy illegally. There's a possibility the Carabinieri were specifically looking to hassle them, one of the country's least favorite immigrant groups. Whatever the case, the technique always seemed like a missed opportunity to me (if you've ever driven in Italy, you know what I'm talking about).

One time when I was driving through Faleria with Omar, they stopped us. "*Documenti*," one of the sunglass-clad, iron-lipped policemen demanded. I didn't have my passport on me. Just my driver's license, which allowed them to take twice as long. Omar and I sat in the car waiting for them to do their fake checks on us to make sure we weren't criminals. "The funny thing is," Omar said to me, "I was just joking around with these guys this morning at the bar here in Faleria. And now they act like they've never

seen me before." Another time, during one of my first reconnais-
sance missions to Paolo Portoghesi's studio to see if I could score
an interview with him, I walked by a roadblock. The police,
standing around and looking bored at the light traffic day, spotted
me. "*Vieni qui!*" screamed one of them, ordering me to come
over. "*Documenti!*" As they thumbed through my passport—the
same guys who'd stopped me with Omar the week before and
the same guys who had stopped me with Pancho the week before
that—they asked me where I was coming from. "Portoghesi's studio," I said.

"Oh, you know the Architect?" one of the policemen asked.

I nodded with caution, since I hadn't actually met Portoghesi
at this point. "Yes, I'm—I'm interviewing him for a story I'm
writing for an American newspaper." The policeman, who had
stopped scrutinizing every stamp in my passport as soon as I had
mentioned the architect's name, handed me back my document
and thanked me for my cooperation. I was stopped two or three
other times after that and before handing them my passport, I
always said I was on my way to see Portoghesi. They'd wave
me on.

Just before Elena and I could ring the buzzer on the thick
metal gate of the Carabinieri compound in Faleria, Gemma
stomped out wearing a deeper frown than usual. As she passed us,
she mumbled something about having just filed a *denuncia*, a report, on Giorgio il Matto. It seemed like you weren't really a true
Calcata resident until you'd filed a *denucia* against the man who
shuffled around the parking lot annoying people on a daily basis.

Inside, Elena explained to the man at the front desk why we
were there and then he asked us to take a seat. The clinical-
looking lobby, complete with faded linoleum floors and professional pictures of policemen wearing Napoleon hats and thick
epaulet-shouldered jackets, was entirely charmless. I tried to ease
my nerves about being in the headquarters of the men who'd
stopped me so many times by making jokes to Elena about the

Carabinieri Monthly magazines spread out on the table in front of us, but Elena would only tersely smile at my attempts at humor. She was nervous too. About forty-five minutes later, we were waved down a hall and into an office. Behind the big wooden desk was Luigi D'Oria, also known by his title Maresciallo Capo (Head Marshall). I'd seen this stocky, thick-necked man with black curly hair before; certainly it was one of the times I'd been stopped. He had an aloof but friendly demeanor. He motioned for us to have a seat and then asked who we wanted to file a *denuncia* against. I thought about jokingly suggesting Giorgio il Matto, but I resisted. Elena began explaining that we wanted to see the *denuncia* that Don Dario had filed when the relic was stolen in 1983. I expected the police captain to shake his head or wave his finger at us, saying it was classified information, but instead he called out to his assistant and barked, "Bring me the file on Don Dario, the priest in Calcata." Elena gave me a surreptitious eyebrow raise. And then we sat there. In silence. The captain looked straight on, tapping a pencil against his desk. I tried breaking the uncomfortable stillness by asking Elena if she'd ask him how long he'd worked here. She just shook her head and mouthed, "No." I looked around at his walls, which were decorated with a mishmash of disparate symbols: a crucifix hung next to an Italian flag, next to framed pics of important Carabinieri higher-ups, next to a couple etchings of Calcata by Giancarlo Croce.

About fifteen minutes later, the assistant set a manila folder in front of the captain. He slowly leafed through the paperwork and announced what each document was. "Here's a *denuncia* about two cups that were stolen from the church in Calcata in 1995. Here's one from the late seventies about some damage that was done to Don Dario's car. Here's a newspaper article about the disappearance of the relic." He got to the end of the folder. "There's nothing here. Nothing about the relic." Then he barked for his assistant again and a few minutes later, he returned with a jaundiced folder. It contained the files on the general thefts in the early and mid 1980s. "If he filed a *denuncia*," the captain said, "and it's not in the first file I just looked through, then it would be here." He began flipping through, shaking his head from side to side with each flip of the page. After he turned over the last document, he said, "Well, I'm sorry, but perhaps the priest never made a *denuncia* about this theft. Do you know for sure that he made one?"

"He said he did," Elena responded.

The captain shrugged and said, "It's a *giallo*," using the Italian word for yellow, which also means "mystery."

He was right. It was definitely a *giallo*.

I hadn't seen Paolo much since the vegetarian meeting and walk down in the valley. He hadn't been basking in the late-afternoon sun on the square. I went to his house, just outside of the village walls, but there was no answer. I asked Lorenzo, a piazza fixture, if he knew where I could find him and he told me to look in Paolo's "cantina," or storage room. He told me the whereabouts of the place and I found it right away.

"Ah, so the energy has led you here," Paolo said, smiling widely, and closing his book on Hindu philosophy.

"Uh . . . yeah," I said. "The energy just pulled me right here."

Paolo nodded at me and smiled.

"I've been doing a lot of reading about the *prepuzio*," I said. "But I still am having a difficult time finding leads on where it could have gone."

"Even if you are not a believer in the Christian god," Paolo said, "the foreskin is important for Calcata. The foreskin was a sacred fertility-giving object. And Calcata was for the Faliscans a sacred fertility-giving place. For this reason, it was destiny that the relic came to Calcata."

I had to admit that the fertility connections between Calcata and the Holy Foreskin were intriguing: Besides the sculptures of fertility goddesses that had been unearthed near Calcata, there's also the phallic Shiva linga shape of the rock. And up until the early 1970s, the church in Calcata (spurred by the avaricious Don Antonio) sold plaques that featured a drawing of the foreskin reliquary looming about the clouds; the priest said he'd rubbed each plaque up against the Holy Foreskin and that if you bought one, you'd have a good chance of bearing children.

Paolo switched gears from the nether worlds of energy to reality (or at least a semblance of reality). "In the late nineteen seventies and nineteen eighties, I worked as a journalist and wrote some stories about the relic for newspapers in Rome. So did some of my journalist friends. If I can find the articles, I will make a copy for you."

I paused for a minute, wondering why he hadn't told me this earlier. What else did he know? "So you were writing about the relic just before it disappeared?"

Paolo nodded his head and smiled.

"Do you think you had something to do with the disappearance?"

Paolo nodded again. This opened up all sorts of possibilities. Perhaps Paolo's "advertising" of the relic caught the attention of interested parties. Or perhaps of the Church itself. After all, the relic was basically forbidden after the 1900 decree, but because of Calcata's near inaccessibility few people knew about it. As the century went on, however, and communication became better and roads were paved, Calcata became less isolated. And with a group of hippie leftist radicals cohabitating with a piece of flesh that was, at one time, one of Christianity's most sacred relics, is it any surprise the relic went missing—especially with people like Paolo writing about it in the Roman press?

"Yes, it's possible," said Paolo. He started laughing, seemingly amused that it had taken me this long to figure it out.

It didn't tell me any more about who had taken the relic, but it did make clear the connection between the Holy Foreskin's mysterious exit from Calcata and the repopulation of the village with hippies and artists. It's as if the foreskin's fate was put in motion the moment the village came under the Messina Law in 1935. No one could have necessarily predicted the relic would eventually vanish, but I was about to learn of someone who predicted the relic's disappearance at least a decade before it went missing.

Chapter 23

THE CONFESSION

I t was a normal Tuesday afternoon in Calcata and Jessie and I had just trudged up the hill to Calcata Nuova to buy some food in Zio Avelio's limited corner shop. On our way down, our arms full of pasta and bread and cheese and six-packs of bottled water, we passed by Capellone's cantina. As was always the case when we walked by, a voice from inside the dark hovel screamed at us. "Hey! Davide!" And soon enough, the bearded man himself, hunched over, emerged from the blackness like some kind of cave-dwelling hermit, imploring us with a wave of his hand and some incomprehensible grunts to come inside—just for a *goccione*, a sizable drop. I looked at Jessie and she gave a hesitant nod. Capellone was a fascist and possibly a white supremacist; he'd been accused of poisoning dogs; and he made terrible wine. But at the same time he was warm and welcoming and generous.

Jessie and I sipped the putrid wine as Capellone grunted out stories about something we could barely understand. Suddenly two silhouettes appeared at the door of his cantina and Capellone jumped up to greet them. We followed. They wore light-pink button-up shirts and dark sport jackets. I peered up the hill and saw at least ten more, all identically dressed, marching toward us, followed by Zio Avelio (Uncle Avelio) himself and Cesare, the sweet but mentally slow Calcata Nuova inhabitant, carrying tin containers of food.

Without knowing it, we'd stumbled upon a party. Capellone dispersed his trademark cheap white plastic cups, the aluminum foil was ripped off the tin food containers. The men roared with laughter and slapped each other on the back. "Hey, check out the two Americans here," yelled Capellone with a sense of pride, almost like we were his exotic pets on display. The men began introducing themselves.

"So, what's going on here?" I asked. "Why the party?"

"We love funerals in Calcata Nuova," one of the guys said, holding a glass of wine in one hand and a paper plate of mixed seafood with the other. "We do funerals all over the area, but when we hear of a job in Calcata, we always call Capellone ahead of time and he's waiting for us here at the cantina with food and wine."

"So, the funeral is over and now you're celebrating a hard day's work?" I asked.

"No, the funeral is happening right now," the man said, looking at me like I'd just said something absurd and pointing up the hill in the direction of the cemetery in Calcata Nuova. "We don't have anything to do until it's finished. Then we have to drive back to Civita Castellana."

The instant party continued, as Jessie and I straddled our grocery bags and sipped wine. We watched Cesare, his bulging hands looking like they'd been sculpted in a Soviet propaganda artist's workshop, shoveling calamari and unidentifiable fish parts into his mouth with the determination of a competitive eater. Cesare was sweet, but so mentally slow I wondered if it would take hours before his stomach would finally be able to get the message to his brain that it was full. Six and a half feet tall and balding, Cesare spoke in a slow, grinding, and slurred monotone that made understanding him impossible. Moreover, he spoke *Calcatese*, a clipped dialect that sounds nearly incomprehensible to most other native Italian speakers. I once asked Elena what had happened to him and she said he'd been in a car accident.

"Oh, that's terrible," I said. "So he was normal before the accident?"

"No," she said with a straight face. "He was pretty much the same. He just didn't limp."

After about ten minutes of Cesare chomping down, the front of Capellone's cantina became an arena for his eating prowess, the funeral workers having paused their own partying to gawk. "He's an eating machine," one of them yelled out. "Hey, Cesare! Why not save some for the rest of us?" another screamed in a jovial tone, for which Cesare cracked a smile and grunted, keeping his intent stare on the tin container of seafood.

I'd logged more time in Capellone's wine cellar than I cared to remember. Maybe it was a sense of gratefulness to him and Mario and Piero for having taken me in my first afternoon in Calcata, but I'd find it difficult to keep walking when I'd pass by the open cantina. By the time I'd step in, everyone would have been in wine for hours, their speech slurred beyond recognition, their heads heavy and wobbly.

Omar hated hanging out in Capellone's cantina. It was less his politics and more the verbal grip in which Capellone would put you. My egregious speaking skills gave me a pass. A couple weeks after that impromptu party, having talked Omar into translating for me while I interviewed some of the old inhabitants in Calcata Nuova, we trekked up the hill to the new village and noticed the swastika-adorned doors open. Before I said anything, Omar stopped and with his index finger almost touching my chest, said, "No. We can't go. Okay?"

"Okay, okay," I said. Secretly I wanted to go. I rarely understood anything Capellone was saying and it would have been nice to have Omar with me to translate. But he was adamant. Right on cue, Capellone rushed out of his shack, waving for us to come in. I remained uncommitted, figuring I'd let Omar give a reason why we couldn't come in for a plastic cup of wine. But perhaps Omar had a hard time saying no, too, because much to my surprise he agreed and soon enough we were firmly planted on a wooden-beam-cum-bench, spiders dangling over our heads, sipping paint thinner disguised as wine. Capellone asked what we were up to and I said, through Omar, that we were on our way up to the new village to interview some of the old inhabitants about their memories of the relic.

"The *prepuzio*?" Capellone suddenly lit up. "Why didn't you come to me earlier?' he asked.

I'd never even thought to ask the fascist about the relic, but he'd lived here all his life and certainly would have something to say about it.

"I can tell you something about the *prepuzio*," he added. His normally buoyant face fell and he shook his head back and forth with regret. And then he started in. I could only understand certain words of what he was saying: "*Vescovo . . . prepuzio . . .* Civita Castellana." Finally Omar looked at me. I could see he was trying to restrain a smile. "Dude, you're not going to believe this," he said to me, and then he began reciting what Capellone had just told him. The teenaged Capellone had gone to school in Civita Castellana. He'd hated it. And he often skipped class to hang out at the bar and drink—what else?—wine. But then, somehow, he'd struck up a friendship with the bishop, one Roberto Massimilliano. Twice a week he'd skip class and head over to the bishop's office or house, the bishop believing that if Capellone was going to skip school, his place was a lot better than the bar. At least then he could lecture him on God. Through the years, they remained close, even through the long illness that would eventually kill Massimilliano. One day, Capellone received a call. It was Bishop Massimilliano on the other end. "Listen to me," he said. "I'm not going to last much longer and there's something I have to tell you. That relic you have there in Calcata . . ."

"Yes," Capellone said.

"As long as I've been bishop here—since 1948—I've always made sure the relic in Calcata remained. But let me tell you that when I'm gone, the relic won't be around too much longer either. You can be certain of that." The bishop died a few weeks later. It was 1976. The relic disappeared seven years afterward.

When Omar finished telling me, my mouth hung open. I looked at Capellone, who was nodding his head at me. He continued. "It was like he needed to make a confession—like he had to get it off his chest," he said. "And he trusted me."

I asked him who took it and he soberly said, "Who do you think? The Vatican, of course. They couldn't stand to have such a precious relic in a crazy little town like this. A piece of our hearts went with that *prepuzio* when it was taken away." He went on to say that he believed agents of the Vatican showed up at Don Dario's house and asked for it back. "Everyone in Calcata Nuova knows the Vatican has it. Everyone."

On the side of the twelfth-century Duomo—the large Romanesque church in Civita Castellana—there's a plain white door and a buzzer next to it that says "PRETE," priest. I couldn't find the bishop's office, so I figured I'd ask the local cleric. I bit down on my lower lip, stuck out my index finger, and pressed it. I waited about five seconds, thinking that any time now I'd hear some shuffling on the other side of the door and someone with an incredulous look on their face would stand there as I requested in my halting Italian if it would be possible to see the bishop. But that rustling behind the door never came. So I pressed it again.

Which was about the time I heard a slurred voice behind me say, "The priest? You're looking for the priest?" I was afraid to turn around, but I did anyway and immediately regretted it.

"The priest isn't there," said the toothless man, who was pointing a one-foot-long knife in my direction. Civita Castellana, about ten miles north of Calcata, is relatively large for the area— the hilltop town of sixteen thousand people was once known as the Stalingrad of Italy because its large porcelain industry was heavily unionized—but I hadn't been expecting to encounter many toothless, knife-wielding people here.

"Actually, I'm looking for the bishop," I said.

"This isn't the bishop's office," the man said to me, in a tone that suggested he thought I was the insane one for ringing a buzzer that said PRIEST while looking for the bishop. "The bishop's office is on the square. Next to the church."

I thanked him and cautiously sidestepped his blade. I'd thought the local bishop's office might be an easier path to official church answers. Apparently, however, this route presented its own hazards. Even though Roberto Massimilliano was long gone and his successor, Bishop Marcello Rosina—the one on whose watch the relic disappeared—died in 1986, I decided to probe the current bishop about the relic. Maybe he knew something about it; maybe there were records in the bishop's office. After Capellone's story about the former bishop's confession, I had to at least try to find out.

On the square, I rang another buzzer that read VESCOVO (bishop) and waited. This time the door buzzed open and I wandered through a Gothic courtyard and up a flight of stairs until I located the bishop's office.

A man with a gray bouffant met me at the door, shook my hand, and motioned for me to have a seat at his desk. He lacked the immediate suspicion that most people associated with the Church revealed when I'd turn up, pen and notebook in hand.

"What can I do for you?" he asked. And just as I began in Italian the ridiculous spiel I'd cooked up on the way over, the phone rang. The Gray Bouffant mostly listened to the caller, nodding his head, and finally put the phone down. "Mamma mia!"

he screamed. "That guy on the phone says, 'My uncle is from Florence, but would like to talk to the bishop.' And I told him the bishop is with the pope today and the guy still asks, 'Well, when can my uncle talk to him?' What does he think this is? Dial-a-bishop?" He paused for a moment and then asked, "So what was it you wanted?"

I hesitated for a few seconds, pleased I had understood him in Italian, but wondering if I should now continue. "I'm writing an article about Civita Castellana for an American travel magazine," I said, which was honestly the truth. "And I'd like to interview the bishop to get his recommendations on where travelers should eat and sleep. You know, his favorite restaurants and so on."

Gray Bouffant had listened to me patiently, nodding, his clasped hands resting on the desk in front of him. "Not everyone," he said, raising his hands up in the air above his head, "can talk to the bishop just because he wants." Then he slapped his hands together, making a loud clapping noise. He smiled at me deviously as he rubbed his palms together as if he were smashing a bug. I felt like I was watching a geriatric version of those old-time professional wrestlers who, before the big match, would stand in front of the camera in a back room and blusteringly announce how badly they were going to smear the opponent. "Now," he said, placing his hands back on the desk, "let's get back to why you're here. The bishop doesn't concern himself with such things like restaurants. He's a holy man." And then he launched in to a long soliloquy about what a bishop does, waving his arms in the air (and yes, it was like he just didn't care), and often using his fist to emphasize a point. I wondered how such an insane person had gotten a job as an adviser to the bishop. I realized I had little chance of outmaneuvering him, so I decided to go for broke and ask directly about the foreskin.

"So, I'm living in Calcata."

He cocked his head.

"You know this village, yes? It's not far from here," I said. "And it's famous because there are many hippies who live there."

"Of course, of course. Yes. I know Calcata."

"Do you know about the relic that was there?"

This time he squinted one eye, as if he knew the answer but couldn't think of it right away.

"The Holy Foreskin," I said. "It disappeared in the eighties."

"Yes, I remember this now. The foreskin of our Lord, Jesus Christ." Gray Bouffant grew silent, staring off into the distance.

I interrupted. "This sounds really crazy, but do you know what people in Calcata think about the disappearance of the relic?"

"What?"

"That the Vatican took it."

Here's when I expected I'd be shown the door. Or at least a finger-wagging or vehement denials. Instead, I got this: He shrugged and said, "The relic was controversial. Relics like the foreskin of Christ are not to be taken lightly. Besides, why would they want such an important relic in an obscure village like Calcata? So . . . yes, probably they took it back. Why not?"

He was clearly speculating, but I was dumbfounded by his candidness. The Vatican wouldn't even give the courtesy of a no or acknowledge my existence when I asked if I could talk to someone about relics in general. And here's this guy with gray bouffant hair claiming to be the bishop's adviser talking about the Holy Foreskin and agreeing with the theory that the Vatican had taken the relic.

He then walked me around the palace, revealing private chapels and high-ceilinged rooms, before showing me the door. We shook hands and I'd begun walking to the bar across the square to collect my thoughts, when I realized there was something I had forgotten to ask him. "Wait!" I screamed, just as the door was about to shut. He stuck his head out, his eyebrows raised, anticipating my question. "So, can I have a meeting with the bishop when he's finished talking to the pope?"

Gray Bouffant stared back at me with a blank look. And then slowly shook his head from side to side and mouthed, "No." The door creaked shut and I heard the automatic locks click into gear and the shuffling away on the other side.

Chapter 24

THE DAY CALCATA
CAVED IN

December 13 started off as any normal day. I caught the ten o'clock bus to Rome and idly strolled over to the Vatican. I pored through manuscripts and turned in a few copy requests. On my way out, I was cutting through an inner-Vatican courtyard—which also doubles as a parking lot for employees—when I heard someone yelling a name. It took a while before I realized that the screamer was trying to get my attention. "Gary," the man called out from across the courtyard, waving his left arm over his head at me. "Gary Coleman! Hey. Gary Coleman. It's me. Remember me?"

I did remember. It was the Czech priest whom I'd met while I was in line for my interview to get access to the Vatican Library. I turned and walked toward the priest; we met in the middle of the courtyard. "Are you still doing research about the Holy Foreskin?" he asked in Italian.

"Uh . . . yeah. Sort of," I said, trying to remain cryptic.

"I have a few good friends here and I've asked about what happened to it. I can't give you an exact answer—because I couldn't get one myself."

"Okay," I said, staring back at him, waiting for what was going to come out of his mouth next. I gave him a slight nudge in the form of a slow and subtle eyebrow raise.

"The only thing I could find is that you're in the wrong place," he said. "Stop looking here." He smiled and nodded.

"What does that mean?" I asked.

"I don't know," he said with a hint of a smirk. "That is what I was told." And with that he said "*Na shledanou*," good-bye in Czech, and then took a few steps backward, his smile intact, his eyes still planted on me, before he turned around and walked back to the Vatican Library.

On the bus ride back to Calcata, I thought about every possibility. Had this been a veiled threat? Was he saying the relic wasn't in the Vatican? Or that it could be here, but I wouldn't find any clues in the library? Maybe he just trying to distract me because I was so close? Once I hopped off the bus, passed by Giorgio il Matto tacking up a new poster in the parking lot, and trudged up the passageway to the square, there were other things to worry about. Such as the fact that the square had just caved in. There were about ten people standing around, their arms resting on top of a newly constructed five-foot wooden fence that lined the circumference of a hole that occupied half the square, going from the church steps all the way across to the Indian clothes shop on the opposite side. As I approached, I noticed everyone staring down into the ten-foot-deep crater in a kind of hushed haze. One of the people not so hushed was Patrizia, who was yelling at the workers. "You're not respecting the historical integrity of the square," she screamed at the men, who didn't know what to do at this point except push rocks around. She pounded her foot on the ground for emphasis, making me fear the rest of the square was going to plunge.

The implosion of the square was unfortunate—it took away Calcata's main social meeting point—but it revealed something that the people here had been saying all along: that Calcata sits on a rock honeycombed with ancient passageways and caves built by the Faliscans. Some of the caves were already well-known and had even been put to use by the Calcatesi. Athon had one in her cave house; it descended about twenty feet into the core of the rock, where the room opened up and the air took on a stale chill. She mostly used the space to stage winter and summer solstice rituals. Giancarlo Croce's Porta Segreta gallery was linked to a cavern twice as deep as Athon's. Part of the reason for all these passageways descending deep into the rock was the search for material. In the Middle Ages and earlier, the people here needed *tufo* stone to build. So they dug. And since in doing so they had just created a nice cool cellar, they stored their wine there. But the horizontal passageways underneath the square, with an underground archway and steps leading farther into the rock, were now being splashed with sunlight for the first time in God knows how many centuries, revealing the foundations of an ancient town. In a short lane just off the square (near Il Gato Nero) there was an open doorway that led down below the village. It was partially blocked by tall potted plants. I'd always wanted to venture below in my quest to find the relic. I'd figured it was probably a long shot that the relic might somehow be there, but in an attempt to exhaust all possibilities (not to mention out of genuine curiosity about what was down there), I sometimes considered taking the plunge. Omar rejected the idea. And there was no way of ever talking Jessie into going, so I'd abandoned the idea.

But now part of that cave was revealed. I was standing there, like everyone else, staring at the hole when Jessie approached. "He did it," she said. "He did it."

"Who did what?" I asked.

"Alessandro. He cut our phone line."

This wasn't the end of the world, but it did mean we couldn't talk to our families and we wouldn't have Internet access anymore, which meant I couldn't file any articles that were due.

Alessandro had been so generous in the beginning by hooking up a phone line that ran from his apartment, about seventy-five feet away, to ours. The only problem was that it was the same line. So sometimes we'd pick up the phone and he'd be in the middle of a conversation with someone. And much to his displeasure, we'd often be on the Internet when he'd want to make a phone call. Maybe it was the day that Abraham Lincoln bit his daughter Aman after one of our English lessons. Or it could have been the time Abraham Lincoln bit him when he was getting up from our couch. But relations somehow went sour between us. Then, the day before the square caved in, I reminded Alessandro that we had friends coming from England in a week and we had reserved one of his rooms for them. But he informed me that he had given it to someone else, claiming I'd never really confirmed.

I suspected his about-face with our friends' reservation had less to do with our supposed lack of confirmation and more with something else. So, I convinced Jessie that we should go talk to him, that person to person we could sort this out. Wrong. We stood there on the ledge that led to Alessandro's front door, as I asked what had happened.

"*Boh*," he said, shrugging shoulders. "I don't know what you're talking about." He was playing dumb. I don't actually remember what escalated our conversation, but before I knew it Alessandro was yelling at Jessie. His chest was protruding and she had backed up to the four-foot wall above the twelve-foot drop to the cobbled alley below. Perhaps as some kind of defense mechanism, he switched to Italian, screaming that he spoke English to us as "a courtesy" and that from now on we'd have to communicate with him in Italian. To protect Jessie, I put my arm in between them, but I feared I was about to get into a fistfight with Alessandro, which I really didn't want to do.

"Go," I screamed at Jessie. "Just—just let Alessandro and me speak, okay?"

"Fucking asshole," Jessie said to Alessandro when she turned away. I thought this was going to be it, but instead he gave her a look of incomprehension.

I stayed there for about two minutes, begging for Alessandro to open up with me, to tell me what had gone wrong between us, and he kept saying that he didn't know what I was talking about. Finally, defeated, I left.

As the days had grown shorter and the air chillier, Calcata had begun to morph into a menacing place. Most days it was too cold to loiter outside near the square and there were fewer tourists, making the village feel abandoned. There was less contact between people, and the raucous dinner parties of the summer died out. Restaurants were now open only on weekends.

About an hour after our confrontation with Alessandro, the village lampposts went out. Everyone still had electricity inside their houses, but the alleyways were nearly pitch black and quiet. I walked through the lanes on my way to the Grotta (hoping, of course, that big brother Pancho could help me sort this out). But I feared running into Alessandro and that my very presence would make him snap; and so I traversed Calcata cautiously and in fear. I thought about how my mood, too, had changed about Calcata. Gone was the bliss I had felt when sitting around this tiny, womb-like fortress town. I felt my confidence in the place had been stripped from me. Maybe, I wondered, the village's supposed malign energy was real and it was finally seeping into me. Before I could consider the idea any more, I turned the corner and almost ran into someone. "Waaah!" I screamed. It was Athon. She began laughing.

After catching my breath, I asked what was going on.

"I don't know. It's very peaceful," she said.

I couldn't agree.

"Where are the wolves?" she asked—rhetorically, I hoped. And then she belted out her wicked bird laugh, each whoop and warble echoing down the alleyways.

When I strolled into the Grotta, Pancho had just finished delivering some steaming pasta dishes to the table by the door. Before I could tell him about the encounter with Alessandro, he said, "Patrizia wants to ask you something." I followed him back to the

kitchen and there, gobbling up a plate of brownies at the bar that
overlooked the cooking area, was Patrizia, sitting like some kind
of Godfather, probably wanting to know what I'd been up to on
the foreskin front.

"Did Sandro tell you the Holy Foreskin wasn't in the Vatican?" she asked, referring to the husband of Simona Weller, who'd
been promising to help set up an interview for me with a Vatican
official—until Pancho assailed those American priests in the supermarket in Rome a few months before.

"Yes," I said. "He did tell me that."

She rolled her eyes and said that he'd told another person recently that it *was* in the Vatican. Then, out of the blue, she said, "I
think you're being secretive with me."

Secretive? I was bewildered.

She continued, "You haven't told me everything you're doing.
You didn't tell me that you went to Fabrica di Roma to see Don
Mario. Nor did you tell me that you went to see the bishop in
Civita Castellana. You didn't tell me that you asked Sandro to get
you an interview at the Vatican. I also don't like that you've been
going around with him."

"Going around with him?" I said. I hadn't been going around
with him. In fact, I explained, he wasn't even talking to me anymore. And how did she know about all these places I'd gone?

I tried pleading my case one last time that I hadn't been hanging out with Sandro. "*Giuro*," I said. I swear.

Patrizia shook her head from side to side, still chewing on the
remnants of a brownie. "I don't believe you," she finally said.

Rather than linger at the Grotta for hours like I usually did, I
went back to Ca' Dante. On my way back, a large beast trotted by.
At first I couldn't make out what it was, but then I realized it was
Willie—the wolf-dog owned by the so-called village burglar,
Angelo. This was the first time I'd ever seen him off the leash. If
there was ever a fitting night for Willie, the killer wolf-dog, to be
running around looking for prey in Calcata, it was tonight.

"Hey," I said to Jessie in a monotone voice when I walked through the door, looking to make sure Abraham Lincoln was inside. Once I saw him curled up on his rug, I let myself plop onto the couch.

"What's wrong?"

"Everything," I said.

She put the photocopied newspaper article she'd been trying to read in Italian on her lap.

"I think this place is starting to drive me crazy," I said. "Everything just seems to be falling apart here at the same moment—and I don't necessarily mean the piazza."

Jessie stared back, waiting for me to say more. So I did.

"I'm sick of this place!" I screamed, even surprising myself. There had been some good times. Dinner parties on the square; long, wine-fueled meals with Paul at the Grotta; Tuesday argument-filled lunches with Pancho and Paul. Sitting around with Omar, smoking roll-up cigarettes and teaching him slang; driving around with Elena; hanging out with Athon in her bird cave. But Italy wasn't necessarily everything I'd expected either. I'd occasionally stumble upon that Italy I'd read about in the pages of travel magazines and books—that much-revered paradise on earth of long days in villas eating simple, savory meals; the one where everyone gracefully strolls down the street sporting designer suits; the one where the locals teach me, the uptight urban dweller from across the sea, how to slow down and appreciate a bit of La Dolce Vita.

But I'd been living in this other Italy. This bizarre quest I'd put myself on and living in an isolated village was starting to take its toll on me. Though I was taking the bus into Rome a couple days a week in order to do research at the Vatican, I was starting to get cabin fever, especially now that the weather made it too cold to linger outside. And now that Patrizia had sworn me off and Alessandro and I were no longer talking, this place had just become even smaller.

And then there was the reason I had come here in the first place: the relic. I'd exhausted every foreskin-finding route I could imagine and only taken the equivalent of baby steps.

"What a day," I said to Jessie. "The square caves in, we have a fight with Alessandro, the lights go out. I haven't even told you what Patrizia just said to me."

"Well," Jessie said, "I have one piece of good news. The phone line is working again. I don't think Alessandro actually cut the line. Maybe it just went out for a while, like the lights."

That *was* good. I had imagined Alessandro, in a fit of anger, ripping out the phone line he'd installed for us.

"Oh, yeah," she said. "I tried reading some of these old newspaper articles on Calcata that Portoghesi gave you. Check this one out." She handed it to me. "Last paragraph."

I began reading, but I didn't have the patience at the moment, so Jessie took it from me and began reading it for me: "Though the relic is long gone, there's a theory that if you do the New Year's Day procession in the name of the relic, it will hasten its return."

The Feast Day of the Holy Circumcision, which was celebrated on January 1, was removed from the calendar after Vatican II. There was no official word as to why, but given the Church's evolving posture toward the foreskin, it isn't much of a surprise that the holiday was phased out. Not that this kept the people of Calcata from their January First procession with the relic, anyway.

On the first of January, 1984, many of the villagers had sat out the procession, protesting the relic's recent disappearance. They'd stood on the sidelines and watched a smaller-than-usual group march by with their wooden crosses. Today, the relic might be gone and the day of the Holy Circumcision replaced, but there's still a pious procession on the first day of the year, starting at the church in the old village and ending in Calcata Nuova. Thanks to that article that Jessie found, I had had thoughts of doing my own procession, of draping a white robe over myself and brandishing a wooden cross—and maybe trying to get some of the locals to go along with me. I asked Pancho what he thought of the idea.

"We've tried so hard to find a peaceful coexistence with the people in Calcata Nuova. Right now, relations are better than ever. Look how the town government has begun cooperating with us. For example, Halloween. But if you go and do something like that, they'll just think you're making fun of them and it'll set our relations back to the days when they were suspicious of us."

Okay, so I didn't want to be public enemy number one for both Calcata and Calcata Nuova. This meant I had no other choice but to join the regular procession and, surreptitiously, meditate on the Holy Foreskin's return.

Did I really believe it would work? Not really. But if the people believed there was an energy flowing out of this chunk of rock we were living on and that the Holy Foreskin would help make you fertile, then why not try this? Besides, I was desperate. That day, the members of the marching band, waiting on the square, kicked in with a tune as soon as they saw the procession pouring out the church doors. The band took the lead, marching down the S-shaped ramp toward the parking lot; the cacophonous song echoed off the *tufo* and probably rang far throughout the valley. The mayor, Don Dario, and a well-dressed couple designated to hold a staff capped by two six-inch bronze sculptures of Calcata's patron saints, Cornelius and Cyprian, followed. The rest of the Calcata Nuova villagers trampled after. I jumped in next to the mayor and marched down through the parking lot. Before I had left Ca' Dante I had taken a postcard-size picture that Giancarlo Croce had managed to snap of the reliquary in 1983 and taped it to my stomach. I could feel the tape tugging at my body hair with each stride. With my hands clasped in a prayer position, I tried thinking about the relic, but I actually wasn't sure how or exactly what I should be concentrating on. I settled on a Hare Krishna–style prayer and repeated the name of the relic: "*Santo Prepuzio, Prepuzio Santo, Santo Prepuzio* . . . With my hands steepled and my eyes half shut, I walked along mumbling the words. That is, until I glanced to the side and saw the mayor looking at me. His look was more of surprise than suspicion at my act of piety. He returned my nod and smile in kind and I went back to my chanting until we reached the end of the parking lot. Then I quietly veered from the procession route and headed back home.

"Well, that's it," I said to Jessie. "I've officially gone insane." In the days that followed, Jessie and I began discussing our return to New York. We didn't have an exact date yet, but we decided it would be in a few weeks.

But a few days after I did the procession, something happened. Was it a sign? Or a coincidence? Had my participation in the procession actually triggered something? Whatever it was, I had a new reason to keep looking for the relic. I encountered Marijcke, the Dutch puppet maker, sitting on the steps of the Granarone.

"Anything interesting?" I asked, referring to the piece of paper she was reading.

"Yes, you'll find it very interesting," she said, and handed it to me. "Ever since you got here and started asking around about the *prepuzio*, everyone else has taken an interest in it again."

I looked at the paper and read about a symposium that was being held in Calcata. "*Dal Santo Prepuzio al Santo Graal*," the headline at the top of the paper read. From Holy Foreskin to Holy Grail. I looked back at Marijcke, who was waiting for my reaction. "Can I take this?" I asked, and then headed back to my apartment. I didn't know that this symposium was about to challenge everything I'd thought about the relic's disappearance and whereabouts.

Chapter 25

SYMPOSIUM AD NAUSEAM

I read every word of the announcement, stopping to look up any words that were beyond my vocabulary. Here's what it said: In the coming weeks there would be a talk on the topics of the foreskin and the grail—held, appropriately enough, at Graal (which means "Grail" in Italian), a Calcata restaurant about thirty feet from my apartment. The organizer? Paolo D'Arpini.

The pairing of the Holy Foreskin with the Holy Grail wasn't lost on me. The two objects, the literal representations of the flesh and blood of Christ that he ordered his disciples to eat at the Last Supper, had come up together from time to time in Calcata, where conspiracy theories are spoken about as matters of fact. I'd heard the canon of conspiracy tales since arriving in Calcata: The Jews, the Freemasons, and the Vatican secretly rule the world; September 11 was a hoax, perpetrated by the Bush Administration; and the Jews control all the media in America. One couple I was friends with—both educated and, I thought, informed about the world—were convinced I was Jewish. Why? They thought my last name sounded Jewish, but the most decisive fact for them, they told me, was that I had written for *The Washington Post*.

This foreskin/grail symposium, however, wasn't actually going to argue a link between the grail and the foreskin. Instead, Paolo (not Patrizia, the self-proclaimed Holy Foreskin expert) would give a talk about the foreskin and a scholar from Rome would then give his theory about the grail, claiming that it was actually buried in a church in Rome.

When the day arrived, I was giddy. The tables in Graal had been arranged to form a large U. Paolo and the grail scholar were seated at the front of the room. About twenty people were sitting around them. Gianni Farauti, representing the town of Calcata, was seated next to Paolo and was already looking about as excited as when he had shown me around the archives. Among the others were Marijcke and Mimmo, Pancho, Capellone's wife, and Omar. There were a few people, perhaps residents of Calcata Nuova, whom I didn't recognize. The conspicuous absentee was Patrizia. I couldn't believe she wasn't in the front row, but she was likely bitter about the fact that she hadn't been asked to lead the conference. She frequently complained that people didn't take her seriously as a scholar and researcher and whenever someone came around looking for an expert on Calcata and/or the relic, they forewent asking her. Which was partly true. She so rarely opened up about the relic and her research that she made it nearly impossible to establish herself as any kind of expert on the relic's history. She was mostly helpful to me, pointing me in certain directions and helping me locate a few historical documents on the relic at the Vatican Library; though later on, she would cravenly claim *everything* I had uncovered about the relic was because of her. She was determined to "own" the subject of the foreskin.

At the conference, Gianni Ferauti got things started by thanking, on behalf of the town of Calcata, everyone for coming and Paolo for having organized such a unique event. Then Paolo took over. "I haven't done a lot of research on this topic," he said, which obviously wasn't an auspicious sign, but given Paolo's proclivity for using energy to learn things, I wasn't surprised. "But I have done some experiments to see if the relic is believable." Then he gave the history of the relic, starting with the 1527 Sack of Rome. "My theory about the relic is not in the mainstream. I want to emphasize the incongruities and mystification of the relic, confirmed by the Church itself. From 1527, Calcata had this relic which added value to the village. Pilgrims would come from all over to worship and give their energy to the relic. This happened until the 1980s. In Naples they believe in the blood of St. Januarius, which liquefies before everyone's eyes one day per year; in Calcata they believed in the foreskin and this belief made the relic perform miracles. The importance they gave to the relic made the relic perform miracles. Climatic miracles. Fertility miracles. Therefore, the object was charged with power—much like what happens in shamanism. That's why many people connect the disappearance with Satanism—that a Satanic sect, perhaps based on Monte Soratte, stole the relic, advised by a branch of Satanists in Calcata."

Depending on your approach, nearby Soratte, rising majestically next to the Tiber River Valley, looks like a gigantic pyramid, the face of Benito Mussolini, or the scaly back of a sleeping dinosaur. The mountain had been used as a sacred place since Etruscan times; the Romans put a temple of Apollo at the top. According to a legend that Dante recounted in his *Divine Comedy*, the man who would become Pope Sylvester fled persecution by taking refuge on Soratte in the fourth century (then he was named pope by Constantine, the very man he'd been running away from). Given its spiritual pedigree, it's no surprise to hear people thought a Satanic sect was operating on or around it. What surprised me more was what Paolo said next.

"When I spoke with Don Dario about the disappearance of the relic, he told me about the couple who had come to see it. They asked to see it, and after some convincing and pleading, Don Dario eventually showed them the foreskin. The next day the relic was gone."

Paulo paused for a second and looked around the room. "We don't know precisely who took it. But what is true is that the relic was really charged with power," Paolo said, "thanks to centuries of veneration and energy being put forth to it. For this reason, it doesn't matter if the piece of flesh inside the reliquary was the real flesh of Christ. It became like the flesh of Christ because we believed in it and we gave it that power. For this reason, it's very clear to me the relic and its reliquary weren't stolen only for material value; they were taken for their spiritual power."

I wanted to stop the symposium and ask more about this couple who showed up at Don Dario's house the day before the relic supposedly was stolen. Could I have been wrong all along about the possibility that the Vatican took the relic? Paolo kept talking, eventually wrapping up by saying that the minute the foreskin left Calcata, he could feel a noticeable drop in the energy of the place. "I noticed the decadence of the people's thoughts. We lost a point of reference after that. But we can bring the Holy Foreskin back—at least in spirit. That's because the rock we are living on, Calcata, is a spiritual place, and always has been, even thousands of years ago with the Faliscans. And now instead of mourning the loss of a powerful object, whose energy is still inside the walls of Calcata, we have to therefore venerate the whole of Calcata; we have to give it our power by venerating it. And then all of Calcata will be the Holy Foreskin."

Everyone in the room nodded thoughtfully at Paolo's idea of praying for the transubstantiation of Calcata. Paolo then nodded at Marijcke to talk, beginning his usual practice of making everyone present say something on the subject. Marijcke said she agreed with Paolo, noting that a yoga retreat had just taken place in Calcata. "And why," she asked, rhetorically, "would they just randomly choose Calcata? It's not a coincidence." Mimmo jumped in, hoping to corroborate by adding that a talk on world religions had just taken place in the village the previous Sunday (forgetting to mention the talk had also been organized by Paolo). Then he went on and on—eye rolls and yawns commenced, just like the time he'd MC'ed the talent show at the Granarone a few months back—about what happens to a human's energy after they die and something about how, with that energy, we could rewitness the crucifixion of Christ. "There was a monk who studied a time machine," said Mimmo, whose wild gray hair makes him seem a bit like a mad professor. When a few people snickered after his time machine comment, he said, "No, really, and this time machine could bring images of things that had not happened yet."

Each person got the opportunity to speak and no one really said anything aside from supporting Paolo's theory. Someone evoked the writer Gurdjieff, who is incredibly popular in Calcata. The conversation finally came full circle when a guest of Paolo's, a scholar who'd done some research on the Holy Foreskin, was talking about the reliquary that housed the prepuce. "It's significant that the gems on the reliquary were green and red because—"

"The Holy Foreskin has always been the focal point of the Church!" screamed a booming voice from the back of the room, cutting off the scholar in midsentence. Patrizia. She was standing by the door, arms akimbo, and as soon as all eyes were on her, she strutted in to the middle of the U-shaped configuration of tables and began ranting about the relic, pacing back and forth. She was staging a coup. "In the nineteenth century, because of the presence of other foreskin relics in the world, the foreskin of Calcata lost some of its spiritual weight. Then the pope issued that decree in 1900 saying anyone who spoke about it would be excommunicated, which is why they kept the relic relatively under wraps. But the pope and other church officials knew this was the real relic."

At this point, I could see Paolo getting a bit shifty. Patrizia was taking over the meeting. Perhaps this was the reason he hadn't invited her in the first place. "Which is why," she continued, "Calcata came under the Messina Law in 1935 and was scheduled to

DAVID FARLEY

be destroyed after it was abandoned. It was part of the conspiracy: to try to sink the Holy Foreskin into further obscurity. But the problem was that even the people of Calcata began to lose faith in it, since they could only now see it once per year, from a distance, and weren't allowed to talk about it and therefore they assumed it wasn't the real relic anymore, that the church had taken it away and left the reliquary empty. Even in the 1970s, after the relic and reliquary were taken to the Vatican for a show on the treasures of the Church, the people believed that Don Dario's annual procession was with an empty reliquary."

Patrizia finally stopped her soliloquy and huffed out of the room, leaving a void of silence. Paolo turned the discussion back over to the scholar who had been talking about the gems on the reliquary. I could see Patrizia pacing in the next room, just waiting to hear something she didn't like. She came out a couple more times before the conference was over, even interrupting the planned talk of the other scholar on his theory that the Holy Grail was buried beneath a church in Rome. Ultimately the conference ended when people began to get up and slowly drift away. Patrizia had never left the floor. As I departed, I could hear Patrizia yelling at someone, "Why don't I get invited to these events? I know more about this than anyone. I've been studying it for years." Omar and I looked at each and laughed, knowing she'd just demonstrated exactly why she hadn't been invited.

There were, it was certain, holes in Don Dario's account of what had gone on the day the relic disappeared—the supposed police report (or lack of one), for example—but after the *prepuzio* symposium, I wondered if the key to the disappearance really lay with that "strange" couple who had visited the priest. They were, by now, over two decades later, nearly mythologized: Two smartly dressed strangers stroll into town, beg to see the relic, and then the next day it's gone. I started asking around and heard a few different takes: They were Satanists, some people told me. Others claimed they were neo-Nazis. *No, no, no,* people said, shaking their finger at me: They were from the Vatican.

My head was spinning from it all. Nazis. Satanists. The Vatican. What was I going to hear next—that the Vatican had taken it in order to clone Jesus, thus hastening the Second Coming? Well, yes. That's what I did hear when I met Alessandro Scannella, whose novel tells just that story. According to his novel, *La Maledizione di Cristo* (*The Curse of Christ*), the Church spirited away the sacred foreskin to its secret state-of-the-art laboratory underneath the Vatican in order to clone Jesus. Alessandro met me for lunch, and as we sat in the Grotta, we talked about the Church. The muscular, long-haired writer explained the premise of his novel.

"But do *you* actually believe that?" I asked in Italian.

He shrugged and gave back a sheepish smile.

"Okay, do people believe there's really a laboratory underneath the Vatican, and as we sit here and eat this gnocchi, pious scientists are cloning Christ?"

Alessandro's response: "*Si dice, si dice.*" One says, one says.

After wishing Alessandro a fond farewell back to his home in Rome, I ran into Patrizia hanging around the square. I'd just spent the entire afternoon speaking in Italian with Alessandro and felt confident I could muster a conversation with her.

"So . . . what about that symposium?"

"No one knew what they were talking about," she said. "*You* don't even know what you're talking about. You don't know the whole story of the relic. No one does. Except for me."

"So you don't agree with Paolo—and everyone in Calcata—that the Vatican has the relic?"

Patrizia wisely didn't give me a straight answer, but she did tell me something enlightening: "A few years after the relic disappeared, Tom Ponzi came to Calcata for a while and did an investigation."

Tom Ponzi, now deceased, was your classic trench-coat-clad

detective. Not to be confused with Charles Ponzi, the pyramid schemer, "Peeping Tom Ponzi" founded his detective agency in 1948 and went on to international fame. Patrizia, perhaps feeling ornery because of the conference, was in the mood to talk, maybe to establish that she was the reigning monarch of Holy Foreskin knowledge in Calcata. Next she told me that Tom Ponzi undertook the investigation with his daughter Miriam. And, after a month of being here, their conclusion was: Don Dario sold the relic to someone who took it to Turin.

Turin? My memory raced back to the first few weeks I was in Calcata when Stefania told me she thought the relic could be in Turin because of the city's long-standing link to the occult. I had dismissed it as "hippie talk." But could I have been looking in the wrong place all this time? I had learned to take everything Patrizia said about the foreskin cautiously, realizing that her theories sometimes involved the Holy Grail and off-the-wall conspiracies. But this was a real tip.

Costantino walked up just then and he and Patrizia began talking about something else. I, on the other hand, stood there in a cloud of wonderment, trying to connect the dots: the mysterious couple, Turin, Tom Ponzi's conclusion about the priest's possible sale of the relic. After all, there was a history of priests selling church valuables in Calcata. I went back to the apartment and got online, going straight to the Italian railways Web site.

I needed to get on the next train for Turin.

Chapter 26

THE CAPITAL OF MAGIC

As I rode the tram into the center of Turin, the sun had just set over northwestern Italy. The blocks-long former Fiat factory buildings of the neighborhood where my hotel was located, the buddingly hip Longetto, were fading, replaced by nineteenth-century apartment houses, as we were inched closer to the historic center. I could already tell there was something different about this city. Relief sculptures, tagged to the side of buildings, for example, boasted cherubs, their wings not gracefully feathered but bat-like and Gothic. Wrought-iron lampposts took the form of dragons.

Before I left, I had called Tom Ponzi's daughter, who took over the agency after the great Italian detective's death and changed her last name to Tomponzi. Miriam Tomponzi, based in Rome, spoke English quite well but she didn't want to say much. I asked her about the investigation she and her father had undertaken in Calcata years back and she surprised me by saying that the case was still open.

"Do you believe the relic is in Turin?" I asked.

"Yes, I do," she said. Then when pressed on why she believed this, she would only say she had a trusted source who had told her so; nor would she tell me who it was. She also said she was suspending her investigation until she had the approval of the Church to continue.

"Approval from the Church?" I said. "Do you really think the Church is going to give you permission to investigate the whereabouts of Jesus' foreskin?"

"Yes," Ms. Tomponzi said without pausing. "They'll approve it. And quite soon."

"Will you talk to me about your investigation after the Vatican gives you the approval?"

Ms. Tomponzi let out a soft groan. "No. I—I don't think I can speak about it then either."

"Okay. What about after the investigation is complete?"

"Maybe then," she said.

But I didn't want to wait until then. The fact is, I found it hard to believe she'd asked for—moreover *expected*—the Vatican's blessing to search for the missing foreskin of Christ. So, before I departed for the city, I started doing my own research. Internet searches perpetually turned up stories that focused on the city's occult connection and its supposed spot as a geographical bull's-eye on the axis of white and black magic. There were also plenty of Christian Web sites warning readers about the vast number of Satanists who lurk in Turin. Newspaper Web sites reported that the Gran Madre di Dio church in Turin had been recently burglarized; the thieves took some holy water and the missal, the book used for daily prayer. Police immediately suspected local Satanists of the crime, saying they needed the missal and water for one of their black masses.

This was the Turin I was hoping to find; this was the side that would help me uncover evidence that the Holy Foreskin was here. I just had to find someone who would talk about it. Which, actually, wasn't too difficult. It turned out everyone I met there knew a little something about the city's historic flirtation with black magic.

The first people I approached, sitting in a candlelit wine bar in the Quadrolatero Romano, the city's hip district for wining and dining, were two twenty-something women, and when they heard the word "occult" come out of my mouth, one of them asked if I had a map. Grabbing the pen from my hand, she began connecting various famed landmarks until she had a pentagram. A growing chorus of dissenters began to surround our table, everyone throwing out their own versions of the five-pointed star.

Finally, the bartender, shaking his head, silenced everyone. "No, no, no! The Mole isn't part of the pentagram," he said, referring to 530-foot tower that dominates the city's skyline, as he came around the bar and grabbed the pen out of someone's hand. After drawing lines on my map between squares, churches, and monasteries to form a five-pointed star, he handed the pen back to me and said, "There. You want another glass of Barolo?"

I did want another glass of Barolo, but I had a tour to get to. I had signed up for a guided tour called Magic Turin, which shuttled the occult-curious around the city to all the sites that supposedly had a connection to the mysterious and the netherworldly. My guide, Emanuela (who was not clad in goth gear, by the way), commenced the tour in front of the small pond next to an Art Deco pyramid-shaped monument on Piazza Statuto. The dark-angel-topped monument, with graceful sculptures of men trying to reach the peak, was a memorial to the workers who died building the Fréjus Tunnel, which finally linked Italy to France. For others, according to my guide, it was a clue to what lies beneath: the Gates of Hell. The esoteric Masonic symbols (that it was a pyramid, apparently, was one tip-off) and the five-pointed star at the top of the angel's head hinted at something darker. "Many people believe the angel is Satan himself," she added.

"However you interpret this monument," said Emanuela, "there's no denying that on and around this square, bad things have happened." The Roman and medieval-era gallows were just beyond the square and the ground we were standing on was a millennia-old necropolis, the Romans—according to Emanuela—adhering to the Egyptian concept that the western side, where the sun sets, was the most appropriate place to bury the dead.

We had begun our tour on the dark side of town, but once we hit the plus-size Piazza Castello, Emanuela announced we'd crossed over. "Here, supposedly, is the highest concentration of positive energy—mostly because of the Shroud." Pointing to an iron gate that separates the square from the grounds of the ornate Royal Palace, Emanuela said the shroud was publicly displayed here (it's now housed in the nearby Duomo and isn't scheduled to be shown to the public again until 2025). Then she nodded to a sculpture with a five-pointed star on its head at the top of the gate. "Note the direction the figure is looking in," Emanuela said. "Many people believe this figure—a symbol of white magic—is looking toward the image of Lucifer back on Piazza Statuto. Their eyes are meeting and good and evil marry together. It's like Turin itself, a duality of good and bad; one cannot exist without the other."

The tour concluded across the Po River, at the neo-Classical Gran Madre di Dio church, the one that had recently been burglarized. Fans of the film *The Italian Job* would recognize it as the church whose steps were subject to a MINI Cooper joyride. Others, however, saw the church as being a key to unlocking one of the great mysteries in the history of relics. On one side of the grand steps that create an approach to the building was a larger-than-life nineteenth-century sculpture of a woman extending a large cup. This cup—or, if you will, grail—was supposed to be a hint that the Holy Grail was buried nearby. How and why such a relic got to Turin, I wasn't sure. But it gave me an opening to ask Emanuela, a lifelong Turinese, about the Holy Foreskin.

She shrugged and then said, "You know, it's possible it ended up here. Perhaps someone could have wanted to create a trinity of Christ relics here." She paused for a second to stare at me, perhaps wondering if I could figure out what they were. There was the famed Shroud, of course, and this supposed Holy Grail, but if no one has found it does that count as a relic in Turin?

"You know about the Shroud, obviously," Emanuela continued, "but in the Basilica of Santa Maria Ausiliatrice there's an enormous relic collection—about five thousand in all. One of their most prized relics is a piece of the True Cross. But if your relic, the *prepuzio*, is in Turin, there's a good chance it could be there."

I woke up early the next morning and hopped back on the tram to the center of town. Santa Maria Ausiliatrice, a massive mid-nineteenth-century church, was built after local priest-cum-saint Giovanni Bosco had a dream in which the Virgin revealed that on this spot three ancient saints had been martyred. I hopped off the tram and huffed it across the historical center. Inside, a few devotees to Bosco were praying over his casket, which was made of transparent glass, revealing the waxy cadaver of Bosco himself. I couldn't find the church's chapel of relics, so I wandered into a back office and asked an ancient nun sitting at a desk.

"It's closed," she said, slicing her hand through the air for emphasis.

"Will it be open later this afternoon?" I asked.

"No," she said. "It's being renovated. It'll be open again sometime next year."

I felt myself sink a little. I needed to get into that chapel. I needed to exhaust every possibility while I was here. "But—but I came here all the way from New York *just* to see the chapel of relics. Please. You have to let me in."

She stared back at me, perhaps digesting my desperation, and then said, "*Momento,*" holding up her index finger. She disappeared behind a door. A minute later she reappeared and waved for me to come forward. I did, and within seconds I was standing in an office talking to Don Sergio, the resident priest. I explained to him that I was in Turin to write something about relics and the city's spiritual side and that I'd heard Santa Maria Ausiliatrice was a great depository of holy relics.

He nodded and then told me what the woman at the front desk had already said. I pleaded, asking if there was any way I could still see the chapel of relics while it was under renovation.

Don Sergio gave me a sorrowful look and slowly shook his head no.

I'd been doing well in Italian so far, but for some reason I couldn't remember how to say "It's a shame," so instead I said, "*Adesso sono triste.*" Now, I am sad.

The priest flashed back a sympathetic look. "What is your interest in relics?" he asked. I went on a rather long and grammatically incorrect spiel about how I was raised Catholic and that I'd been interested in relics since coming to Europe for the first time when I was twenty years old.

By the time I finished, he had perked up a bit. Perhaps he'd just wanted to make sure I was there for the right reasons. So, I decided to take the conversation a step further. "I'm especially interested in Christ relics."

The priest nodded, as if he were impressed. So I continued. "The Holy Shroud, the Grail, the Holy Blood. Especially, the Holy Foreskin." I stopped, expecting the priest to put his hands up, palms facing me, begging me to stop. But he didn't flinch.

"Well, then," he said, "I have something locked away in the next room that I think you'll find very interesting. It's very special. One moment." And with that, I watched him take out his keys and open up a breadbox-size wooden container and pull out a large skeleton key. He stepped out, but I could hear clinks and clangs coming from another room. *Is this really happening?* I thought. Did I just mention the Holy Foreskin and he said he has something to show me? My heart began pounding. Is my search for the relic going to end right here, right now?

The priest was gone another three minutes before I heard his feet slapping against the tile floor. Clasped in his left hand was an object covered with a thick white cloth. He set it on the desk in front of me and grabbed the cloth at the top of the object, ready to unveil whatever it was. First, though, he looked at me and gave a faint smile and an ever-so-subtle eyebrow raise. "Okay, *eccolo*," he said, here it is, and whisked away the cloth.

There, before me, was a baroque silver crucifix topped, oddly enough, with a hen and three pairs of dice showing the numbers five, three, and one. Embedded inside the middle of the two-inch-thick cross and covered by glass was an object, a relic. But I couldn't identify what it was. It was dark and small. And just when I was going to ask, the nun from the front desk called for Don Sergio. He excused himself, leaving me alone with the cross and the relic that was embedded inside. Could this be the Holy Foreskin? I bent down, putting my hands on my knees, focusing on the dark object in the center of the cross. It *was* about the size of a chickpea, as the ancient documents attest. I couldn't believe it. The theory could be right—that someone had wanted to unite a relic of Christ's birth with a relic of Christ's death. Fantasies about grabbing the reliquary and making a beeline for my hotel started to run through my head. I could take it back to Calcata and reunite the village with the relic. Was this all happening, I wondered, because of the procession that I'd done a few weeks earlier?

"*Eccomi*," Don Sergio said, announcing himself as he reentered the room, interrupting my illicit thoughts. "It's quite a spectacle, isn't it?"

"*Certissimo*," I said. Most certainly. "So, is this the Holy Foreskin?" I asked.

He began laughing. "No, no, no. This is a piece of the True Cross. The Holy Foreskin," he said, waiving his hand, "—that's just a medieval fantasy."

I explained that I had heard maybe the relic was here in Turin and figured it could be in the church's chapel of relics. He laughed again and I thanked him for showing me a piece of the True Cross and headed for the nearest wine bar.

The next morning, my head slightly stinging from thoughts of what could have been that afternoon at Santa Maria Ausiliatrice and from having drunk too much Piedmontese wine, I hopped back on the tram to the center of town for more investigating. Thanks to Valeria, a friend in New York who was a native to Piedmont, I had a few more interviews set up. On this day, my third in Turin, I had a date with the city's most renowned writer on the occult, Giuditta Dembech.

I took the elevator up to her apartment, which was located in the center of town, and found Ms. Dembech waiting for me at her door. Her red hair and eyeliner reminded me of Athon and made me wonder if they knew each other somehow. Her apartment was crammed with crystals and images of angels. Ms. Dembech tried to explain the complex theory about energy and its relation to Turin. I mostly wanted to ask her about the foreskin, but I thought I'd hear her theories first, which included the energy grid. She said that sometimes the natural landscape—mountain ranges, for example—can block the movement of these forces. But in some cases, particularly in places that are rich in granite, the energy flows out of the earth like a spring. "Just look on a map," she said. "There are a lot of spiritual places that follow this same line—Stonehenge, Turin, Jerusalem, and Mecca."

When I brought up the foreskin, Dembech, like Don Sergio from the day before, didn't flinch, making me think they were used to this sort of thing in Turin. She thought about it for a long second and then slowly shook her head no. "I don't think it's here," she said. "I probably would have heard about it."

I thanked her and headed to my next interview. Professor Bruno Barberis was the director of the Centro Internazionale di Sindonologia (*Sindone* is the Italian word for "shroud"). He lived in a tall apartment block not far from my hotel. To the people of the twentieth and twenty-first centuries, the Shroud was the most famous Christ relic. Might Professor Barberis know something about our Christ relic and its relation to Turin?

The hirsute professor appeared suspicious of me when we sat down at his dining room table. Much like Patrizia with the foreskin, the professor insisted I remain earnest in my dealings with the relic. "If you're not going to take the Shroud seriously in whatever it is you're doing with this information, then please don't include my name," he said. I assured him that I'd make no jokes about the relic he'd spent the majority of his life studying and, it seemed, defending. Besides, I wasn't there to find out about the Shroud; fearing he'd think it was a prank call when he heard the person on the other end asking about a "sacred foreskin," I decided to wait until our tête-à-tête before mentioning the relic.

Not that I had any wiggle room for foreskin querying. Professor Barberis, having probably talked to scores of journalists during his tenure as one of the world's most renowned Shroud experts, launched into a thirty-minute soliloquy about the large piece of cloth that had supposedly covered the dead, preresurrected Christ. He never came out and said that it was for sure the real thing, but it was clear he'd spent a lot of time defending the relic against skeptics. When he finally took a second to breathe, I broke in. "For the last year, I've been living in this village near Rome called Calcata. And in this village was a very interesting Christ relic: the foreskin."

Barberis clicked his tongue. "Relics like this are nonsense," he said. "In the Middle Ages there were a dozen foreskins. It's not like the Shroud!"

"Wasn't there a shroud that was in Constantinople and it was possibly different from the one that is here in Turin?" I asked.

"Well, okay, there have been a couple shrouds, but those were obvious fakes and quickly disappeared as soon as they were proven to be fake."

"Well, whatever the case," I interjected, hoping to forestall another long monologue, "apparently the foreskin of Calcata was sold to someone here. Have you ever heard of anyone in Turin who claimed to posses the Holy Foreskin?"

"No," he spat back, "let me be clear about this: There is no Holy Foreskin in Turin. There is only the Shroud!"

I left Barberis's apartment soon after, convinced he regretted having granted me an interview. But maybe he felt that way with all journalists, many of whom come to him with a sense of incredulity about the Shroud. It was proven to be a medieval fake after tests in 1988, but recently those results have been called into question. So, the verdict is still in limbo. It does seem fitting for the Shroud to be in Turin. The more I read on the history of this city, the more I realized that its reputation was manufactured, mostly out of the nineteenth-century battle for Italian unification. Out of benign tolerance or just a flip of the nose at the Vatican, the Savoy family's policy of letting non-Catholics reside in Turin resulted in a mass immigration of peoples from all over Europe, looking for a haven to safely practice their beliefs. Mormons, Jews, and Protestants all flocked to Turin. The Savoys also jailed cardinals, creating a standoff between themselves and the Vatican. The papal propaganda machine was revved up and soon Turin was being painted as a place filled with Satanists and other cults. But did Turin's reputation as a city of magic and the occult solely depend on papal propaganda? And what would this mean for the theory that the foreskin was here? I didn't have much time left in Turin, and the only thing I'd learned so far was that the foreskin wasn't there. I felt like I'd talked to people who would have at least heard of the relic if it was, in fact, in this city.

I had one more interview set up. Dr. Massimo Introvigne's name kept popping up in pretrip research I'd done on Turin and religion. The director of the Center for Studies on New Religions (or CESNUR), Introvigne was one well-connected and accomplished man. He'd written about forty books about religion and religious cults, as well as tomes attacking secular humanism. He was a lawyer as well as a member of Alleanza Cattolica, the Catholic Alliance, a pro-Church activist group. I made sure to show up on time, since I had been granted only thirty minutes with Introvigne.

Before he arrived, I sat in front of an empty desk surrounded by floor-to-ceiling shelves filled with books on Freemasonry and the Maya and files labeled Jonestown, Lutherans, Punk, Loch Ness, Opus Dei, Islam, Ramtha. It seemed Introvigne didn't let any movement escape his attention. When Dr. Introvigne strode into the office, he gave me a firm handshake and sat down at his desk. He was built like a soda can, and had a perfectly round head. I explained to him my interest in Turin's "shady side" and he started in, speaking in perfect sound-bite-like sentences.

"Ninety percent of this story about Turin is legend, but it does have a historical grounding," he said, telling me about Turin's role in the unification of Italy and papal propaganda. "There were no Satanists in Turin. That is, until the nineteen sixties when a few people, relying on this false pedigree with the occult, opened up two small Satanic churches here. There were about a hundred fifty to two hundred members. At the same time," Introvigne continued, "some pranksters created documents claiming there were forty thousand Satanists in Turin. *La Stampa*"—Turin's daily newspaper—"published it, even though the journalists knew it was a false document."

"So," I said, "all this stuff about the occult and Satanism in Turin is fake?"

"Ninety percent. The remaining ten percent of the story is true—that in the nineteenth century the city was a free zone for spirituality."

"And what about the two axes of black and white magic?"

"Yes, that also is a fake from the nineteen sixties," Introvigne said, smiling wryly.

That Turin's occult/black magic landscape had been forged doesn't necessarily mean that people here didn't believe in it. It was true that everyone I'd met in Turin said they didn't know any Satanists in the city. But, real or not, given the city's reputation, perhaps some Satanists or dabblers in black magic had bought into this idea and those people would be attracted to Turin. And maybe some of those people would want the Holy Foreskin.

Our thirty-minute meeting, which largely consisted of an interesting history lesson by Dr. Introvigne, was nearing an end. But I had to ask about the Holy Foreskin still. So far, I had struck out with all my religious and occult experts in Turin. But Introvigne was an active and (I suspected) high-ranking member of the Catholic community. I was hoping he'd offer as much enlightenment about the foreskin's whereabouts as he just had about Turin's sham Satanic scene. I introduced the topic the same way I had with Barberis, telling him about the foreskin's disappearance from Calcata and the belief it had been sold to someone who took it to Turin.

Introvigne, his hands folded in front of him, nodded and then said, "After I heard about the relic's disappearance from this village where you live and having read Roger Peyrefitte's book *The Keys of St. Peter*, I called up my friends at the Vatican and asked them what had happened to the Holy Foreskin."

I stopped writing in my notebook and leaned in.

Introvigne continued. "They said it's under the church."

"Below St. Peter's," I said. "In Rome, right?"

"No," Introvigne said, unfolding his hands and leaning back in his chair. "Below the church in Calcata."

"Wait," I said. "The Holy Foreskin is still in Calcata?"

"Yes," he said. "My friends at the Vatican said it's really quite a simple matter: They decided to retire the relic since there was no way to prove its authenticity. They ordered the priest to put the relic away. It's there in Calcata in some room underneath the church."

I nodded at Dr. Introvigne and swallowed hard. My throat felt like it had just closed up. I thanked him for his time and left the office. I walked down the street with no particular direction or destination. I was in a serious daze. The Holy Foreskin, it turned out, had never left Calcata at all.

Chapter 27

HOLY FEAST

"If you need directions to the place you're going, then you will never get there," said Paolo when I ran into him in his little hermit room a few days after I got back from Turin. Jessie and I only had a week left in Calcata and this was going to be one of the last times I would get to hang out with Paolo. I rarely understood what he meant by these grand, innocuous bong-philosophy statements, and at first this one was no exception; except that when I really thought about it—which is what I did as we sat in his incense-filled rabbit hole of a room—this statement seemed to encapsulate my time in Calcata quite well. When I arrived, I knew no one. Nor did I have a clue about where to start looking for the lost foreskin. No one of any consequence would talk to me about it. And I didn't even speak Italian very well. So, even if I needed directions, I didn't even know how to ask for them. But I got there. At least I think I did. Plus, I made some great friends here and, I believe, I found out what had happened to the Holy Foreskin; of course, I'd had to go to Turin to find out that it was in a place we all least expected.

At least, it seemed no one expected it to be where Dr. Intro-

vigne claimed his Vatican friends said it was. So I asked Paolo.
"Have you ever thought that maybe the *prepuzio* could still be in
Calcata? Maybe in the church or in Don Dario's house?"

"No!" Paolo exclaimed. "Don Dario was too embarrassed
about the relic. He wouldn't have kept it in his house. I am ninety
percent sure the Vatican has it. He also went to Rome the day the
relic supposedly was stolen. Many people—including myself—
believe that he probably delivered the relic to the Vatican. But," he
added, "wherever it went, that is where it is now."

"Why didn't you tell me earlier about the couple from Turin
or the fact that you had written about the relic in the late nineteen seventies and early nineteen eighties?" I asked.

Paolo looked to the ground, thinking about his answer. "Why
should I have told you? I said to you from the very beginning
these things will come to you, if you feel the energy of the place.
There was no need to tell you. And look what happened: You
learned these things."

I suppose in a twisted form of logic, he was right. "By the
way, how can I find out more about this energy?" I asked. I was
still intrigued about this connection between the Calcata energy
theory and the foreskin. "Do you have any documents that give
evidence that Calcata was this spiritual place?"

Paolo paused again before answering. This time, however, he
stared at me until a slight smile came across his face. "No, there
isn't any such documentation. That's because I invented it."

"You invented what?" I asked.

"I invented all the information about Calcata as a spiritual
place for the Faliscans."

I didn't know what to say, I just stared back at him.

"But don't get the wrong idea," he said. "Calcata is a spiritual
place with much energy. But I created these stories so that other
people would be inspired to put more energy toward Calcata.
This way, the entire rock will be a center of energy."

I was amazed and a little bit annoyed that he'd been stringing me along this entire time about Calcata's supposed ancient history. In a way, though, his theory had worked: People were always talking about the energy as a matter of fact and I always felt like there was something wrong with me because I'd never felt it. The next time I was up in Calcata Nuova I asked several of the residents who had grown up in the medieval village if they had ever felt an energy there. Not one person knew what I was talking about.

I wanted to probe more people about energy, but I was more interested in looking around the church in Calcata for a door to the basement. When the next Sunday came—the day when Don Dario opened the church—I tiptoed through the church, trying every door I could find. I tried the door to the sacristy, but it was locked. On the other side of the room, there was another door. I tried it and it opened. The light from the main room illuminated what turned out to be a storage room for church-related junk: old robes worn at mass lingered with brooms, and silver-plated cups rested on tables. I doubted the relic was in there, and there were no other doors in the room that would take me down to the basement. But when I left the church, I saw Gisa, my landlord. She was, along with Don Dario, one of the key holders to the church. So I asked about the possibility of a basement.

"I don't think so. The only thing under the church, I believe, is the crypt."

That was it. If the Holy Foreskin remained in Calcata, it was in the crypt.

"Is there any way to get down there?" I asked.

Gisa shrugged and said she didn't know. She suggested that Don Dario might be the only person who had access.

If what Dr. Introvigne had heard from his Vatican friends was true, then some of the dangling mysteries that emerged during my quest made a bit more sense. Bishop Roberto Massimilliano's statement, for example, that once he was gone, the relic would be gone: He knew the Church wanted to retire it, but understood what it meant to the community, so he'd insisted it remain, perhaps arguing that the village was so isolated that few people outside of the area really knew about the relic's existence. That is, until Paolo D'Arpini began writing about it. That was when, it could be argued, the Church decided they needed to do something about it.

And the story about the "strange" foreign couple who came to Don Dario's door asking to see the relic? They were, I came to believe, a figment of Don Dario's imagination. Blaming it on "foreigners" or slyly mentioning that their accents sounded like they came from Turin, a place whose reputation would make the theft more believable, now smacked of a fine work of fiction. Which was why there was no police report: It would be illegal to file a report for a crime that never happened. Yet it was necessary for Don Dario to cook up such a story—he had to save face; if he had told the villagers the truth, that he was ordered "from above" to put the relic away, he would have been run out of Calcata for good. And then there was the Czech priest I had met at the Vatican whose advice, telling me to look elsewhere, I had feared was a veiled threat. But now it appeared more like he might not have known himself where the relic was but had at least been tipped off it really wasn't in the Vatican, as many Calcatesi assumed.

And what would one now make of Don Dario's supposed trip to Rome, the one during which many villagers believe he hand-delivered the relic to the Vatican? Was that trip part of the priest's contrived tale? Here's a possibility: Considering Dr. Introvigne's tip that the foreskin was still in Calcata, could it be that once the Church decided to "retire" the relic, they just wanted back their valuable reliquary and didn't care so much about the piece of shriveled flesh that was inside it? Perhaps they decided the best thing for it would be to keep it in—or, rather, below—the church in case they ever needed it again. Could it be that Don Dario went to Rome that day to give back the reliquary and then, by orders from above, placed the actual foreskin in the crypt of the church?

Maybe I'd never learn the truth, but with my time winding down in Calcata, there was only one way to find out. Ask Don Dario. I just had to get him to sit down with me—and in a talkative mood.

I had a plan.

✦

As Omar and I stood in front of Don Dario's gate—just as we had months earlier—I took a deep breath and rang the buzzer. After two rings, the priest popped his head out of his door and then stepped out. Omar reintroduced himself and the priest opened the gate and waved for us to come in.

"I'm not sure if you remember," Omar said, "but my friend here is still very interested in speaking to the various people of Calcata about their memories of the village."

Don Dario looked at me and then nodded his head. I think he had no idea who I was.

"So, we would be honored if you would be our guest for dinner. At the Grotta dei Germogli."

Don Dario stood up and excused himself, saying he'd be right back. Omar and I flashed looks at each other, wondering if he was going to return. Bea, Pancho's sous chef, had recently told me that it was impossible for Don Dario to refuse a meal. After my few encounters—and particularly the last one, in which I'd questioned the date the relic disappeared—I didn't have much hope. But, a minute later, the priest reappeared, flipping through his day-planner.

"How about Friday evening at eight o'clock?" he said.

We were on.

✦

It was Friday night—the big dinner with Don Dario. I had come early to set the table, uncork a bottle of wine, and choose some

nonintrusive music to play. At twenty-five minutes past eight
o'clock, Don Dario was a no-show. Omar too. He had said that
he might be a few minutes late because he was having pictures
taken of himself for a portfolio that he hoped would launch him
out of Calcata and into the world of acting. I began to get nervous. The only thing I could do was pace.

Then, a few minutes later, Omar strode in from the photo
shoot, his face caked with makeup.

"What's with the makeup?" I asked.

"What?" said Omar. "You can see I'm wearing makeup?"

Just then, the heavy glass door of the Grotta opened and there
he was: Don Dario, with his crooked smile, black golf shirt covering his rotund belly, and thick glasses smeared with grease. I
couldn't believe he was standing before me. "Okay," he said, clasp-
ing his hands together, "I'm ready to eat!" Then he let out a huge
guffaw. We sat down at a table and Pancho arrived to greet Don
Dario and pour us some wine. My strategy was simple: Get him
as drunk as possible and wait for him to talk.

We began with his own beginnings in the Church. Don Dario
took us through his life, starting with his childhood in the mountains of Le Marche. By the time we got to Calcata in his story, I
was starting to feel bad for him. He'd joined the ranks of the
church to get out of the obscure village in which he grew up, just
to get stuck in another obscure village (albeit one with a Holy
Foreskin).

Which, by the way, I had no idea how I was going to bring up
in conversation. That is, until about twenty minutes later when
he said, "Few outsiders would show up in Calcata when I first
moved there. Just pilgrims now and then."

Omar and I gave each other quick sideways glances, both rec-
ognizing the window of opportunity Don Dario had opened for
us. And before I could direct the next question for Don Dario,
Omar said exactly what I was going to tell him to ask: "Don
Dario, why would a pilgrim come to Calcata?"

"Oh," the priest said, leaning back in his chair in an attempt to look casual, "just for the relic we had here. Nothing much."

Pancho came up to take the dishes from our first course. I surreptitiously touched the rim of the empty wine bottle and nodded at Pancho to bring a second bottle. He nodded back.

Once again, Omar took the lead. "What was the relic?" he asked.

Don Dario continued. "Oh, just the foreskin of Jesus."

"Wow," I said, disingenuously. "The Holy Foreskin? That's incredible." At that moment, I realized the error of my previous ways. Instead of trying to build up to a moment when we were comfortable enough to bring up the relic, why not let him lead us into it and then play dumb, like we'd never heard of such a relic before? Looking at Omar—so he'd know where I was going with this—I added in Italian, "I had no idea such a relic was here. How interesting. How did it ever end up in Calcata?"

Don Dario, disarmed when he thought I knew nothing about the relic, launched into a long history of the Holy Foreskin, complete with the German soldier and the seven-year-old Clarice.

Pancho delivered our next bottle of wine and when he heard the topic of our conversation, he gave me a slight smile and a quick raise of his eyebrows.

Because of Don Dario's thick accent, I didn't understand everything he was saying at the moment, but Omar would occasionally look over at me and say, "You already know this." So, I sat there, watching Omar nod and Don Dario speak. I refilled everyone's wineglass to the rim. Omar was really coming into his own as my translator. Maybe it was the makeup that he could hide behind, giving him a new confidence, but gone was the sheepishness he'd had whenever the subject of talking to Don Dario would come up. After a few minutes, Omar glanced over at me and, in English, said, "Why don't I ask him what happened to the relic?"

"Please do," I said.

Don Dario responded, "It was stolen in 1986."

Omar pressed the priest for more details. Don Dario launched into the story of the 1900 decree warning excommunication to anyone who spoke or wrote about it. Unlike the time we'd accosted him in the church, however, Don Dario kept talking. "Times were changing," he said. "And the Church needed to change too. So by the time I arrived in Calcata, I was told that I couldn't show the relic to anyone. But I did anyway. Just to a few people now and then." The first couple people he said he showed it to were locals. They pleaded with him because they needed a miracle. One of those people was the grandmother of Avelio, the guy who ran one of the two markets in Calcata Nuova. A friend of hers had possibly fatal meningitis. And, he added, it worked; the very next day, the friend was cured. "The third time I showed it was the last time," he said, his voice growing grave. "A couple came to my door begging me to see the relic. They had foreign accents, like maybe they were from Turin. And they seemed so desperate, so I invited them in."

"So," I interjected as soon as Omar had translated for me, "this was a man and a woman?"

"No," he said, "two men in their late thirties. Anyway, the next day I went to Rome and when I came back I noticed my window was open and I went over to the wardrobe and the relic was gone. Someone told me later that as soon as I drove away that morning, they saw a woman running toward my house. And even below the open window where she climbed in and out of my house, there was a footprint—of a woman's shoe. I am convinced," he added, "this was the couple that came to my house the day before."

"But you just said they were two men," I said.

"Yeah," Omar added. "I was just thinking the same thing."

Don Dario got flustered. He leaned forward, resting his elbows on the table and began fidgeting with the wine bottle. "Well, perhaps she was an accomplice," he said. "The two men begged their way into my house, watched as I took the shoe box out of the wardrobe and then the reliquary and relic out of the shoe box, and then they told their friend—the woman—where it was and she went and got it."

"And how did you know it was a woman's shoe print on your wall?" I asked.

"I don't know," Don Dario replied. "You could just tell." Then he mentioned that he'd gone to the police station in Faleria to report the theft.

"Did they come and do an investigation?" I asked.

Don Dario shook his head no.

"Why wouldn't they at least come out to see if they could find any evidence?" I asked.

"Do you know how small the *prepuzio* was?" he said. Then he picked up three blackened bread crumbs from the table and held them in the palm of his hand. "Like this," he said. "Just three little black balls."

I looked at Omar and said, in English, "Okay, the relic may have been dubious, but the reliquary was priceless." He shook his head in agreement. There was something fishy about this whole story. "And what about the fact that there was evidence—a shoe print? Why didn't police come out?"

Omar translated the part about the shoe print to Don Dario, who was still fidgeting with the wine bottle. The priest shrugged and then—unprompted—showed us his palms and added, "I didn't have anything to do with it." Then he folded his arms.

Omar and I, not sure what to do, both picked up our wine-glasses and took a drink at the same time.

Don Dario cleared his throat. "I never believed in the relic," he said. "I only pretended to. The same goes for my predecessors."

Since Don Dario seemed to be in such a candid mood, I tried leading him into a confession by saying that after Vatican II, relics no longer were front and center in the eyes of the Church. "Don't you think it would make sense that they simply retired the relic and de-manded that you give it back? Or at least give back the reliquary?"

Before the end of the night, I must have asked this question four other times, each time phrased differently, and each time Don Dario denied it. The last time, I made up a story about how, growing up, my church had a relic and the Vatican decided that the saint was more of a legend than an actual person, so they "retired" the relic. After all, St. Christopher, the patron saint of travelers, met a similar fate after Vatican II.

Both Don Dario and Omar asked me who the saint was.

"Um . . ." I paused. I hadn't expected to be asked. "St. Cletus," I blurted out. Omar and the priest both looked at each other. "St. Cletus, St. Cletus, St. Cletus," Don Dario, looking at the ceiling, mumbled to himself as if he were going through the index of saints in his mind. Even Omar was perplexed.

"Where was he from?" the priest asked.

"Mississippi," I said.

"Oh, so an American saint," Don Dario said.

"Yes," I said, deciding now to have some fun with this. There were only three saints who were U.S. citizens—St. Katherine Drexel, St. Elizabeth Ann Seton, and St. Frances Xavier Cabrini—but I figured no one here was really keeping track. "He was the patron saint of trailer parks," I added. Neither Omar nor Don Dario knew what a trailer park was, so I had to stop and explain. "So, this didn't happen with the *prepuzio*?" I asked, taking one more shot.

"The relic did fall out of favor with the Church long ago," Don Dario said. "Much like your relic of St. Cletus. They stopped believing in the foreskin. It was worthless to them. But the priests—my predecessors—understood how important it was to this community, so they didn't do anything about it. And then, as I said, it was stolen."

Bea, the Grotta's sous chef and a lifelong resident of Calcata, walked up to say hello to Don Dario and the topic of conversation changed. Within a few minutes, Don Dario stood up to leave and we shook hands. He thanked me for inviting him to dinner.

And he told Pancho that his food reminded him of the food he'd seen being prepared on a popular cooking show on TV—the Italian version of *Iron Chef*. "It's of a very elevated quality," he told Pancho. "I don't usually eat stuff like that, but I thought your cooking was very good."

Then he looked over at Omar and me and, perhaps suddenly fearful about all he'd said tonight about the relic, added, "Listen, even if the relic had fallen out of favor with the Church, I did believe in the power of the people's belief in it. I think those miracles really happened because people believed in the relic."

Spirituality can make odd bedfellows and right at that moment I pictured Don Dario spooning with Paolo. Catholic belief turns a wafer into the body of Christ and a cup of wine into his blood; and, according to Paolo's lecture at the symposium a month earlier, if you believe strongly enough and put enough energy to something—like a piece of flesh said to be the foreskin of Jesus (or the very rock Calcata sits on)—that object can become charged with power and energy. If you believed it was, then it could do miraculous things. Or, rather, your mind could perform miracles. We have the power within us to perform superhuman feats—lift up an automobile when someone we love is trapped underneath it, cure ourselves of sickness and disease just by concentrating on getting better, or, in the case of many old Calcatesi, miscarry a child by saying you're going to name her Clarice. The sacred objects we prayed to for miracles, it turns out, were—when you really boiled it down—just vehicles for our minds to work that power.

Perhaps someday, thanks to Paolo's philosophy of post-prepuce Calcata, the entire village and the rock it sits on really will have taken in so much positive and spiritual energy that the whole mound will have been incarnated into a giant Holy Foreskin of sorts. And just imagine if Dr. Introvigne was right—that the relic had been underneath the church in Calcata the entire time. If this were true, imagine: Someday far into the future, a Calcatese is going to finally open that crypt below the church in Calcata. Maybe it will be Paolo's grandson, Sava, or even Sava's grandson or granddaughter. And that person will find a silk satchel with perhaps a ribbon tied around it. Maybe the writing on that ribbon will be worn off, revealing only the first few letters: "N. S. . . ." And perhaps they'll even figure out that the next letter to this faded Latin acronym is G, as in N.S.G., *Nostro Signore Gesù*, Our Lord Jesus. If someone there, looking at this small sack, had heard the legends about the curious relic that once had a home in the village, they might exclaim, just like the priest did in 1557 in the presence of Maddalena Strozzi and Clarice: The *Santissimo Prepuzio*. And with that, the Most Holy Foreskin will be resurrected in Calcata again.

Source Notes

Chapter 1
The Prepuce, the Priest, and the Wardrobe

1 **As Don Dario Magnoni draped:** "Conmocion en Italia: Robaron el Prepcio de Cristo," *Interviu,* February 1–7, 1984.

1 **"This year," Don Dario began:** Tana de Zulueta, "Mystery over theft of tiny 'divine' relic," *The Sunday Times,* January 15, 1984.

2 **The Church feared the relic was:** Ibid.

2–3 **The decree also stated:** This is according to Calcata resident Louise McDermott, who claimed to have a copy of the decree.

3 **Several popes wrote about:** Robert P. Palazzo, "The Veneration of the Sacred Foreskin(s) of Baby Jesus—A Documented Analysis," in James P. Helfers, ed., *Multicultural Europe and Cultural Exchange in the Middle Ages and Renaissance* (Turnhout, Belgium: Brepols Publishers, 2005). I'm indebted to Palazzo's exhaustive study of the history of the Holy Foreskin, the most researched study I could find in English.

3 **Christ's flesh and blood are:** Marc Shell, "The Holy Foreskin; or, Money, Relics, and Judeo-Christianity," eds. Jonathan Boyarin and Daniel Boyarin, *Jews and Other Differences: The New Jewish Cultural Studies* (Minneapolis: University of Minnesota Press, 1997).

5 **A group of medieval monks:** Thomas Head, *Hagiography and the Cult of the Saints: The Diocese of Orléans, 800–1200* (Cambridge: Cambridge University Press, 1900).

7   **Though Vatican II didn't address:** Geoffrey Edward Measel, *Domus Dei: A Post Vatican II Look at the Catholic Church* (dissertation, University of Cincinnati, 2007).

Chapter 2
A Piece of God

12   **There's only one way to get:** The account of the relic's discovery in Calcata has been recounted in many historical sources. I mostly relied on: *Breve Racconto della Reliquia del Santissimo Prepuzio di Mostra Signore Gesù Cristo Dato in Luce da un Divoto in occasione delle solenne Consacrazione della nuova Chiesa delli SS. Cornelio e Cipriano nella Terra di Calcata in cui la medesima si venera* (Rome: Nella Stamperia della R.C.A.: 1728); Cesare Sinibaldi Gambalunga, *Narrazione Critico-Storico della Reliquia preziosissima del Santissimo Prepuzio di N.S. Gesù Cristo che si venera nella Chiesa Parochiale di Calcata* (Rome: Presso Vincenzo Poggioli, 1802); Gaetano Moroni, *Dizionario di Erudizione Storico-Ecclesiastica*, Vol. CI (Venice: Tipografia Emiliana, 1860).

Chapter 3
Oh! Calcata!

22   **Who could have known that an earthquake:** William Sinclair, "Peace and Love 30 Years On," *Time Out Roma,* October 2002.

Chapter 4
The Father of All Foreskins

30   **But most relic scholars agree:** James Bentley, *Restless Bones: The Story of Relics* (London: Constable and Company Limited, 1985).

31   **Not that this made relic:** Peter Brown, *The Cult of the Saints: Its Rise and Function in Late Christianity* (Chicago: University of Chicago Press, 1982).

31   **At the time of St. Peter's:** Anthony Doerr, *Four Seasons in Rome: On Twins, Insomnia, and the Biggest Funeral in the History of the World* (New York: Scribner, 2007).

32 **Which is one reason Roman:** Bentley, *Restless Bones.*

32 **At the Second Council of Nicaea:** Patrick J. Geary, *Living with the Dead in the Middle Ages* (Ithaca: Cornell University Press, 1995).

34 **Charles, along with his allies:** Patrick J. Geary, *Furta Sacra: Thefts of Relics in the Central Middle Ages* (Princeton, New Jersey: Princeton University Press, 1978).

34 **According to legend:** The tale of Charlemagne receiving the Holy Foreskin in the Church of the Holy Sepulchre appeared frequently in historical and scholarly sources, including, *Breve Racconto della Reliquia del Santissimo Prepuzio di Mostra Signore Gesù Cristo Dato in Luce da un Divoto in occasione delle solenne Consacrazione della nuova Chiesa delli SS. Cornelio e Cipriano nella Terra di Calcata in cui la medesima si venera;* Amy G. Remensnyder, *Remembering Kings Past: Monastic Foundation Legends in Medieval Southern France* (Ithaca: Cornell University Press, 1996).

34 **An Alternative story of Charlemagne:** Walter Johannes Stein, *The Ninth Century and the Holy Grail* (East Sussex: Temple Lodge, 1996).

35 **After his death in 814:** Remensnyder, *Remembering Kings Past.*

36 **In the late eighth century:** Rudolf Schieffer, "Charlemagne and Rome," ed. Julia M. H. Smith, *Early Medieval Rome and the Christian West: Essays in Honour of Donald A. Bullough* (Leiden: Brill Academic Publishers, 2000).

36 **In actuality, we know:** Alphons Victor Müller, *Die hochheilige Vorhaut Christi im Kult und in der Theologie der Papstkirche* (Schwetschke, Berlin 1907).

37 **Medieval Popes, some harboring:** P. Grisar, "Il 'Sancta Sanctorum' in Roma e il Suo Tesoro Novemente Aperto," *La Civilta Cattolica,* June 16, 1906.

Chapter 5
Family Jewels

43 **The first mention of the Holy:** Müller, *Die hochheilige Vorhaut Christi im Kult und in der Theologie der Papstkirche.*

43 **In fact, so many recently:** Bentley, *Restless Bones.*

43 **One of the most eventful times:** Guy Martin, "Prague Rocks," *Conde Nast Traveler,* November 2006.

44 **A couple centuries later:** Carlos M. N. Eire, *War Against the Idols: The Reformation of Worship from Erasmus to Calvin* (Cambridge: Cambridge University Press, 1986).

44 **The emergence of wealthy:** Jonathan Sumption, *Pilgrimage: An Image of Mediaeval Religion* (Totowa, New Jersey: Rowman and Littlefield, 1975).

44 **But nothing could compare:** For Christ and Virgin relics other than the Holy Foreskin, I've largely relied on: Joe Nickell, *Relics of the Christ* (Lexington, Kentucky: University of Kentucky Press, 2007); G. W. Foote and J. M. Wheeler, *Crimes of Christianity* (London: Progressive Publishing Company, 1887); Patrice Boussel, *Des réliques et de leur bon usage* (Paris: Balland, 1971); and James Bentley, *Restless Bones.*

47 **But no relic could elicit:** Nicolas Vincent, *The Holy Blood: King Henry III and the Westminster Blood Relic* (Cambridge: Cambridge University Press, 2001).

Chapter 8
The Ultimate Circumcision

75 **There wasn't much talk in the Bible:** For the history of circumcision, I relied on Felix Bryk, *Circumcision in Man and Woman: Its History, Psychology, and Ethnology* (New York: American Ethnological Press, 1934); Leonard B. Glick, *Marked in Your Flesh: Circumcision from Ancient Judea to Modern America* (New York: Oxford University Press, 2006); Hayyim Schauss, *The Lifetime of a Jew: Throughout the Ages of Jewish History* (Cincinnati: Union of American Hebrew Congregations, 1950); Michael Signer, "To See Ourselves as Others See Us: Circumcision in Pagan Antiquity and the Christian Middle Ages," in ed. Lewis M. Barth, *Berit Mila in Reform Context* (Secaucus, N.J.: Carol Publishing Group, 1990);

David Gollaher, *Circumcision: A History of the World's Most Controversial Surgery* (New York: Basic Books, 2001); and P. C. Remondino, M.D., *History of Circumcision: From the Earliest Times to the Present* (Philadelphia: F. A. Davis Publisher, 1891).

75 **And thus it became obligatory:** William E. Phillips, *The Sexuality of Jesus* (Cleveland: Pilgrim Press, 1996).

76 **Jesus' circumcision:** "The First Gospel of the Infancy of Jesus Christ," in *The Apocryphal New Testament, Being All the Gospels, Epistles, and Other Pieces Now Extant Attributed, in the First Four Centuries, to Jesus Christ, His Apostles, and Their Companions, and Not Included in the New Testament by Its Compilers* (Boston: N. H. Whitaker, 1832).

77 **But for now what is most:** Palazzo, "The Veneration of the Sacred Foreskin(s) of Baby Jesus—A Documented Analysis."

78 **In fact, Renaissance painters:** Jack M. Greenstein, *Mantegna and Painting as Historical Narrative* (Chicago: University of Chicago Press, 1992).

79 **One author on the subject of Christian phallic worship:** Ian McNeil Cooke, *Saint Priapus: An Account of Phallic Survivals Within the Christina Church and Some of Their Pagan Origins* (Cornwall: Men-an-Tol Studio, 2002).

Chapter 9
CA' DANTE

81 **Calcata's streets follow a:** *Calcata and Faleria: An Urban Study Experience in Northern Lazio* (Brooklyn, NY: Pratt Institute School of Architecture, 1981).

83 **According to a recent survey:** Ian Fisher, "In a Funk, Italy Sings an Aria of Disappointment," *The New York Times,* December 13, 2007

84 **Of course, there's a historical:** For an accessible introduction to Italian culture and history see: Luigi Barzini, *The Italians* (New York: Touchstone, 1996).

Chapτεκ 10
FOR THE BIRDS

92 **With all her eccentricities:** see Athon Veggie and Alison David-
son, *The Book of Doors Divination Deck: An Alchemical Oracle from
Ancient Egypt* (Rochester, Vermont: Destiny Books, 1994).

Chapτεκ 11
LOOKING FOR THE KEYS TO ST. PETER'S

100 **From 1870 to 1929:** Kertzer, David I. *Prisoner of the Vatican: The
Popes' Secret Plot to Capture Rome from the New Italian State* (Boston:
Houghton Mifflin, 2004).

102 **And of course, it has its own:** Robert J. Hutchinson, *When in
Rome: A Journal of Life in Vatican City* (New York: Main Street
Books, 1996)

103 **And twentieth-century British historian:** George G. Coulton,
Five Centuries of Religion (London: Cambridge University Press,
1923).

Chapτεκ 12
ARMIES FOR JESUS

112 **Ever since I'd begun reading:** According to Charles Freeman's
intriguing study of the early Church, *The Closing of the Western
Mind: The Rise of Faith and the Fall of Reason,* references to Mary
in the Gospels are scant; Isaiah prophesizes the birth of Christ,
writing "Behold a virgin will conceive." This interpretation was
taken from the Septuagint (Greek) version, which used the term
parthenos to render the Hebrew for *almah,* which meant no more
than a young girl, so, as Freeman writes, "the scriptural base of
Mary's virginity was shaky, especially as Gospels mention Jesus
and brothers and sisters." Freeman adds: "[I]t is only in the fourth
century that sees the development of a cult of Mary as perpetually virgin—Athanasius was among the first to use the term 'ever
virgin.'" (pp. 241–242).

112 **Plato, whose thought had:** On the formation of the early Church, I'm indebted to Ramsay MacMullen, *Christianity and Paganism in the Fourth to the Eighth Centuries* (New Haven: Yale University Press, 1997), Charles Freeman, *The Closing of the Western Mind: The Rise of Faith and the Fall of Reason* (New York: Vintage Books, 2002); Jonathan Kirsch, *God Against the Gods: The History of the War Between Monotheism and Polytheism* (New York: Penguin Compass, 2005); and Euan Cameron, *Interpreting Christian History: The Challenge of the Churches' Past* (Oxford: Blackwell Publishing, 2005).

Chapter 13
A History of Nothing

119 **On June 1, 1828:** Stendal, *Promenades dans Rome* (Paris: Calmann Levy, 1930).

122 **In March 974 Calcata's:** L. D. McDermott, *Calcata: Some Historical Notes* (Rome: Gufo Editori, 1992).

Chapter 14
The Foreskin Phenomenon

136 **If another village or monastery:** The concept of attributing relics—particularly the Holy Foreskin of Charroux—to Charlemagne is masterfully argued in Remensnyder's *Remembering Kings Past.*

137 **The Holy Foreskin of Conques:** Amy G. Remensyder, "Legendary Treasure at Conques: Reliquaries and Imaginative Memory," in *Speculum,* no. 71, 1996.

138 **The earliest source for the:** Müller, *Die hochheilige Vorhaut Christi im Kult und in der Theologie der Papstkirche.*

139 **Even the architecture:** Remensnyder, *Remembering Kings Past.*

140 **Pope Innocent III had:** Sumption, *Pilgrimage: An Image of Mediaeval Religion.* Also: Palazzo, "The Veneration of the Sacred Foreskin(s) of Baby Jesus—A Documented Analysis."

141 **Which is when St. Catherine:** Bernard McGinn, *The Flowering of Mysticism: Men and Women in the New Mysticism (1200–1350)*

(New York: The Crossroad Publishing Company, 1998); Frank
Graziano, *Wounds of Love: The Mystical Marriage of St. Rose of
Lima* (New York: Oxford University Press, 2004). Catherine's
fourteenth-century hagiographer, Raymond of Capua, found this
detail uncomfortable enough that he translated "Holy Foreskin"
into "bejeweled gold ring."

141 **And Maria said: As my son was:** *The Revelations of St. Birgitta,*
trans. William Patterson Cumming (London: Oxford University
Press, 1929).

Chapter 15
SACRED CHOW

143 **Meet Agnes Blannbekin:** Agnes Blannbekin, *Life and Revelations,*
trans. Ulrike Wiethaus (Cambridge: D. S. Brewer, 2002).

Chapter 16
"PRECIOUS RUBBISH"

157 **Once they penetrated the walls:** André Chastel, *The Sack of Rome,
1527* (Princeton, New Jersey: Princeton University Press, 1977).

157 **The soldiers had marched:** Judith Hook, *The Sack of Rome, 1527*
(London: Macmillan, 1972).

159 **Of a piece of the broiled fish:** Foote and Wheeler, *Crimes of
Christianity.*

160 **The theological debate over:** For information and source material on theological problems and opposition to the Holy Foreskin,
I largely relied on Müller, *Die hochheilige Vorhaut Christi im Kult
und in der Theologie der Papstkirche,* and Palazzo, "The Veneration of
the Sacred Foreskin(s) of Baby Jesus—A Documented Analysis."

Chapter 18
MISSING PIECES

171 **In 1559, two years after:** This tale is often recounted in historical
documents related to the relic, for example: *Breve Racconto della*

Reliquia del Santissimo Prepuzio di Nostra Signore Gesù Cristo Dato in Luce da un Divoto in occasione delle solenne Consacrazione della nuova Chiesa delli SS. Cornelio e Cipriano nella Terra di Calcata in cui la medesima si venera; Gambalunga, *Narrazione Critico-Storico della Reliquia preziosissima del Santissimo Prepuzio di N.S. Gesù Cristo che si venera nella Chiesa Parochiale di Calcata;* and Moroni, *Dizionario di Erudizione Storico-Ecclesiastica.*

172 **Afterward, a series of popes:** Moroni, *Dizionario di Erudizione Storico-Ecclesiastica.*

172 **But the Vatican still wanted:** Giovanni Marangoni, *Istoria dell' Antichissimo Oratorio o Cappella di S. Lorenzo nel Patriarchio Lateranese Comunemente Appellato Sancta Sanctorum* (Rome: Ottavio Puccinelli, 1747).

Chapter 19
ENERGY BOOSTERS

189 **A few millennia before the hippies:** T. W. Potter, *The Changing Landscape of South Etruria* (New York: St. Martin's Press, 1979).

189 **Narce was one of the earliest:** T. W. Potter, *A Faliscan Town in South Etruria: Excavations at Narce, 1966–71* (London: The British School at Rome, 1976).

Chapter 21
RED SKIN

203 **Three years later, on January 14, 1859:** Pierre Saintyves, *Les Reliques et les Images Légendaires* (Paris: Mercure de France, 1912).

204 **The reason for this relic resurgence:** Hugh McLeod, *Secularisation in Western Europe, 1848–1914* (New York: St. Martin's Press, 2000).

204 **In December 1864, Pope Pius IX:** Kertzer, *Prisoner of the Vatican.*

205 **In response to the criticism,** Saintyves, *Les Reliques et les Images Légendaires.*

Acknowledgments

It took a village—a real Italian one and a theoretical one—to write the book you're holding and in no way should I get all the credit for it.

Nearly everyone in Calcata (and Calcata Nuova) gave me a welcome that was more open than I ever could have imagined when I first hopped off that bus one warm early-summer day. Among those Calcatese I'd like to especially thank are John Arnold, Deborah Borghi, Capellone, Giancarlo Croce, Paolo D'Arpini, Alessandro Falcone, Gianni Farauti, Gisa Federici, Wilma de Filippis, Maria Margherita Greco, Gianni Macchia, Marijcke van der Maden, Don Dario Magnoni, Mazzula, Louise McDermott, Scot McFiggen, Sofia Minkova, Costantino Morosin, Mario Panaro, Paolo Portoghesi, Beatrice Roberto, Stefania Scagnoli, Gemma Uyttendaele, Athon Veggi, and Romano Vitali. Patrizia Crisanti gets a big shout-out for helping me locate documents in the Vatican Library and for trusting that I wouldn't make a mockery of the relic she has spent so much time studying. Extra-special thanks goes to my great friends Elena Foschi and Omar Roveri, for making themselves available on a moment's notice to

289

translate for me or drive me anywhere I asked. I owe a lifetime of thanks to Pancho Garrison and Paul Steffen, who took me in like I was part of their families and whose spirits of kindness and generosity I take with me everywhere. For help when I was in Turin, I'd like to thank Carlo d'Oulx.

A few translators did arduous work for generously low fees: Erna Beers (Dutch), Valeria Emma Osella (Italian), Ed Moran (French), Janine Padilla (Spanish), and Ed Stone French (German).

Several scholars offered research advice and lent their historical knowledge to me. They are Professor Robert Crotty at the University of South Australia, Professor Thomas Head at Hunter College, Professor Richard Landes at Boston University, Professor Amy Remensnyder at Brown University, and Thomas Serafin from the International Crusade for Holy Relics. A special thank-you goes out to Robert Palazzo, whose finely researched article on the Holy Foreskin(s) was a beacon for finding historical documents I had been hitherto unaware. Big thanks to the New York Public Library for having just about every book that has ever been published. Also, I'd like to thank the Vatican Library for giving me access. I hope you don't regret it.

I give hearty thanks to several editors whose assignments kept my landlord happy and my tummy full with pasta and wine while I was in Calcata: Mollie Chen at *Conde Nast Traveler*, Melynda Fuller and Norman Vanamee at *Sherman's Travel*, Jeff Hoyt and Alain Gayot at Gayot.com, Gregory Hubbs at Transitions Abroad, Denny Lee at *The New York Times*, Dr. Drew Limsky at *Lexus Magazine*, Barbara Peck at *Endless Vacation*, Thomas Swick at the *South Florida Sun-Sentinel*, and K. C. Summers at *The Washington Post*. Special thanks is reserved for Torie Bosch from Slate.com, whose encouragement to write an article about the relic directly resulted in this book.

Many friends offered wise writing counsel, endured my incessant ramblings about the relic, and shared my enthusiasm for the project, for which I'm eternally grateful: Jim Benning and Michael Yessis at WorldHum.com, Frank Bures, Tom Bissell,

ACKNOWLEDGMENTS

Nichole DiBenedetto, Tom Downey, Arthur Frommer, Pauline Frommer, Nicholas Gill, Olivia Giovetti, Stephanie Elizondo Griest, Matt Gross, Ayun Halliday, John Hayter, Marie Kenny, Abbie Kozolchyk, Jane Kramer, Tim Leffel at PerceptiveTravel.com, Jen Leo, Carol Malzone, Mary Morris, Tim Patterson, Tony Perrottet, Rolf Potts, Erik Olsen, Francis X. Rocca, Alex Steele and everyone at Gotham Writers' Workshop, Cullen Thomas, J. Maarten Troost, Susan Van Allen, and Benjamin Wallace. Big thanks to my friends Alexander Basek, Kate Sullivan, and Tania Grossinger, whose generous feedback on the manuscript helped transform it into a publishable state.

Thanks go to my agent, Jim Rutman at Sterling Lord Literistic, who is about as knowledgeable, trustworthy, and supportive an agent as any writer could wish for. I owe eternal thanks to my alchemical editor at Gotham Books, Patrick Mulligan, who believed in this book from the very beginning. His knowledge and enthusiasm for the subject and his tireless editing and attention have made this a much better book.

I owe everything to my mom, Patricia Farley, whose staunch belief that you really can be anything you want in life gave me the courage to take chances. My family has given me unwavering support throughout my life and during the research and writing of *An Irreverent Curiosity* and I thank them for that. Cathy and Tom Kelly get a special mention for their occasional unsolicited boosters in the form of cash. My in-laws Dan Sholl and Pat Rosaves also deserve a special shout out for their love and support. So does Sheila Sholl.

And last, but never least, to my wife, Jessie Sholl. Without her unyielding support, encouragement, wholehearted love, and willingness to go just about anywhere, I could never have had the courage to begin working on this book and I wouldn't have had the wherewithal to finish it. She's the reason I'm a writer and the best editor any spouse could ask for. This book is dedicated to her.